Praise for *Beyond Baseball's Color Barrier*

"Not since [Robert] Peterson's *Only the Ball Was White* have I read a more complete, thought-provoking history of the Black experience as it pertains to both the Negro and Major Leagues. Even better, in *Beyond Baseball's Color Barrier*, Constantino takes a deeper dive, bringing us full circle from the pre–Jackie Robinson era to today when African American participation in the game is at a multi-decades low. Constantino brings to life the legends and voices of Black baseball—their struggles, their courage, and their oft-untold exploits. A must-read for anyone who wants a more thorough picture of our national pastime—and our country's complicated history. An appropriate story for our current, turbulent times."—Erik Sherman, *New York Times* best-selling author of *Two Sides of Glory: The 1986 Boston Red Sox in Their Own Words*

"*Beyond Baseball's Color Barrier* is an important book because it honors the careers of so many Black players throughout Major League Baseball history. African American ballplayers at the Major League level have played significant role models in the lives of Black youths who have aspired to reach those heights. There are so many Black ballplayers who rank among the greatest players to ever play the game. Recognition of lifelong accomplishments encourages one to dream big."—Andre Dawson, MLB Hall of Famer

"I want to mention to the Afro-American players throughout the Major Leagues that [*Beyond Baseball's Color Barrier*] is outstanding. Jackie Robinson was the first, Larry Doby the second, and if it wasn't for those two individuals, myself as a player, getting an opportunity as a Major League ballplayer it would have taken a monumental task on my part."—Fergie Jenkins, MLB Hall of Famer

"I'm very honored to be in Rocco's book with pitchers like Bob Gibson, Satchel Paige, Luis Tiant, and many others. *Beyond Baseball's Color Barrier* is a great book that honors so many of the game's greatest."—Dwight Gooden, former MLB All-Star Pitcher

"Rocco does a great job of capturing the important history of Black ballplayers in MLB in *Beyond Baseball's Color Barrier*. He honors everyone from Aaron and Mays to Betts and Griffey while also looking to the future. It's a great book."—Shannon Stewart, former MLB outfielder

"*Beyond Baseball's Color Barrier* is a book that honors great Black players through Major League history, including myself. It's important to honor great players such as Jackie Robinson, Willie Mays, Henry Aaron, and so many more."—Willie Wilson, former MLB All-Star outfielder

"Rocco does a great job of capturing the history of black players in MLB while being hopeful about the future. I've been inspired by so many throughout my career, from Jackie Robinson to players like Tony Gwynn and Ken Griffey Jr. It's hugely important to honor them for the sacrifices they made paving the road and for the efforts that went in to progressing the game both on and off the field. It's something that myself and future generations will forever be indebted for, so thank you very much to those players from the bottom of my heart and thank you to Rocco as well for continuing to spread that message."—Greg Allen, San Diego Padres outfielder

"*Beyond Baseball's Color Barrier* honors the great history of Black players in MLB history and also looks toward the future with hope. Rocco creates a detailed history that is very colorful and well researched."—Royce Lewis, top overall pick, 2017 MLB Draft, Minnesota Twins

BEYOND BASEBALL'S COLOR BARRIER

The Story of African Americans in Major League Baseball, Past, Present, and Future

Rocco Constantino

ROWMAN & LITTLEFIELD
Lanham • Boulder • New York • London

Published by Rowman & Littlefield
An imprint of The Rowman & Littlefield Publishing Group, Inc.
4501 Forbes Boulevard, Suite 200, Lanham, Maryland 20706
www.rowman.com

6 Tinworth Street, London SE11 5AL, United Kingdom

British Library Cataloguing in Publication Information Available

Library of Congress Cataloging-in-Publication Data

Names: Constantino, Rocco, 1974– author.
Title: Beyond baseball's color barrier : the story of African Americans in Major League Baseball,
    past, present, and future / Rocco Constantino.
Description: Lanham, Maryland : Rowman & Littlefield, 2021. | Includes bibliographical references
    and index. | Summary: "Beyond Baseball's Color Barrier celebrates Black players throughout the
    history of Major League Baseball. The book not only provides a comprehensive history dating
    back to the 1800s, but also highlights accomplishments, personalities, participation trends of
    African American players, and insight into what the future may hold"— Provided by publisher.
Identifiers: LCCN 2020045290 (print) | LCCN 2020045291 (ebook) | ISBN 9781538149089 (cloth) |
    ISBN 9781538149096 (ebook)
Subjects: LCSH: African American baseball players—History. | Major League Baseball (Organiza-
    tion)—History. | Discrimination in sports—United States—History. | Racism in sports—United
    States—History. | Baseball—United States—History.
Classification: LCC GV863.A1 C599 2021 (print) | LCC GV863.A1 (ebook) | DDC 796.357092/
    396073—dc23
LC record available at https://lccn.loc.gov/2020045290
LC ebook record available at https://lccn.loc.gov/2020045291

CONTENTS

FOREWORD

Luis Tiant

When I was a boy growing up in Havana, I remember baseball players coming around to visit my father, Luis Tiant Sr. Dad had spent more than 20 years as a pro pitcher, including many seasons in the Negro Leagues, and enjoyed seeing his old teammates, but he didn't want me following in his footsteps. He wanted me to finish school and become a doctor or lawyer.

I didn't understand it at the time, but my father was trying to protect me from what he had gone through. It was tough for African Americans, Cubans, and other Black ballplayers in the 1930s and '40s. Dad played year-round and was still never able to save much money. He and his Negro League teammates drove in broken-down buses from one town to another, and when they couldn't find restaurants or hotels that served Blacks—which was a lot—they ate and slept on the bus. Some of them knew they were good enough to play in the majors, but this was before Jackie Robinson broke the color line. By the time he did, in 1947, Dad was too old to get his shot.

But you know what? Even with all the racism they faced, Dad and the other great Black ballplayers knew they were part of something special. Like Bob Feller and Ted Williams, they were the best in the world at what they did. They had loyal fans who packed ballparks to watch them, and they held their own against white big-league clubs. They were poor, but they were *proud.* And in the end, my father saw I had the same love for the game that he did—and gave me his blessing to follow *my* dreams. When I made it to the major leagues, I did it for both of us.

That is what Rocco Constantino has captured so well in *Beyond Baseball's Color Barrier*: the tough times and great times Black ballplayers had during the many long years they were kept out of the majors, and their quick rise to the top when they got their chance. The early success of guys like Jackie and Larry Doby and Roy Campanella in the late 1940s and '50s made it possible for the second wave—Henry Aaron, Willie Mays, Roberto Clemente, Ernie Banks, and the rest—to come up behind them. By the time I played my first game, in 1964, the All-Stars teams were filled with players who 20 years before would have been riding the buses with my father.

In 1975, when Dad saw me pitch in the World Series, African Americans made up 18.5 percent of all MLB players. Black players were constantly among the league leaders in batting, homers, and other stats, and superstars like Jim Rice and Reggie Jackson signed record contracts. They still faced racism, like when Aaron received all that hate mail when he was chasing Babe Ruth's record. But they had made it to the top, and served as inspiration for the next generation of stars like Ken Griffey, Jr. and Frank Thomas.

Now I worry things are going the other way. There are plenty of Dominicans and Cubans and other Latino players in the majors, which is great, but less than 7 percent of MLB players are African Americans. Dave Roberts was one of only two African American managers in 2020, and he won the World Series. What does that tell you? There should be more of them, in the dugout and on the field.

Baseball has gone from the game everybody played in the park after school to a specialized youth sport with expensive travel teams for the best players—most of them white. MLB is making an effort to reach out to young Black kids through initiatives like the RBI Program, and I hope it works. As Rocco shows so well in this book, African Americans have a rich legacy in the major leagues. For the sake of those who paved the way, and guys like my dad that never got the chance, that history needs and deserves to continue.

Luis Tiant pitched in the Major Leagues from 1964 to 1982 and is considered one of the greatest Cuban-born baseball players of all time. A member of the Boston Red Sox Hall of Fame, Tiant is still hailed as a hero in Boston based on his eight years with the Red Sox and his performance in the 1975 postseason.

ACKNOWLEDGMENTS

This book would not be possible without the vision and encouragement of Christen Karniski of Rowman & Littlefield and Curtis Russell, a great baseball fan and president and principal agent of P.S. Literary Agency. I am indebted to them for believing in my writing and supporting my career. I credit my love of baseball history to my father, Rocco, and his twin brother, Canio, who grew up watching baseball in the 1940s and provided nightly history lessons as I learned about the sport in the 1980s.

I also thank my friends and family who help keep that love of the game alive. Baseball is best when shared with other fans, so I thank those who are always ready for a conversation about the sport. These people include, but are not limited to, Daniel Constantino, James Constantino, Pop Roberto, Anthony Roberto, Brian Sheridan, John Engdahl, Mike Mundy, Carmen Pizzano, Mike Jannicelli, Ashton Corley, Aubrey Orr, Veronica Cobos, Chris Vitali, Doug Cancelliere, Alex Flor, Jim Miele, Pat Barbone, Ken Constantino, Ray Monahan, Barbara Monahan, Mary Monahan, Tom Monahan, Irene Constantino, Michael Barbone, Anthony Barbone, Paul Marcantuono, Mike Lamberti, Jim Hague, Dan Tiant, Diego Ramirez, Dave Loveton, Jack Corley, Craig Moropoulos, Jeff Walker, Bill Pintard, Devin Engebretsen, Akil Hill, Mike Medel, and Dave Goss.

I would also like to thank those in the baseball world who participated in the writing of this book, lending their professional insight to this important issue. These people include former pros Jerry Reuss, Jim Campanis Jr., Andre Robertson, Luis Tiant, Brian McRae, and Rudy May; former minor-league manager Tony Barbone; and Bob Kendrick, president of the Negro Leagues Baseball Museum. In addition, thank you to the fantastic photographers whose photos are featured in this book, including Keith Allison, Richard Boudreau, Brad Schloss, Gene Wang, and Michael Baron. I would especially like to thank Bob Cullum, the grandson of famed Boston sports photographer Leslie Jones, whose historic photos are also featured. Mr. Jones had a front-row seat to the baseball world during the first half of the twentieth century, including the entire period of integration. I thank Mr. Cullum and the Boston Public Library for permitting these incredible photos to be used.

A final thank you to the players and people who fought for equality in Major League Baseball and continue to do so. It is my hope that this book can serve as a comprehensive history lesson about the incredible African American players of the past century and a half. No matter what era of baseball fans examine, there were always African American superstars doing great things on the diamond, even during the period of segregation in the Negro Leagues. Participation in Major League Baseball among African Americans may have declined significantly, but that slide has leveled off and there are fantastic efforts being made to reverse that trend. I hope that people can read this book and appreciate the long, storied history of African Americans in baseball and become part of the grassroots efforts to help keep the revitalization moving in the right direction.

INTRODUCTION

The date is well-known and revered annually throughout Major League Baseball: April 15, 1947, the day Jackie Robinson bounded out of the dugout at Ebbets Field for the first time as a Brooklyn Dodger. That event is celebrated as the moment Major League Baseball's color barrier was broken. It's considered a seminal moment in not only baseball history, but also American history. The truth is that the origins of African American history in Major League Baseball are murkier than that, and the future may be even murkier.

In a *New York Times* article on April 11, 1947, four days before Robinson's debut, a headline spanned the top of the entire sports page announcing, "Dodgers Purchase Robinson, First Negro in Modern Major League Baseball." The inclusion of the qualifier "modern" might seem suspicious to today's fan, but the article provides insight. The *Times* gives quick background on a player named Moses Fleetwood Walker, identified in the article as the "last Negro to play in the majors." In 1884, Walker played one season for the Toledo Blue Stockings, where he was joined by his brother, Weldy, before the color line was drawn, not to be crossed by anyone again until that day in 1947.

In 2004, research from Peter Morris, a member of the Society for American Baseball Research (SABR), shed light on William White, who is now recognized as the earliest known "legal" African American Major League Baseball player. White played one game as a fill-in for the Providence Greys on June 21, 1879. White's story is complex, however. He has been confirmed as being the son of a white slave owner from Milner,

Georgia, named Andrew White. William's mother was Hannah White, who has been listed on census reports as "mulatto," making William one-quarter African American, which according to laws in most states at the time meant that a person was "legally" Black. This meant he would have had to abide by the separatist laws of the time. The issue concerning White is that he identified his race as "white" in the 1900 and 1910 census. Whether you can consider White the first African American ball-player is a matter of interpretation. Legally, yes, White is the earliest known African American Major League Baseball player. Socially, how-ever, White probably shouldn't be classified in that way.

The day Robinson debuted was covered as a historic event, but it was not held in the same esteem as it is today. The *Times* article by Louis Effrat carried a bold headline and painted a picture of support, stating that "I'm for Robinson" buttons were sold outside Ebbets Field during that day's exhibition game. It mentioned that the Dodgers' Dixie Walker, someone who two years earlier said he would not play with Robinson and who was the most outspoken teammate against him during spring train-ing, was roundly booed during batting practice and the game; however, the article also hinted at the vitriol Robinson could face. Effrat wrote, "He may run into antipathy from Southerners who form about 60 percent of the league's playing strength. In fact, it is rumored that a number of Dodgers expressed themselves as unhappy at the possibility of having to play with Jackie."

After Robinson debuted during the 1947 season with four other African American players, the league slowly began to integrate. After no additional teams integrated in 1948, Monte Irvin debuted for the Giants in 1949 and as each year passed, the rest of the 16 teams slowly integrated. The Detroit Tigers (1958) and Boston Red Sox (1959) were the last two teams to integrate.

In the 1959 season, the first year of full integration, 8.8 percent of players were African American, according to research by SABR. Throughout the course of the initial integration process, multiple African American players were making baseball history. The 1955 season was a monumental season that may well have catapulted Major League Base-ball from the slow integration era into the boom in diversity of the 1960s and 1970s. In 1955, a 24-year-old Willie Mays followed up his Most Valuable Player (MVP) season from the year before by blasting 51 home runs and playing the flashiest stint at center field anyone had seen. In

Brooklyn, the Dodgers were led by a trio of African American legends as they captured an improbable World Series title. That year, Roy Campanella won the third of his MVP Awards, Don Newcombe became the first African American pitcher to win 20 games, and Jackie Robinson, then 36 years old, was still productive as the team's third baseman.

In Chicago, Ernie Banks emerged as one of the great young superstars of the game. In his second season in 1955, Banks made his first All-Star Game, belted 44 home runs, and drove in 117 runs, while finishing third in MVP voting. Also making waves in the Midwest was a young Hank Aaron, who was a first-time All-Star at age 21, for the Milwaukee Braves that year. Frank Robinson debuted the next season for the Cincinnati Reds, winning the Rookie of the Year Award. For the first time, baseball fans had an influx of young African American superstars as many of the African American players who starred the eight years prior were older veterans or part-timers.

From 1960–1975, the percentage of African American baseball players rose steadily to its peak in 1975, at 18.5 percent. The career of Mays ended in 1973, and Robinson and Aaron said goodbye in 1976. The torch was passed along to a succession of African American superstars like Bob Gibson, Willie Stargell, Reggie Jackson, Billy Williams, and Joe Morgan. Just as the presence of African American stars remained consistent, the overall percentage of African American players in Major League Baseball was stable as well.

From 1975–1994, the percentage of African American players never swayed more than one percentage point from 17 percent. The success and popularity of African American ballplayers from the 1950s through the 1970s buoyed the interest of young African American baseball fans. They had someone to emulate in the streets while they played stickball; they had role models in Major League Baseball. Players who looked like them not only were among the best in the majors, but also were being talked about with the best to play the game. In 1974, when Hank Aaron passed Babe Ruth to claim the career home run title, the time had come for an African American player to hold perhaps the most revered record in sports. The transition from Aaron and Mays to Reggie and Gibson coincided with the childhoods of such players as Ozzie Smith, Dave Winfield, Rickey Henderson, and Tony Gwynn.

As fans can point to the 1955 season as a defining season in the path of African American Major League Baseball history, data can point to the

1994 season as another watershed season. That season, the percentage of African American baseball players was at 17.2 percent, its highest total since 1988. The league was again rife with young African American stars like Barry Bonds, Frank Thomas, and Barry Larkin. Albert Belle was widely considered the game's most feared hitter, and Ken Griffey Jr. was a modern-day Willie Mays in center field.

On August 11, 1994, Major League Baseball shut down for a 232-day players' strike, the longest and most damaging strike in major-league history. Play resumed in late April 1995, and after a slightly abbreviated 1995 season concluded, 16.1 percent of the players who played that season were African American. It was the first time since Jackie Robinson's debut that the percentage of African American players in the major leagues dropped by more than 1 percent from one year to the next. From that point onward, the percentage of African American players decreased in each season through 2010, when it stabilized at about 7 percent. In three of the four seasons between 2013 and 2016, that percentage dropped to 6.7 percent, the lowest number since 1957. In 1957, there were still two teams that had yet to integrate.

The topic of the slow decline of African American baseball players has been well-publicized and well-theorized during the past two decades. There is plenty of valid circumstantial evidence as to why this has happened. Theories include the rise in the percentage of Hispanic players (as high as 27.9 percent in 2006), the increase in popularity of the National Football League and National Basketball Association, the rising costs of playing the sport as a youth, and a generational culture shift. Even the expansion of roster spots taken up by pitchers plays a role. Traditionally, the percentage of African American pitchers is much lower than that of position players, so as pitchers took up more real estate on major-league rosters, one can surmise that may have influenced the drop in participation as well.

Throughout the peaks and valleys of the past seven decades of integrated Major League Baseball, there has been no shortage of role models and icons among African American ballplayers. Jackie Robinson transcends the sport as a cultural giant in American history. Hank Aaron and Willie Mays do as well. Lou Brock and Rickey Henderson are the top two basestealers in the sport's history. Bob Gibson is one of the fiercest competitors to ever wear a major-league uniform, and few in the game's history could wield a bat like Tony Gwynn. Ken Griffey Jr. is among the most graceful ballplayers to play the sport, and few players or managers have commanded respect the way Frank Robinson did.

While the accomplishments of those inner-circle Hall of Famers speak for themselves, there is also a litany of other African American players who have had fantastic seasons, accomplishments, and careers. Vida Blue had one of the great pitching seasons in baseball history as a 21-year-old in 1971. The baseball world didn't see another season like that until Dwight Gooden's historic 1985 season. When Cecil Fielder cracked 51 home runs in 1990, he broke a streak of 13 seasons without a 50-homer player, the longest such drought in major-league history. The beloved Roy Campanella is known for his three MVP seasons but also still holds the highest career caught stealing percentage of any catcher in major-league history, at 57 percent. Curt Flood was a Gold Glove center fielder, but his bigger impact came when he sacrificed his career to challenge the reserve clause in 1969.

Major League Baseball has been around for more than 150 years, and as the sport expands globally, the impact African American ballplayers have had stretches far and wide. It hasn't been just the names in the record books who have blazed a trail through the sport. It was Pumpsie Green finally integrating the Red Sox, Joe Morgan's elbow flap, and Billy Williams's sweet swing in Chicago. It was Dave Stewart glaring at the batter who dared to stand in the box and Vada Pinson gliding around the outfield at Crosley Field. It was Oscar Gamble's Afro, Dave Parker's cannon, Bo Jackson breaking a bat over his knee, and Dick Allen blasting obscene home runs and lighting up cigarettes in the dugout. It was Mookie Wilson's ground ball in the 1986 World Series, and Mookie Betts's heroics in the 2018 World Series. It was Dominic Smith speaking emotionally, tears streaming down his face, during the racial unrest in the summer of 2020. It's Dave Roberts becoming the first African American manager in National League history to win a World Series behind the leadership of Mookie Betts. It's Blue Moon, Mudcat, Oil Can, Bo Knows, and The Big Hurt.

Baseball may have been widely popular in the first half of the twentieth century, but it truly gained its flair in the post–World War II era. Think Jackie Robinson dancing off third base, ready to steal home; Satchel Paige bringing his "Trouble Ball" to the Indians; Willie Stargell whirling his bat; and Reggie Jackson stirring the drink. The flair was Gary Sheffield menacingly waving his bat, Darryl Strawberry's moonshot home runs, and Josh Harrison wiggling out of another rundown. If you are someone who remembers those images, chances are you're smiling as big as Curtis Granderson or Kirby Puckett. While the percentage of African American ballplayers may have steadily decreased in the past 20 years, the impact they have made on the game has not. But before all of that was possible, there was Will White, Moses Fleetwood Walker, and the subsequent rift that divided baseball along the color line for more than 60 years.

I

DRAWING THE LINE

FLEET WALKER AND THE CURIOUS CASE OF WILL WHITE

Column three on page seven of the June 22, 1879, edition of the *Chicago Tribune* offers insight into the racist language that was acceptable at the time, while also verifying that the idea of baseball superstitions extended back to the game's early beginnings. In a collection of unrelated anecdotes appearing under the simple heading "Notes of the Game," a short story tells the tale of Jack Burdock, a second baseman for the Boston Red Caps. On his way to a game against the Cincinnati Reds, Burdock spotted a cross-eyed woman in a window, and after the Red Caps lost, he declared that a hex was put on the team by the woman. The article continues,

> On the first day they played here, a little Negro boy rode all the way out to the grounds on the rear steps of the band-wagon containing the team, and returned to the city in the same way. As the Bostons won a victory, [Charley] Jones pronounced the boy a lucky "coon" and named him. He paid the little snowball a half a dollar, and secured from him a pledge to be around at Gibson House on the following day at 1 o'clock for another ride. The promise was kept, and another victory resulted. On Saturday, there was no "coon," and defeat followed.

The language used in the article in one of the most prestigious newspapers in the country is striking by today's standards, even if it was standard during that era. While it exemplifies normative language of the 1800s, it doesn't carry any historical weight. A brief mention in column one on the same page about a player in a game between the Providence Grays and Cleveland Blues does, however.

The article mentions that veteran first baseman Joe Start took a leave from his team and was replaced for that game by a man named William White, a member of the Brown University baseball team. According to the article, White "played the position with remarkable activity and skill for an amateur." He also scored a run later in the game. White never appeared in another major-league game and would rest in baseball history as a forgotten footnote for the next 130 years.

In 2004, as part of a large-scale project to find accurate personal information for every single person who appeared in a Major League Baseball game, researchers stumbled upon the idea that White might have been the first African American professional baseball player. The National League was just three years old at the time, and although there are records of baseball games involving African American and white players, there had been no known Black Major League Baseball players to that date. When researching White's information, researcher Bruce Allardice e-mailed Society for American Baseball Research biographical researcher Peter Morris, alerting him to the possibility of White's racial makeup. Allardice found that an Andrew (A. J.) White lived in Milner, Georgia, where he owned 70 slaves. The 1860 census listed no children or wife for White. Ten years later, the next census listed a woman named Hannah White, who was living with her mother and three children, one of them a nine-year-old named William White. Hannah was listed as biracial on the census.

That led researchers on a quest to convincingly link Hannah and William White to A. J. White, confirming William's parentage. That objective was realized when reading A. J. White's will. In it, he bequeathed his entire estate to "William Edward White, Ann Nora White, and Sarah Adelaide White, the children of my servant, Hannah." According to racial classifications of the time, William was considered a "quadroon," someone who is one-quarter Black. Complicating things, however, was that William identified himself as a white male on multiple census reports. Calling White the first African American baseball player may be accurate based on laws of the time, but socially it's difficult to make that distinction.

There is one missing piece of the puzzle that could cement this case further. According to the *Chicago Tribune* article, White played well in the game, and it is known that Joe Smart, the man he filled in for, missed a significant amount of time. The next game was three days later in Boston, and White did not play for the team. A plausible theory is that White's lineage was discovered, and he wasn't permitted to play anymore. For now, that is just one unconfirmed theory among others.

In 1908, African American player and scholar Moses Fleetwood Walker authored a pamphlet titled *Our Home Colony*. In it, Walker traces African American history to that point with the ultimate thesis that African American people should consider returning to Africa to populate a "colony of their own." Walker wrote,

> What Negro parent can have the audacity to hold up before his beloved son the possibility of ever becoming president of the United States? Or even a United States senator? If his son is mechanically inclined, how can he stimulate and satisfy his ambition by promising to place him in any of the great machine shops of the land, or on a locomotive engine on the numerous railroads of the country?

In writing about the lack of opportunities for societal advancement among African Americans, Walker failed to include the profession of Major League Baseball player. It is a topic that he would have been fully qualified to speak on, as it was Walker, not Jackie Robinson, who was the first African American to openly play in the major leagues. Unlike William White, who lived his life as a white man, Walker did not and could not hide his identity. White's complexion and 75 percent white parentage gave him the opportunity to claim to be white in social situations, even if he was considered African American by law. Walker also was of mixed race, but his dark complexion left no doubt that he was a Black man. So, when Walker and his brother Weldy played for the Toledo Blue Stockings of the American Association in 1884, they became the first players to openly embrace their African heritage as Major League Baseball players.

The opportunity almost never came to pass, as a year earlier, Walker was the target of the supremely talented, but viciously racist Hall of Famer Cap Anson. Anson's Chicago White Stockings team was scheduled to play an exhibition game against Walker's Toledo team on August 10, 1883. Walker was a star catcher, known for his excellent defense behind the plate and adequate offensive game. In March of that year, a motion was presented to the Executive Committee of the Northwestern League by a member of Peoria's team to bar African American players from the league. The motion was voted down, allowing Walker and a small handful of other African American men to play in the league. By the time Walker's squad was set to face off against Anson's team, the Chicago star tried to take a stand.

As was typical of catchers of the time who did not wear a glove, Walker had a sore catching hand, and it is believed that Toledo manager Charlie Morton didn't want Walker to catch in an exhibition with a hand injury. Morton allegedly planned on holding him out of the game. Anson did not know this and protested Walker's place in the game. After learning of this, Morton entered Walker into the starting lineup in center field as a means of protest against Anson. The game was delayed for an hour while Anson and Morton argued about Walker's participation. Eventually, Morton declared that if the game was canceled, Anson's team would forfeit their share of the game's gate. With no way around this, Anson ordered his team to the field and competed against Morton's Toledo squad.

The incident was well documented in the *Toledo Daily Blade* and painted a picture of acrimony in Anson. The article also celebrates Morton's stand and notes that Walker had the support of the people of Toledo as well. This incident happened less than 20 years after the end of the Civil War and showed the respect Walker carried among those who were familiar with him; however, Anson's stature in the game carried tremendous weight, and he had the support of many. In 1884, Toledo and Chicago were set to play again. By this time, Toledo had joined the American Association, which was considered a major league at the time. For this game, Anson demanded advanced notice that Walker would not play in the game.

Walker didn't play in the game, allegedly due to injury. He was plagued by injuries in 1884, his only season in the majors, and he hadn't played the three previous games, so it is not out of the question that this injury was legitimate; however, it is also plausible that pressure from Anson kept him out of the game, even though the defiant Morton was still manager of Toledo. Walker played in 42 of the team's 104 games in 1884, and his brother appeared in five games that season. The White

Stockings disbanded after that season, and Walker never had another chance to play in the majors, taking a job as a mail carrier instead.

Anson's influence on baseball segregation has been debated. There is no question he refused to play against African Americans multiple times, and there are written accounts of him using horrendously racist epithets; the debate lies in just how influential Anson was. There are no accounts of leaders citing Anson as their motivation for segregation. While he was undoubtedly an influential player-manager, the real power and fault in the segregation of the International League lies with the owners. After the incidents between Anson and Walker's teams in 1883 and 1884, participation of African Americans in the high minor leagues actually increased.

While there were no additional African American players in the majors after Walker, there were seven African Americans playing in the International League, which was the highest level of Minor League Baseball at the time. On July 14, 1887, in the face of growing numbers of African Americans playing, owners of the teams in the International League brought forth a vote on the future of integrated baseball. The owners voted six to four to ban future contracts for African American players in their league. The six teams who were all white were the ones to approve the measure, while the integrated teams all voted against it. African American players like Frank Grant, George Stovey, Bob Higgins, and Walker were allowed to remain, but no new players could be signed. Although the vote was not part of recorded league business, it existed as a "gentleman's agreement" from that point onward. Other high-level leagues and the major leagues followed suit, and a segregation line was drawn, informally on record but steadfast in practice.

BASEBALL'S WHITE ERA

The Syracuse Stars were a fledgling team in the International League in 1887, when management attempted a bold move to boost the team's production. Ownership signed seven players from the Southern League, which had folded after the 1886 season. The group of Southerners and their racial prejudices made the trip north, and while it may have seemed like a good plan to infuse the team with new talent, it ended up drawing a deep divide within the roster. The former Southern League players banded together to influence who would manage the team before the season started, and when games began, the Southerners sabotaged the performances of players who were not part of their group. The team atmosphere was so toxic that manager Jim Gifford resigned on May 17, to be replaced by "Ice Water" Joe Simmons.

Simmons had managed current Syracuse player Fleet Walker the year before in Waterbury and was familiar with many talented African American ballplayers who many teams wouldn't consider signing. In an attempt to bolster his roster, Simmons's first move was to sign Robert Higgins, a left-handed African American pitcher who was 19 years old. Not only was Higgins a talented pitcher, but also he was promoted as an adept hitter and speedy baserunner. Considering the rift already in place and the large influx of Southerners on the team, it's no surprise that this move was akin to throwing a lit match into a powder keg. In Higgins's first start, the Southern players on the Stars intentionally botched numerous plays throughout the game to make him look bad. The Stars lost, 28–8, with 21 of the runs being unearned.

Coverage of the game was plentiful considering the era, and publications castigated the Stars for their play behind Higgins. The *Toronto World* newspaper ran a headline that simply read, "Disgraceful Baseball," and *Sporting News* ran an article under the headline, "The Syracuse Plotters; the Star Team Broken Up by a Multitude of Cliques; the Southern Boys Refuse to Support the Colored Pitcher." A Syracuse reporter even went as far as to call the Southern League players the "Ku-Klux coterie." Whether it was the well-earned backlash from the media and fans or the stewardship of Joe Simmons, the subsequent games in which Higgins pitched were played squarely. The next problem came when the Stars were set to take their team picture. Many players bristled at the idea of being in the team photo with Higgins, but almost everyone lined up for the photo anyway. Two players, Henry Simon and Doug Crothers, flatly refused to be in the team photo, leading to a physical altercation in which Crothers punched his manager.

The team photo incident was also covered by the media, and Crothers attempted to explain himself in an interview. Crothers said,

> I don't know as people in the North can appreciate my feelings on the subject. I am a Southerner by birth, and I tell you I would have my heart cut out before I would consent to have my picture in the group. I could tell you a very sad story of injuries done my family, but it is

personal history. My father would have kicked me out of the house had
I allowed my picture to be taken in that group.

Crothers was initially suspended for the season, reinstated two weeks
later, and then ultimately released two weeks after that. Simon faced no
punishment for refusing to sit in the team photo, partially because he was
one of their top players and also because he did not punch his manager.

While the Stars were drowning in controversy in 1887, the Newark
Little Giants were dominating the International League thanks in large
part to pitcher George Stovey and catcher Fleet Walker. Although professional baseball was two decades old, Walker and Stovey comprised the
first African American battery in professional baseball history. The Little
Giants won the International League title in 1887, on the strength of
Walker's leadership and Stovey's masterful season, in which he went
35–14 (sometimes debated as 33 or 34 wins), with a 2.46 ERA.

Still reeling from the mess of the 1887 season, the Stars hired Charlie
Hackett away from the Little Giants to manage them in 1888. Despite the
racial unrest, Higgins was asked back to the Stars in 1888, and in an
attempt to protect and mentor the young Higgins, Hackett brought the
respected Walker over to the Stars from the Little Giants. Walker's presence and popularity with fans helped subdue the outward racial hatred of
his teammate, but it did not fully eradicate it. Despite going 17–7 in 23
starts (reported in 1888, by *Sporting Life*, as 20–7) through the first half
of the 1888 season, Higgins eventually tired of the racial strife and left
professional baseball altogether before the season ended. Walker remained and helped the Stars to the International League title. Walker
returned in 1889, and had built up a fantastic reputation in the town and
among fans. He served as a team spokesman and leader, and was a popular figure in the Syracuse business community. His play on the field was
not up to his typical standard, however, and Walker was released on
August 23, 1889. No African American would appear in an International
League game again until a 27-year-old Jackie Robinson joined the Montreal Royals in 1946, after batting .414 for the Kansas City Monarchs of
the Negro Leagues the season before.

BLURRED LINES

By all accounts, Charlie Tokohoma was an outstanding ballplayer who played at the turn of the twentieth century. In fact, some opined he was one of the best of his era. He was a well-rounded second baseman and a deft baserunner, and had the leadership acumen to be named team captain on one of his teams. He even led his 1896 squad to a championship. The reason he is a nearly unknown blip in baseball history is that Tokohoma only existed for a short period of time. In actuality, Charlie Tokohoma was Charlie Grant, star second baseman for the Columbia Giants, a professional all-Black baseball team that predated the Negro Leagues. But briefly in 1901, Grant was on the cusp of becoming the first African American baseball player to break the understood color barrier of Major League Baseball.

Prior to a 30-year stint as manager of the New York Giants that would land him in the Hall of Fame, John McGraw helmed the Baltimore Orioles for two seasons in the newly formed American League. It was during that time that the first documented interaction between McGraw and Grant occurred. There is plenty of conjecture about how Grant and McGraw became acquainted. Grant was the star of a popular barnstorming team in the late 1800s and a well-known player in those circles. McGraw could have known him from those games and conceivably even played against him. Hall of Fame player-manager Clark Griffith could have also played a role. He was a player for the Chicago Colts and Chicago Orphans during the same time when Grant was starring for the Columbia Giants in Chicago. It is well documented that Griffith attended many all-Black baseball games and was likely very familiar with Grant. It is also known that Griffith was in Hot Springs, Arkansas, at the same time as McGraw and Grant when the plan was hatched. The logical explanation could be that some preexisting relationship or knowledge brought McGraw and Grant together, and that Griffith, at a minimum, had knowledge of the situation.

Famed sports columnist Bill Bryson Sr. relayed a folksier story of Grant and McGraw in his column in the *Des Moines Tribune* on July 6, 1962. Allegedly, McGraw traveled to Hot Springs to scout potential baseball players when he saw a group of African American men playing baseball. The group consisted of employees of the Eastman Hotel, and Grant was among them. McGraw was widely known as a person who would bend (if not break) baseball rules, and he used his expertise in finding loopholes to try to get Grant onto his team.

The story goes that McGraw knew Grant had the talent to play in the majors and met with him in the Eastman Hotel lobby. McGraw told Grant that he wanted to sign him for his team, but African American players weren't allowed in Major League Baseball. At some point in that lobby, McGraw was looking at a map and noticed the Tokohoma Creek, a name with a clear Native American etymology. McGraw then decided that Charlie Grant, the great African American second baseman, would become Charlie Tokohoma, the mysterious Native American ballplayer. Although African American players were banned from playing in the major leagues, Native Americans were not. Louis Sockalexis, a Penobscot Indian from Maine, was teammates with Cy Young on the Cleveland Spiders from 1897–1899, and although he faced discrimination, American Indians were not outwardly banned the way African Americans were. In fact, Sockalexis was a celebrated athlete who did nothing to hide his American Indian heritage. McGraw figured that Grant's lighter complexion and straight hair could help in passing him off as a Native American, and the two moved forward with their plan.

Dave Wyatt, another African American ballplayer, later worked as a sportswriter and claims the idea of Tokohoma originated with him. Wyatt knew McGraw and Griffith, and in an article he wrote in the *Indianapolis Freedom* on February 19, 1910, Wyatt claimed he approached one or both of the men with the idea of passing off Grant as an American Indian to get him into the major leagues. Wyatt also cautioned that many major leaguers, including influential Hall of Famer Roger Bresnahan, knew exactly who Grant was, so it would be difficult to pull off. Wyatt wrote,

> Grant was one of our greatest baseball players. Some years ago, he accompanied the writer [Wyatt] to Hot Springs, where we hatched a plan to better the condition of colored players. I placed the same before McGraw, whom I knew personally. We manufactured [a name]— Grant-a-Muscogee.

According to Wyatt, however, a different newspaper reporter heard of the plan to sign the mysterious American Indian superstar and reported that his name was Tokohoma. If Wyatt's version is to be believed, the reporter overheard a conversation about the plan of a player named Grantumuscoge from Tokohoma, mistook his name as Tokohoma, and ran with the story. Whatever the origin was, the subsequent details are a little clearer. McGraw signed Grant and billed him as a "full-blooded Cherokee Indian from Oklahoma." The signing was well-publicized for the time and drew the attention of fellow major-league managers and administrators.

McGraw moved forward, and word spread about Grant. The *Baltimore Sun* mentioned Grant in an article on March 10, 1901, just six weeks before Opening Day. The article focused on the brooding conflict between the American League and National League before they were combined to form the major leagues. The article segued into a discussion about the Orioles preparing for the season. It mentioned that team captain Wilbert Robinson and some players were working out at Johns Hopkins to prepare for the season, to be "in form to keep pace with the manager [McGraw] when he appears with the Cherokee Indian player Grant."

Two weeks later, the *St. Louis Post-Dispatch* mentioned Tokohoma again, this time in more detail. In an article under the header "Current Sporting Comment," Tokohoma is referenced as a "utility man signed by the impresario McGraw for his Baltimore American Club." The article continued, "He is an Indian, whose previous career on the diamond is not familiar to St. Louis fans." The article theorized that Tokohoma may be used as a utility man but also speculated another use for Tokohoma that painted a picture of the cartoonish ways Native Americans were viewed during that time. The article suggested that Tokohoma would "possibly do war-dance stunts on the baselines when his fiery little chief [McGraw, who was player-manager at the time] is at the bat or on the bases." This didn't seem to be a tongue-in-cheek suggestion either, as the paragraph ended by intimating that Tokohoma could "fill the interesting role of mascot."

The article continued and drew parallels between Tokohoma and Sockalexis, who had been out of baseball for two years at that point. The interesting part is that there was no hint whatsoever that this was all a ruse. The *Post-Dispatch* article imagined Tokohoma's popularity among fans and compared his potential to that shown by Sockalexis during his short career.

> But whatever his part, he is destined to become conspicuous in the baseball world if he holds his job. The small boys in the bleachers will at once develop a particularly friendly interest in him, call him, "To-

kie, old boy," and direct him every time he steps to the plate to make a "homa."

For the sake of other noble red men who contemplate deserting the reservation for the ballpark, his tribe earnestly hopes Tokohoma will eschew the picturesque precedent set by that other famous Indian, Sockalexis. Tebeau trotted out that reformed man of the blanket and head feathers as right fielder on his star Cleveland team, and, for a time, he threatened to put Willie Keeler and others "out of business." But firewater was his undoing, and "Socks" has been permanently wiped off the baseball map.

As far as records show, the scheme lasted a few more days before suspicions were raised, most notably by Charles Comiskey, the Hall of Fame owner of the Chicago White Sox. On March 30, the *Topeka State Journal* reported that Comiskey claimed that "Indian Grant" was African American. Grant still tried to play along, however.

According to the article, Grant insisted that his mother was a Cherokee Indian and his father a white man. He said his mother lived in Lawrence, Kansas, and that McGraw can get proof that he is "Indian and white-bred." The article concluded by declaring that Tokohoma was set to play second base on Opening Day, which was now less than three weeks away.

Whether it was Comiskey's charges, Clark Griffith's probable knowl-edge of the situation, or, as Dave Wyatt claimed, the idea that many major leaguers already knew of Grant based on his play for the Columbia Giants, McGraw relented and didn't include Tokohoma on his Opening Day roster; however, it appears that McGraw had a change of heart a month later. On May 20, the *Baltimore Sun* interestingly reported that Charlie Grant had been ordered by McGraw to report to Boston, where Baltimore had been playing a series against Cy Young and the Boston Americans. This time, however, there was no attempt to masquerade Grant as a Native American. The press release was straightforward, casu-ally mentioning his fleeting identity as Tokohoma, but didn't reference any controversy about McGraw adding an African American to his roster. The release did say there was ongoing discussion as to whether Grant was Native American or African American.

The exact date of the transaction isn't known, but circumstances relat-ed to Baltimore's game against Boston on May 17, could have provided a clue. While Baltimore was in Boston, American League president Ban

Johnson issued a suspension of McGraw for five games. In the previous series against the Philadelphia Athletics, McGraw argued vehemently with umpire John Haskell. Some accounts said that McGraw tried to stamp on the umpire's feet, causing McGraw, who was the team's starting third basemen, to get tossed from the game. Two innings later, Baltimore pitcher Crazy Schmidt was ejected by Haskell, causing McGraw to return to berate Haskell once again. It was after McGraw's suspension that the Orioles attempted to sign Grant, most likely as McGraw's replacement. Grant never did officially report to the Orioles. There are no records as to what kept Grant from replacing McGraw in the lineup, but one can surmise the league put an end to that idea just about as quickly as it was hatched.

The bizarre plans to have Grant play for the Orioles on two separate occasions possibly marks the closest any African American ballplayer came to appearing in the major leagues in the decades between Moses Fleetwood Walker and Jackie Robinson. That is, unless you believe claims that some African American players were snuck into the league under the guise of being Cubans.

Baseball in Cuba is said to date back to at least the 1860s and has remained a passion among Cubans ever since. The United States and Cuba have had a reciprocal baseball relationship dating as far back as 1899. John McGraw frequently visited Cuba while scouting, and many American professionals played winter ball in Cuba since the advent of the major leagues. The first documented Cuban to play professional ball in the United States was Esteban Bellan, who played for the Troy Haymakers in the National Association (the precursor to the National League) in 1871 and 1872, well before the color line was drawn. The color line wasn't so much broken in one fell swoop by Jackie Robinson. More accurately, it was eroded away in the years before Robinson shattered it for good. Pitcher Luis Padron was asked to try out for the Chicago White Sox in 1909, and that was where the lines started to blur.

The complexities involving racial heritage in the United States and Cuba were inconsistent, so ballplayers fell into different categories depending on where they were playing. In the United States, players were categorized by what was colloquially known as the "one drop" rule, which stated that if there was any African American ancestry in a person's lineage, a person was considered African American. "One drop" referred to the idea that if a person had "one drop" of African American blood, he or she should be considered African American, no matter how light or dark that person's skin was. In Cuba, however, they used a spectrum, as people fell into different racial classifications based on skin color. So, a person in Cuba with African ancestry and light skin was treated differently than a person with African ancestry and dark skin.

The big difference in baseball in the two countries when it came to race was that in early Cuban baseball, every race were permitted to play professional ball, while African Americans were barred from playing amateur ball. In the United States, when the color line was drawn, if a person had any African ancestry, they could not play. That started to change when Cubans and Latin Americans began to get opportunities in the majors. Participation rules started to change, and the color of a player's skin started to play a role, in addition to his ancestry. Padron was a light-skinned left-handed pitcher who could also play the outfield.

He is a member of the Cuban Baseball Hall of Fame and was well-known during his playing days. But his potential track to the major leagues is unclear and inconsistent. At the very least it is known that Padron played for the New Britain Base Ball Club in 1908. An article from the *Springfield Republican* from July 24, 1908, gives some insight into Padron's case but also that the idea of color line was still on the collective minds of the baseball world.

The seemingly innocuous resignation of the Connecticut League treasurer prompted coverage by the *Springfield Republican*, and while that was the focus of the story, it was the fallout of that resignation that is important to historians. The article announced that P. H. Prindiville resigned from his position and would be replaced by early baseball legend and Hall of Famer Jim O'Rourke. The article then stated that league business was on hold, including the case of Padron's ethnicity.

There is nothing in the winds just now to stir up the league directors to meet. Even the question of the race of pitcher Padron of New Britain has been dropped. The league officials say that Padron's color was never a subject of talk at the league meetings, and they claim there is nothing to indicate that there will be a discussion of the point. It is ticklish to business to bring up racial talk—a fact which the directors recognize. Padron may be a Negro, as many players and fans claim, but such an expert as James H. O'Rourke does not know of any written baseball law that would deny a negro the right to play. Of course, there is an understanding that Negroes will not be hired to play in organized leagues, and sentiment is strongly against the Black man in league baseball. If Padron is a Negro—and this has not been proved—he is the first to play in the Connecticut League. Mr. O'Rourke says that in his years of experience he has heard of but one man in league baseball, Grant, who was believed to be a Negro.

The fact that league officials seemed blasé about Padron's race might be the first evidence that there was a grey area developing when it came to the color line. It is acknowledged that fans and players have made claims that Padron was African American, and the "gentleman's agreement" understanding is referenced as well; however, despite the topic clearly gaining attention, league officials didn't want to pursue an investigation. Whether it was because of the "ticklish situation" regarding racial discussions or Padron's playing ability, league officials were fine with him playing in the league. In July 1908, the *Hartford Courant* reported that Dan O'Neil, the manager of the Springfield club in the league, angrily protested that he was going to pursue a ban on Padron at an upcoming league meeting. Apparently, Padron had beaten Springfield's club twice, and O'Neil was not happy about that. Likewise, manager Allie Paige, who had been fired by New Britain just prior to this, claimed he completed his own investigation and found that Padron was not a Cuban. But Paige made this revelation after he was fired by New Britain, and his argument did not carry much weight. The matter was never formally introduced at the meeting, and Padron remained in the league for four seasons.

Jim O'Rourke's involvement is interesting as well. O'Rourke was one of the first players from baseball's earliest days to be inducted into the Hall of Fame and was considered an icon at the time. O'Rourke's career as a player began less than a decade after the end of slavery, and he was a widely respected leader throughout his career. O'Rourke was also known as a civil rights supporter and even signed Harry Herbert to play for the Bridgeport Victors in 1895. Herbert was the first African American player to play professionally for Bridgeport and was with the team for four seasons. It is known that O'Rourke had progressive views for his era, so it is not surprising that he saw no fault in Padron's participation and was dismissive of the color line.

On July 23, 1909, the *Chicago Tribune* reported that Padron tried out for White Sox player-manager Billy Sullivan. Three days later, the *Washington Post* reported that Padron was signed by the White Sox, and "under the guidance of Comiskey, the veteran baseballist, there is no doubt but that Padron will be looked upon as a phenom." There were no other reports of Padron signing or reporting to the White Sox, however, so that report is thought to be inaccurate. Instead, it is believed that Padron's ancestry was unproven and Comiskey chose not to sign him due to the pushback he received about the possibility of Padron being of African descent. Padron continued to play professional ball in both Cuba and the United States until 1916. Some of his final days playing were spent toiling in Jersey City, New Jersey, for the Jersey City/Poughkeepsie Cubans in the Independent League. Thirty years later, Jersey City would be the site of a monumental event in the course of racial milestones in the baseball world.

While Padron never got his chance in the major leagues, two of his Cuban teammates on New Britain had similar dreams and, more importantly at the time, lighter skin than Padron. Armando Marsans and Rafael Almeida were young, 20-year old teammates of the veteran Padron on the New Britain Perfectos in 1908. They were considered excellent players in their native Cuba and had caught the eye of legendary manager Frank Bancroft, who frequently took teams of professional ballplayers on barnstorming tours in Cuba. Bancroft was considered a pioneer in scouting Hispanic and Latino players. Years before Marsans and Almeida were on Bancroft's radar, he was manager of the Providence Grays in 1884. Bancroft's first year as manager happened to be the year of Old Hoss Radbourn's famous 60-win season. Perhaps the second-most historically significant player on that team was backup catcher Sandy Nava, who is believed to be the first player of Mexican descent to play in the majors.

Bancroft recommended Marsans and Almeida to the Reds as early as February 1911. A surviving letter from Almeida to Reds president August "Garry" Herrmann from February lists his uniform measurements, showing that the process of bringing Almeida and possibly Marsans into the fold was in place long before the season started. On June 16, 1911, the *Norwich Bulletin* reported that the Cincinnati Reds had purchased Marsans and Almeida from the New Britain Perfectos for $7,500. The article made mention that Marsans and Almeida had established themselves as stars in the league and referenced that they played winter ball in their native Cuba.

Two weeks later, a widely published national press release stated that Almeida and Marsans reported for duty with the Reds and mentioned that the two would be the first two Cubans to be signed by a major-league club. On July 4, Marsans and Almeida made their debut in the first game of a doubleheader against the Chicago Cubs. In an 8–3 loss, Reds manager Clark Griffith emptied his bench, including Marsans and Almeida, as the Cubs' lead grew. Marsans and Almeida both went 1-for-2, and Marsans even batted against Hall of Famer Three Finger Brown, grounding out to Joe Tinker, another Hall of Famer, for the last out of the game. Coverage of the game in the *Cincinnati Enquirer* and *Chicago Tribune* didn't make any mention of the cultural significance of their debut, but renowned sportswriter Harry Neily did tackle the subject in an opinion piece in the *Butte Daily Post.*

In an article titled "Baseball to Lower Color Line," Neily wrestled with the topic of baseball's color line being blurred. His subheadlines read, "Signing Two Cuban Players Step Toward That End" and "Whites Only in the Past." The article doesn't come out in favor of or against Marsans and Almeida, but it does provide insight into the issue as it happened. It starts by declaring, "Clark Griffith has signed two Cubans, who may or may not be part Negro." Neily further explained that Cuban culture is complex because some Cubans have African descent, while others have Spanish descent, and that Cuban lineage is difficult to track. Interestingly, Neily examined the hypocrisy of baseball and the players who uphold ethnic restrictions. He pointed out that some of the major leaguers who speak out in favor of the color line will then go off to Cuba to play in the offseason with and against African Cubans. He even identified Ty Cobb as someone who was fine with segregation in the major leagues while then going to Cuba in the offseason to make money playing against Cubans and African Americans. In addition, Neily wrote that the Cuban teams had plenty of Black players from the United States who were posing as Cubans.

Neily also reiterated the "gentleman's agreement" and that "there has never been any legislation against the black man in baseball, but it has always been understood that no Negro should play in the major leagues." Neily then considered a more diverse league and wrote in favor of it.

> The addition of the gentlemen of color from Cuba adds zest and variety to the national pastime, regardless of how much it helps the poor old Reds. We now have red men, yellow men, white folks, and Black men, in conjunction with a few very green ones who stroll up from the bush

leagues. All of which goes to show the cosmopolitan aspect of base-ball, as well as everything else in this great and noble country.

However, just as it seemed Neily would come out in support of the Cubans, his concluding paragraph called for Cincinnati owners to "inquire diligently" if Almeida and Marsans were Spanish Cubans or African Cubans. He then commented that African Americans are permitted to be stage actors but aren't allowed in the grand opera and opined that baseball cannot afford to "let the bars down."

In addition to Marsans and Almeida, 16 other Cubans played in the major leagues between 1911–1929. By the end of the 1929 season, 31 Native Americans had also played in the majors, including popular Hall of Famer Chief Bender, legendary athlete Jim Thorpe, and Pepper Martin, one of the leaders of the champion Gashouse Gang Cardinals teams of the 1930s. The participation of Native American, Cuban, and Latino players in the majors divided fans. Some were fine with nonwhite players participating, no matter how dark or light their skin was, as long as they weren't African American.

Nonetheless, there was a more vociferous sentiment that baseball should remain "whites only," causing the minorities to face taunting, discrimination, lower salaries than their white contemporaries, and segregation. Even the highly successful Bender was the frequent subject of racist caricatures in news publications and racist remarks from fans, opponents, and even teammates. At the time, referring to a Native American as "Chief" could be construed as a derogatory epithet, even if history shows that Bender embraced the moniker. Interestingly, Bender's long-time manager, Connie Mack, always referred to him by his middle name, Albert, in a sign of respect by the iconic skipper. No matter what side of the debate people were on regarding nonwhite players playing in the major leagues, both sides had one thing in common: They agreed that the major leagues should be closed to African Americans.

2

PUSHING AGAINST THE COLOR BARRIER

THE FIRST STEPS TOWARDS INTEGRATION

Buck O'Neil, the irreverent Negro League legend, is one of the great baseball ambassadors in the game's history. A captivating speaker, O'Neil was always able to paint a picture, create a mood, and uplift the spirits of anyone who listened to him speak on baseball. For a man who did a lot of public speaking in his 94 years, perhaps his most poignant line came during one of the most solemn times of his life. O'Neil gave the eulogy at the funeral of his friend, Negro League legend Satchel Paige, in 1982. He has told the story many times and the exact wording of his line changed from time to time, but the sentiment always remained the same. As O'Neil tells it, after the service, a reporter was reminiscing about Paige and said to O'Neil, "It's a shame Satchel didn't get to play against the best baseball players in the world." O'Neil responded with five powerful words in his calm voice: "Who's to say he didn't."

In the 1930s, the United States was experiencing a time of economic crisis. The Stock Market Crash of 1929 spurred the Great Depression, plunging the U.S. economy into a decade-long abyss. In every corner of the United States, people suffered mightily. As families struggled to put food on the table, disposable income evaporated from American society and attendance at Major League Baseball games plummeted. Baseball had been enjoying a tremendous popularity boom throughout the 1920s, thanks largely to the celebrity of Babe Ruth and other great stars of the era. The United States became a playground during the Roaring Twenties as the economy blossomed in the post–World War I era. Such pop culture and technological developments as radio, the automobile, aviation, and the telephone ushered in a new world. This made things more depressing when it all came crashing down in 1929.

As one would expect, the accompanying attendance crash at major-league stadiums caused the sport to struggle like every other industry in the United States. Attendance throughout baseball dropped 13 percent for the decade compared to the 1920s, and for the entire 1933 season, the average attendance at major-league ballparks was less than 5,000 per game. Teams struggled to find creative ways to stay in business, with the Depression hitting minor-league parks first. The Independence Producers, a Class C team, installed lights on their field and played the first professional, organized night baseball game on April 28, 1930. The idea caught on quickly in the minor leagues, as it made it possible for fans with daytime jobs to go to a game to escape their problems at home for a few hours. On May 24, 1935, Major League Baseball played its first night game at Crosley Field, as the Reds beat the Phillies, 2–1. The most important stat of the game was attendance, which was more than 25,000. The Reds played eight night games in 1935, one against each team in the National League, and as a result, their average attendance rose 117 percent from 1934. Sometimes the best innovations are born through crisis.

Teams did everything they could to earn money. Some teams began to sell broadcasting rights to their games to radio stations; the Cubs started "Ladies Night," allowing women into the games for free; and the Cardinals expanded their farm system and used those clubs to generate money to support the major-league team. The first All-Star Game and the opening of the Major League Baseball Hall of Fame also happened during this decade. There was no shortage of legends who played in the 1930s as well. Babe Ruth, Lou Gehrig, and Lefty Grove were the stars at the advent of the decade, and by the time it was over, they had passed the baton to Joe DiMaggio, Ted Williams, and Hank Greenberg. For all the change and innovation, however, one thing remained the same. Owners still refused to sign African American ballplayers, and it wasn't for a lack of candidates. The owners remained stubborn in excluding African Americans, even if it meant that it would have brought an influx of African American fans and their money to their ballparks. Just as Babe Ruth ushered in the 1930s for Major League Baseball, Satchel Paige and Josh Gibson did the same for Black baseball. Iconic innovator Rube

Foster led Negro League baseball through the early part of the twentieth century, the first golden era of organized leagues and teams featuring African Americans; however, as with the major leagues, the Depression had a major effect on the Negro Leagues, and teams began to collapse. When it was announced in March 1932, that the Negro National League would fold, professional Black baseball seemed doomed. A new Negro National League formed in 1933, and it would not only survive the decade, but also last through World War II before being absorbed by the Negro American League in 1948, after Major League Baseball integrated.

Barnstorming was a way for professional baseball players to make money and promote their sport outside of their regular season whether they were Black or white. The earliest roots of barnstorming date to at least the 1860s, when the Brooklyn Excelsiors toured New York state, bringing the sport to many towns that had only read about it in newspapers. It became a popular practice through the closing decades of the nineteenth century and gained even more notoriety in the 1920s when Babe Ruth became a popular barnstorming attraction. In the era before television and radio, the only way a majority of the country learned of Ruth's mythical exploits was through articles in newspapers and magazines, and some silent newsreels, if they were lucky. Ruth's incredible ability and playful nature were perfect for the traveling exhibition of barnstorming, as the pressure to win was much less significant than in the major leagues. Ruth and Lou Gehrig's barnstorming tour of 1927, featuring the famous "Bustin' Babes" against the "Larupin' Lous," is perhaps the most well-known barnstorming tour in baseball history among white players. But if Kenesaw Mountain Landis had his way, it never would have taken place. He began enforcing a rule that had been on the books since 1910, against barnstorming. The rule tempered barnstorming but didn't end it. If players played offseason games after the rule was in place, it was up to the individual teams to discipline their own players, and most owners just looked the other way—that is, until Landis came to power.

Landis was known as a strict federal judge before he was named commissioner of baseball in 1920, in the wake of the Black Sox Scandal. That same year, Rube Foster formed the Negro National League in addition to the barnstorming tours that had already been taking place. Landis thought barnstorming would devalue the World Series. To that point, the World Series was billed as the grand culmination of the baseball season.

In the eyes of owners and the commissioner, barnstorming was also considered postseason play, which meant that the World Series wasn't a culmination, it was simply just another postseason series. Owners also cited the risk of injury to players as a reason against barnstorming. Moreover, there was a sentiment that major-league ballplayers losing to barnstorming teams would "cheapen" the major-league brand. In an editorial in the *Evening Star* in Washington, DC, written on January 16, 1910, and titled "Barnstorming Hurts Standing of Clubs," the writer reported that Pittsburgh Pirates owner Barney Dreyfuss asked his team to cancel a postseason barnstorming trip. It was written that many times, pitchers would play the outfield and other players would play out of position, risking injury. Also, while the highly paid superstars may not be playing and some nonprofessionals would fill spots, the team was still billed as the "Pittsburgh Pirates," and subsequent headlines about them losing to minor-league and independent teams was embarrassing.

When Landis took office, he threw down the gauntlet on barnstorming. One of the first to test him was a 25-year-old Babe Ruth and Yankees teammate Bob Meusel. Ruth and Meusel ignored Landis's threat of suspension, but that just provided the new commissioner an opportunity to establish his power right at the start of his reign. When Ruth laughed off Landis's threat and played in a short tour following the 1921 World Series, Landis responded by suspending Ruth and Meusel for the first six weeks of the 1922 season. Ruth returned after his suspension, and by July of that season, the barnstorming rule had been softened. The new rule allowed barnstorming for players who weren't involved in the World Series. Players who participated in that year's World Series could barnstorm with permission of their team president and the commissioner. With Landis's position softened, Gehrig and Ruth took their tour west of the Mississippi River in 1927, after their "Murderers' Row" season, and it was wildly successful. While the tradition of barnstorming wasn't new, the success of the 1927 tour further popularized the practice and whet the appetite for baseball fans nationwide. Barnstorming teams led by Ruth, Bob Feller, Dizzy Dean, Satchel Paige, and Jackie Robinson came to diamonds for the next two decades but lost popularity after integration and amid growing radio and television coverage.

While Ruth and Gehrig's 1927 tour was an offseason hit, barnstorming baseball in the pre–World War II era is most associated with Negro League players and teams. Typically, Negro League teams would barnstorm through the Midwest during their offseason, and the general reception of fans when the teams came through stood in contrast to the racism African Americans faced in society during that time. It wasn't uncommon for a Negro League team to go into an all-white Midwest town and beat a group of local white players in front of white-dominated crowds. Sometimes after the games, fans and promoters would even hold dinners with the players and fans as a means of celebration and appreciation. But when players ventured into town to eat dinner or look for a place to stay, they faced the same racial roadblocks as other African American people of the time.

Monte Irvin, a Hall of Famer who was able to bridge the gap playing in both the Negro League and the major leagues, recounted a story from his barnstorming days. In the book, *Invisible Men: Life in Baseball's Negro Leagues*, author Donn Rogosin relayed a story from Irvin during his time barnstorming with the Newark Eagles. The Eagles made a stop in Birmingham, Alabama, looking for some refreshments, but the owner of a café stopped them before they could even enter the establishment. According to Rogosin, Irvin interacted briefly with the café owner, who had told them they couldn't enter.

"Why are you saying 'no,'" asked Irvin, "when you don't even know what we want."

"Whatever it is, we don't have," she responded.

"Won't you sell us some soft drinks, some Pepsi-Cola or Coca-Cola?" he asked again.

"No," she said bluntly.

"How could she hate us so?" he lamented. "She didn't even know us."

No matter how much the players may have been cheered during the games, they were still treated like second-class citizens when they returned to everyday life. As unfair and disgraceful as the players were treated, Negro League barnstorming remained highly popular among players and fans. Aside from being starved for professional baseball, fans of the towns where the tours stopped were struck by the dynamic way the Negro League stars played the game. Satchel Paige, Cool Papa Bell, Josh Gibson, and so many others were supremely talented and knew how to put on a show. Their brand of baseball was exciting and aggressive, their athleticism was always on display, and major-league players took notice.

Pepper Martin, the colorful shortstop for the St. Louis Cardinals, turned in what John McGraw called the "greatest individual performance in the history of the World Series" in 1931, and Martin attributed this to playing against Negro League teams while barnstorming. The Philadelphia Athletics had won the previous two World Series and were heavy favorites to capture a third against the Cardinals in 1931. The Athletics were led by Connie Mack and featured five Hall of Famers, including the great Jimmie Foxx and pitchers Waite Hoyt and Lefty Grove. By and large, the Athletics outplayed the Cardinals, holding them to a .205 team batting average, but Martin was the difference. The firebrand shortstop batted .500 in the series while stealing five bases. Martin stretched singles into doubles, ran the bases with aplomb, advanced around the bases on sacrifice flies, and executed squeeze plays throughout the series. In an article in the *Pittsburgh Courier* in 1939, Martin communicated his inspiration for his rousing play.

> In the latter part of 1930, I was playing with a group of All-Stars which included Diz Dean, Paul Dean, and a number of other big-leaguers, and we had a game with the Kansas City Monarchs. We were winning the game 4–1 in the last of the ninth. The colored team came to bat three runs behind, and we were sure of victory; however, the first man up got a hit, and then it was on. The man on first streaked for second just as our pitcher threw to the batter. The batter laid one down the first-base line and beat it out.
>
> The man who had streaked for second went all the way to third. From that time on, they drove us nuts. Every man that got on ran like they were wild around the bases, and they finally won, 5 to 4. That aggressive type of ball, the type that Ty Cobb always advocated, impressed me, and I made up my mind right then that I would play that type of ball in the majors. I did it all that next season and throughout the World Series against the Athletics.

Major leaguers played with and against African American players throughout the height of barnstorming in the 1930s and 1940s, and more often than not, the Black ballclubs topped the white teams. Hall of Famers like Ruth, Gehrig, Dizzy Dean, and Bob Feller had some of the more popular barnstorming teams of that time, and their games against Negro League stars were widely successful. They played games in Brooklyn's Dexter Park, Yankee Stadium, and just about every place in between. No matter if it was a public park or major-league stadium, fans came out to see the games, sometimes in larger numbers than for major-league games.

Most accounts say that the Negro League players and major-league players got along cordially, even if they didn't socialize after they left the ballpark.

Dizzy Dean, who for years teamed with Satchel Paige to form a widely popular barnstorming rivalry, was one of the high-profile exceptions. Dean's shoddy, double-speak vocabulary, a dumbed-down version of the folksy Yogi Berra, was often littered with every racial epithet one could imagine and some he likely invented himself. In one barnstorming game, Dean was so appalled that Clint Thomas of the New York Black Yankees stole home against him that he chased him out of the ballpark and protested wildly that the umpire blew the call intentionally. He also threatened physical harm to the home plate umpire. Dean, who dropped out of school in second grade while growing up in rural Arkansas during the era of the Jim Crow laws, knew no other way of acting.

In an article in the *Brooklyn Daily Eagle* on October 18, 1934, Dean recounted his incident against the Black Yankees, saying he baited the runner into trying to steal home.

"I invited him in," said Dean. "I see him coming, and then when he's on his way, I fog that ball in with plenty to spare. He is out a mile, but that crooked umpire beat us. Can you imagine that? That is the first home that was ever stoled on me, and one of them Black Yankees has to do it."

THE *PITTSBURGH COURIER* SURVEY

Work, integrity, tact, temperance, prudence, courage, faith. These are some of the words that can be used to describe people like Jackie Robinson, Roy Campanella, and Hank Aaron; however, they held even more weight four decades before Robinson debuted for the Brooklyn Dodgers. Those were the words emblazoned on the masthead of the *Pittsburgh Courier*, a newspaper for the African American community established in Pittsburgh in 1907. The *Courier*, which ran weekly until 1966, was one of the most influential newspapers of the twentieth century, as it reported on news that was widely ignored or misrepresented by mainstream white newspapers of the era. The paper covered mostly African American issues and accomplishments, and reached a circulation of more than 350,000. The issue on October 7, 1961, was released six days after Roger Maris broke Babe Ruth's home run record, a feat that drew intense media coverage nationwide. There was one baseball article in the four-page sports section on October 7, and it discussed the possibility of Frank Robinson winning the National League Most Valuable Player (MVP) Award, which he did two months later. There was no mention of Maris breaking Ruth's record. This was not the place for that.

In 1939, the *Courier* ran a fascinating series examining the sentiments of Major League Baseball players regarding the possible integration of their sport. The *Courier* interviewed prominent players, managers, and coaches of the eight National League teams and published their findings, along with player remarks, during a two-month stretch in the summer and fall of 1939. It is perhaps the most extensive look at the opinions of the baseball world at that time when it came to integration. The paper promoted the series as the "most exclusive, startling, and revealing expose of the major-league players and managers themselves, ever written," and the *Courier* was right. Everyone interviewed believed that the stars of the Negro Leagues were good enough to play in the majors, and many commented that they would have no issue if they did. This included the managers that were interviewed as well.

The project was spearheaded by legendary writer Wendell Smith, who would recommend Jackie Robinson to Branch Rickey as the best candidate to integrate the major leagues less than a decade later. Fittingly, the Brooklyn Dodgers were the first team featured, and manager Leo Durocher spoke with the most conviction of those surveyed. Pictures ran on the page of the seven Dodgers who were interviewed, with Durocher scoring the largest photo and his own headline. The simple headline above the grainy photo read, "'I've seen a million'—Leo Durocher," and was taken from the first paragraph of his interview. In full, the quote read, "I've seen plenty of colored boys who could make the grade in the majors. Hell, I've seen a million!" Durocher continued,

> I've played against some colored boys out on the coast who could play in any big league that ever existed. [Satchel] Paige, [Bill] Perkins, [Mule] Suttles, and [Josh] Gibson are good enough to be in the majors right now. All four of them are great players. There are plenty of colored players who should be in the big leagues right now; however, that decision is not up to the managers. Personally, I have a liberal attitude toward the Negro ballplayer. I certainly would use a Negro ballplayer if the bosses said it was all right.

Durocher's strong statement was not only echoed by the players he managed on the Dodgers, but also repeated weekly throughout the entirety of the series. Dolph Camilli, the popular star who would go on to win the 1941 National League MVP, was equally complimentary, especially when it came to Satchel Paige. Camilli said, "I played against Satchel Paige out on the coast, and I think he's as good as any pitcher in the majors. He threw the fastest ball I ever looked at." Camilli was someone who batted against eight different Hall of Fame pitchers, notably Carl Hubbell and Dizzy Dean, whose fastball was said to approach 100 miles per hour.

Pitcher Luke Hamlin echoed those sentiments.

"I also played against Satchel Paige, and he could have made it any day of the week," said Hamlin. "I swear, I don't see how in the world he could throw a ball so fast. They say you can't hit 'em if you can't see 'em. Which means that Paige doesn't have a worry in the world. Very few batters see his fastball when he lets it fly."

Other Dodgers rattled off familiar names of other stars they felt would be successful major leaguers. Tuck Stainback named Paige, Mule Suttles, Cool Papa Bell, Felton Snow, Sam Bankhead, and Pullman Porter. Chuck Dressen, who was a coach with the Dodgers and played for the Cincinnati Reds in the 1920s, spoke of some of the earlier Negro League stars. He named Oscar Charleston, Martin Dihigo, and Cristobal Torriente among the best and said, "They were good enough to play in any big league that ever existed."

The next entry in the series confirmed the thoughts expressed by the Dodgers. The following Saturday, the *Courier* published the results of their interviews with players on the Chicago Cubs. Manager Gabby Hartnett, a Hall of Fame catcher who spent 19 seasons with the Cubs starting in 1922, grabbed headlines when he declared that there would be a "mad scramble" to sign Negro League players if they were permitted. Hartnett's extensive interview not only listed some players he thought could succeed, but also gave additional insight on the topic within his ballclub. After stating that Rube Foster and Smokey Joe Williams were two of the "best ballplayers who ever lived," Hartnett admitted he hadn't seen many of the current top Negro League stars because he was too busy managing, hunting, and fishing. He did, however, say that his players spoke frequently about Josh Gibson and Satchel Paige. Hartnett said that the day before he was interviewed, the Homestead Grays and New York Black

Yankees played a night game at Forbes Field, and many of the current Cubs took the day off to go watch the game. They came back the next day raving about Josh Gibson.

Dizzy Dean relayed a story about playing against a team of Negro League All-Stars with his team of major leaguers. Dean, who also said that some of the toughest games he ever played were against Negro League teams, commented that his team of big-leaguers didn't think they stood a chance against the Negro League All-Stars. When the major leaguers ended up winning the game, Dean said they felt like they "accomplished something." Wendell Smith relayed a story to Dean about the immortal Walter Johnson, who proclaimed that Josh Gibson was a better catcher than Bill Dickey and would be worth a $200,000 salary if he was in the majors. Dean, the uneducated Hall of Fame Southerner who was known to use racist terms liberally, concurred that Gibson was worth the salary, which would have been astronomical at the time.

Perhaps the most interesting part of the Cubs interviews was that they took place while the players were in the stands as fans watching the Grays play the Black Yankees. Smith not only got to interview them on their opinions, but also was able to report about their behavior and fan reaction during the game. Smith wrote that at one point, a foul ball landed in the stands next to the Cubs players, and they stopped the fan who caught it so they could examine the ball. They concluded that it was the same ball they played with in the majors, as if they expected it to be altered in some way to allow for longer home runs or more movement on pitches. Smith also reported that the crowd was about 90 percent Black, and when they recognized the Cubs stars, they mobbed them for autographs until the crowd became too large, forcing them to leave.

The Cardinals feature came the following week, and if any city was going to contrast the flowery comments of the Cubs and Dodgers, it would likely be St. Louis. At the time, Sportsman's Park in St. Louis was the only stadium in the majors that still had segregated seating. Smith described St. Louis as a "metropolis of Dixie that lives by Southern tradition." Pepper Martin and Daffy Dean were the only two players interviewed, as was manager Ray Blades.

Like most respondents, Blades lauded Paige, Charleston, and Gibson, saying that Charleston was one of the best ballplayers he'd ever seen. Blades said he played against the early Negro League star in the 1920s and "declared right then that he was good enough" to play in the major leagues. While those thoughts were common among the players inter-viewed, Blades gave further insight as to what was keeping these players from playing in the majors, despite the players and managers wishing they could. Blades put the onus directly on the league's owners.

Blades concluded that there is "no doubt that there are plenty of Negro players capable of playing major-league ball, and a number of them would be outstanding stars. But as yet the owners have not seen fit to put any of them on their teams." Smith wrote that all eight managers inter-viewed blamed the owners for keeping African American players out of the majors. The manager said, "It is not up to the managers or players but up to the men who pay out their salaries. We are hired to win a pennant. That is not a problem for us to decide on." Blades didn't seem optimistic that would happen anytime soon, especially in St. Louis. He was asked when he thought the game would integrate, and his response was sobering in comparison to the compliments the Negro League players had been receiving.

> I cannot venture to say because I don't know how the owners look upon the question. Right now, I would say the chances are very slim. In that I might even say that they might never be admitted; however, they might change their minds tomorrow and give the Negro players a chance. You know, prejudice and other social factors must be over-come before Negro players are admitted. In St. Louis, for instance, it might be a difficult problem right now because it is a Southern town, and although they seem to be changing slowly, I don't think they are ready for Negro players. Another thing, baseball has survived 100 years without a Negro player, and that alone may convince the owners that it is not necessary to hire him.

Blades's comments may have been deeply discouraging, but they were also informed. In his mind, he thought the bigger social issues of racism needed to be improved upon first before the majors were integrated, and he didn't seem too optimistic that St. Louis was changing fast enough when compared to other National League cities. Smith wrote that atten-dance in St. Louis was feeble, and the town had trouble supporting the Cardinals in the National League and the Browns of the American League. By integrating one of the teams, it would bring an influx of fans to the park. Blades circled back to the existing racism in St. Louis, however. He said, "Before Negro players are admitted I think that the social prejudice that exists right now will have to be broken down."

As the series continued, the chorus from major-league players and managers remained the same. The headline on the Pittsburgh Pirates entry was a quote from Hall of Famer Pie Traynor that read, "No Need for Color Ban in Big Leagues—Pie Traynor." Among those surveyed was Honus Wagner, who was one of the game's biggest stars in the early twentieth century. Wagner was a coach on that Pirates team and was 65 years old at the time. Described as the greatest shortstop of all time in the article, Wagner told the story of hearing about Pop Lloyd and how he was referred to as the "Black Wagner," which prompted the icon to go see him play in person.

Wagner said, "Another great player was John Henry Lloyd. They called him the 'Black Wagner,' and I was always anxious to see him play. Well, one day I had an opportunity to go see him play. After I saw him, I felt honored that they should name such a great ballplayer after me."

In addition to Lloyd, Wagner rattled off six more names of Negro League players he thought highly of. He even claimed that Rube Foster was the "smartest pitcher I have ever seen in all my years of baseball," which at that point was nearly five decades. Wagner wasn't alone in declaring that some Negro League stars were the best they had seen in different baseball capacities. Other Pirates and players from other teams felt the same way. Danny Bell of the Pirates said that Turkey Stearnes was the "best all-around player I have ever seen anywhere." He added, "He was a big-leaguer from every angle." He also described Cool Papa Bell as the "fastest thing that ever stepped on a basepath" and declared that Bell was "so fast it was a shame." Teammate Jack Brubaker concurred, saying that Bell was the "fastest man I have ever seen in baseball." He said that he had seen Bell score from second by tagging up on a routine fly ball and that he "musta' had wings on his feet."

The *Pittsburgh Courier* study gives fantastic insight into many aspects of the color barrier and the power structure of Major League Baseball at the time. The most powerful people in the game at the time were not the players, managers, or front office staff. Even the power of iron-fisted commissioner Kenesaw Mountain Landis likely did not match that of the owners. Everyone had clearly defined roles during this time. Players were at the bottom of the totem pole, and managers were not that much more powerful than they were. In fact, many clubs simply had active players fill the role of manager. The way they saw it, they were hired to do their job, and that was all they did. They couldn't hold protests or demand trades. In the era before free agency, their only real option was to just play baseball for whatever team owned them until that team didn't want them anymore. Then they were traded, fired, or released. Judge Landis may have been the strictest commissioner in the sport's history, but his role was that of rules enforcer. He was named baseball's first commissioner after the Black Sox Scandal in 1919, as someone to clean up the game. The role of commissioner at the time was not to advance the sport or innovate within the sport. He was merely tasked with enforcing the rules that were on the books.

By and large, the onus of perpetuating the ban of African Americans in baseball fell to the owners, and that was clear in the *Pittsburgh Courier* survey. Also clear in the survey was that players and managers in the survey were unanimous in saying that there were many African American players in the first half of the twentieth century who were good enough to play in the majors. The message came across loud and clear among players, coaches, and managers; Buck O'Neil may have been right in his retort to the reporter who lamented that Satchel Paige didn't get to play against the best baseball players while he was in his prime. Paige pitched against Josh Gibson, who many said was the best catcher they had seen; Mule Suttles, who many called one of the best power hitters they had witnessed; and Cool Papa Bell, who was roundly cited as the fastest player to ever play the sport. Paige pitched against players like Pop Lloyd, who Honus Wagner said he was honored to be compared to; he pitched against Cristobal Torriente, Biz Mackey, and Martin Dihigo, who would have been superstars in the majors according to their white peers. The list isn't short by any means. As O'Neil intimated, who's to say Satchel Paige didn't get to pitch against the greatest players to ever play the sport?

THE MURKY ROLE OF JUDGE LANDIS

In 1864, Civil War surgeon Abraham Landis nearly lost his leg to a cannonball in the Battle of Kennesaw Mountain. Two years later, when his son was born, Abraham decided to name him after the place where he almost met his untimely end. Thus, the story of Kenesaw Mountain Landis began. Landis would rise to become one of the most respected judges in the country and was hailed as a hero in 1907, when he ruled against John Rockefeller and Standard Oil in one of the biggest court cases in U.S. history, breaking up their monopoly and setting precedent against future conglomerations. His decisions were swift, and he was viewed as a coldhearted enforcer of the letter of the law. Landis wielded unquestioned power from the bench and carried that authoritativeness to the commissioner's office.

As the person who presided over nearly the entire segregated era of baseball, it is easy to place a large portion of the blame on Landis for perpetuating segregation. If we're going to judge Landis honestly, the best-case scenario was that he was at fault for never challenging the gentleman's agreement and standing up to the stronghold of the owners. At worst, he was complicit in outright keeping Major League Baseball white. At this point, it's up to fans to do their own research and make their own determinations.

By today's standards in professional sports, a commissioner could step in and order teams to operate in a certain way, while also working with the players' associations. Commissioners have almost unilateral power in their sports, but that wasn't the case during Landis's tenure. It's true that there isn't any record of Landis approaching owners about a conversation regarding integration, and in today's society, such inaction would be seen as supporting the status quo of inequality. But trying to answer hypotheticals from the early 1900s using today's standards is not a way to draw accurate assumptions. A common chorus for people who brand Landis as a racist is that he simply could have declared that African Americans were now allowed in baseball and that he could have encouraged teams to sign them. He most certainly could have said that, but the owners of that era were not likely to take him up on his suggestion. It could be assumed that if Landis did put pressure on owners to sign African American stars, the owners could have simply removed him from his office and installed someone else who would temper the subject of integration, which seemed to be gaining momentum in the 1930s. The owners controlled Landis's contract as commissioner of baseball, so a simple vote could have easily removed him from the position while elevating one of the league presidents into the role. If Landis was to challenge segregation, that would have likely been the scenario, but we'll never know because Landis never did attempt to coerce the owners to integrate.

Those are hypothetical assumptions based on the chain of command in baseball at the time. On the other hand, it is feasible to say that Landis could have pressured teams to integrate, and they may have complied. One can picture a scenario whereby if Landis wanted to integrate the sport, he could have used his legal expertise to do so. If Landis could successfully take on John Rockefeller and Standard Oil, it's safe to assume he could have used his legal background to force owners to integrate if he really wanted to. The problem with the power structure at the time was that everyone answered to the owners, including the commissioner.

Landis's legacy on this topic is best described as murky. In his time, he was viewed as someone with liberal beliefs on race relations, and there are multiple instances of his support of African Americans throughout his life. There was an incident in 1938, where Yankees outfielder Jake Powell said in a radio interview that in his offseason job as a police officer, he enjoyed using his baton on African Americans. Landis swiftly suspended Powell for 10 days. In another case in 1942, Dodgers manager Leo Durocher said publicly that he would like to see baseball integrated, but that it was up to the commissioner. Not the first manager to claim this, Durocher was called into a meeting with Landis and then recanted his claim that the commissioner was blocking integration. Landis issued a public statement about his position on integration. The statement read as follows:

> Certain managers in Organized Baseball have been quoted as saying the reason Negroes are not playing in Organized Baseball is that the commissioner would not permit them to do so. I have come to the conclusion that it is time for me to express myself on this important issue. Negroes are not barred from Organized Baseball by the commissioner and never have been during the 21 years I have served. There is no rule in Organized Baseball prohibiting their participation and never has been to my knowledge. If Durocher, any other manager, or all of them want to sign one or 25 Negro players, it is all right with me. That is the business of the managers and the club owners. The business of the commissioner is to interpret the rules of baseball and enforce them.

This was not the only time Landis took this public stance. While he was someone with tremendous power and a strong-willed reputation, it was entirely within his character to rule baseball the way he ruled his bench as a federal judge; strictly as an arbiter of rules. Nevertheless, an argument can also be made that it would have been on-brand behavior for Landis to decree that baseball should integrate. In the Durocher statement and other public comments, Landis remarked that there was no written rule segregating baseball and that if a club wanted to sign African American players, that would be fine by him. What isn't known, however, is what he said behind closed doors. One could speculate that he could have taken a different stance in private conversations with owners. There is no concrete evidence one way or another to corroborate or deny those claims; at this point it is just hearsay.

Bob Kendrick, the highly respected president of the Negro Leagues Baseball Museum in Kansas City, noted the conflict of Landis's actions.

"He had a good relationship with Rube Foster, and it is kind of conflicting from the standpoint that he was so adamant about keeping separation in our sport," said Kendrick.

> Although you could clearly tell that he had a working relationship with Rube Foster and there was a level of respect for these Black athletes, but he wasn't going to allow whatever affinity he might have to move over and across and beyond his hard-line stance on not allowing Blacks into the major leagues, so it is conflicting from that standpoint.

The *Pittsburgh Courier* survey also provides interesting insight into Landis's role in segregation. There wasn't one respondent who blamed Landis for segregation. In addition, the writer who conducted the study, Wendell Smith, never mentioned Landis as the culprit for segregation. Every finger pointed from those interviewed was aimed decisively at the team owners. Those fingers came from various backgrounds as well. There was Wendell Smith, the widely respected and learned African American writer. Current players, both young and old, supported integration, and those who commented mentioned the owners as shouldering responsibility, not the managers or commissioner. Old-timers who played in the early days of segregation, for instance, Honus Wagner and Casey Stengel, also clearly identified this responsibility as falling to the owners. The entire study, coupled with Landis's "Durocher statement," can either be interpreted as a strict case of everyone involved in the sport "staying in their lanes" or a well-crafted situation of everyone "toeing the company line" in a well-orchestrated enunciation of league-wide talking points.

On September 2, 1939, the *Pittsburgh Courier* published its final entry on the investigation into the sentiments of baseball personnel regarding integration. As was mentioned frequently in the series, the managers and players interviewed were unanimous in supporting integration. Smith wrote a short concluding statement on his findings, largely letting the previous extensive interviews speak for themselves. His statement kept with the common theme of laying blame on the owners and did not mention Landis at all. Smith wrote,

> And there you have the opinions and testimonials of the Pittsburgh Pirates, the eighth and last team in this series on the National League. Looking back on the comments made by eight managers and scores of players, it appears that the big-league owners have misinformed the public by stating that their employees would object to Negro ballplayers in the majors. Negro ballplayers deserve a place in big-league baseball. It is time the closed-door policy were done [*sic*] away with and this undemocratic custom of barring Negro players were smashed forever. Open your doors, Mr. Owner, the time has come.

Despite his public stance that there was no written rule, there always was that lingering "gentleman's agreement" in which the owners understood that there should be no African Americans in the sport. Kendrick also brought up another important factor regarding the owners' refusal to integrate. The Negro Leagues were successful and drew thousands of fans to their games. If Major League Baseball would integrate, they would potentially siphon the top Negro League stars, putting the Negro Leagues in serious jeopardy of folding.

"There was no written rule, but the owners were in lockstep," said Kendrick.

> They didn't want this, even though some of them I think secretly did want this. But you can't be the first guy to bring it up because they look at you differently now, which again makes Branch Rickey stand out even more. There had been other owners who wanted to sign Black players. Clark Griffith, who owned the Washington Senators, was watching the Homestead Grays play in his home ballpark and would outdraw his own Senators team. More importantly, he was watching Buck Leonard do these incredible things in his ballpark, and he was watching Josh Gibson hit balls where no mere mortal had ever hit them. It has long been referenced that he wanted to sign Leonard and

Gibson well before Rickey made the move to bring Robinson. But he wouldn't pull the trigger. My speculation is the fact that he was struck by two things. He knew if he signed Leonard and Gibson, his Senators would move instantly into contention; he also knew he would be ostracized too. The question is, "Is it worth the risk I am going to take?"

The second dilemma I think he had was the same mindset that others had: "If I put the Negro Leagues out of business, I am going to take away a source of revenue for me." The Homestead Grays were filling up his ballpark. He's getting a percentage of the gate and in likelihood all of the concessions from those games. That's a pretty significant flow of revenue. By putting the Negro Leagues out, he'd lose that.

The case of Kenesaw Mountain Landis is probably best left for individual interpretation based on the available facts. If someone was to say that Landis's inaction served to perpetuate institutional racism, it would be hard to argue against that. Theories about Landis's public statements serving as a guise for collusion with owners to keep the game integrated can be justified as well. It is curious that not one owner tested Landis's claim that there was no ban and any signing of an African American would not receive pushback from him. The players, managers, and coaches agreed that preintegration Negro League stars absolutely had the talent to excel in the majors, and Landis said publicly that it was fine to sign them. So where is the disconnect that kept the burgeoning movement at bay?

The sentiment expressed in the *Pittsburgh Courier* survey in 1939, was loud and clear: The stars of the Negro Leagues were good enough to help ballclubs, and the players and managers largely wanted them in the league, even if there were plenty who weren't interviewed who did not. For support to be that strong, those beliefs had to be in place years before the *Courier* survey. These weren't just the sentiments of a new age of ballplayer either. While there were many younger players surveyed, there were also veteran baseball lifers, legends of their time like Honus Wagner and Casey Stengel, supporting integration. Fans will never know what would have happened if Landis or the owners were significantly pushed to integrate. There is plenty of blame to be shared for keeping African Americans out of the game, and the main culprits are clearly the owners and Landis. The debate is about how to divide that blame. Is it equally divided between Landis and the owners? Was it Landis as the strong-willed ruler and his years of inaction? Or were the owners so powerful that even Landis couldn't make progress if he wanted to? As fans, all we can do is sift through the evidence and informed opinions, and draw our own conclusions on where the blame lied. And there was plenty to go around.

BUILDING UP TO JACKIE

On August 16, 1942, the Negro Leagues held their 10th annual East–West All-Star Game in front of 50,000 people at Comiskey Park. As usual, the rosters were rife with talent, including Josh Gibson, Satchel Paige, Sam Jethroe, Hilton Smith, Leon Day, and 30 other stars of the Negro Leagues. The East–West games had become wildly popular and held the interest of baseball fans of all races. As they had done in 1939, the All-Stars were set to play two All-Star Games that season. The 1941 game drew more than 50,000 fans for the first time, and looking back, the early 1940s were the peak of popularity for the game.

Building off of the strength of the 1941 game and with the exciting pitching matchup of Leon Day against Satchel Paige, anticipation for the 1942 game was feverish. Unsurprisingly, the *Pittsburgh Courier* led the charge in promoting the game. In an issue that was released two days before it was to be played, the weekly paper provided a preview. The game was billed as a "Dream Game" in the lead headline and described as the "blue-ribbon classic of the horsehide world." In addition to the typical pregame coverage, columnist Wendell Smith continued to bang the drum for the integration of Major League Baseball. Smith wrote that in addition to being a "colossal spectacle," the East–West game was "Negro baseball's answer to owners and managers in the majors who insist[ed] that the time [was] not ripe for the inclusion of sepia stars in the big leagues." Smith also mentioned that the "50,000 spectators is proof enough that the Negro players are tops with the public."

Smith went on to write that there wasn't a pitcher in the majors with more talent than Satchel Paige, and he named seven other players in the prime of their careers who would succeed in the majors. That didn't even include Ray Dandridge, who had recently left the Negro Leagues to play in Mexico, and the legendary Roy Campanella, who had been suspended for playing in an exhibition game without permission. Smith also mentioned that Campanella had been frequently identified for a major-league tryout. The game ended up drawing 45,179 spectators, and Day's East squad topped Paige's West team, 5–2. While the outcome was important to those who played and cheered that day, there was a more important lesson learned based on the context of the times. Eight months earlier, Japan bombed Pearl Harbor and Major League Baseball had already begun to lose stars to the service. Between Pearl Harbor and the time of the East–West game in 1942, the majors had already lost Bob Feller, Hank Greenberg, and other players not in the Hall of Fame. Owners also knew that the United States was likely headed for a lengthy involvement in the war and they would lose more players to the military.

Major-league owners had an answer sitting right in front of them for the inevitable loss of talent that was about to hit their sport. Integration would have given the sport not only an influx of talent, but also a boost in attendance. In addition, it could have helped show that the country was uniting in these difficult circumstances. After all, if white and Black soldiers were both able to fight for the United States in the war overseas, shouldn't they also be able to play ball together on the homestead? Unfortunately, owners tried every other means to make up for the dearth of ballplayers as more and more men were sent off to the war. According to the U.S. Navy, more than 500 major leaguers and 4,000 minor leaguers were forced to put their baseball careers on hold or end them altogether to fight in World War II. Moreover, such Negro League stars as Monte Irvin, Jackie Robinson, Leon Day, Buck O'Neil, and Larry Doby also served overseas.

The lack of talent in the major leagues caused owners to scramble while filling their rosters, as many of the able-bodied men who were also good baseball players were sent overseas. Owners did just about anything they could to fill rosters, except integrating the sport. The St. Louis Browns used one-armed outfielder Pete Gray for the 1945 season. The immortal Jimmie Foxx was coerced out of retirement after two years away from the sport to play for the Boston Red Sox. The Sox even used Foxx as a pitcher for nine games, and he registered a 1.57 ERA against the watered-down competition. Dodgers manager Leo Durocher was so disturbed by his incompetent infield when the team was preparing during spring training 1944, that he activated himself with the intent to play second base that season; however, a broken thumb prevented him from ever taking the field in the regular season. Joe Nuxhall pitched for the

Reds as a 15-year-old; Babe Herman came out of an eight-year retirement in 1945, to play for the Dodgers; and Ben Chapman, who was a teammate of Babe Ruth and Lou Gehrig, came out of retirement and batted .296 in three seasons during the war. Clyde Sukeforth, who was teammates with Deadball Era stars Eppa Rixey and Edd Roush, played in 18 games for the Dodgers in 1945, after an 11-year retirement. Perhaps the most unlikely player to return to the majors during the war was Paul Schreiber, who pitched two games for the Yankees in 1945. Schreiber had last pitched for the Brooklyn Robins in 1923, facing off against hitters like High Pockets Kelly, Frankie Frisch, and Casey Stengel. During the course of his career, Schreiber pitched against players who played as early as 1912 and as late as 1964.

While Major League Baseball owners were trotting out one-armed players, teenagers, and players who had been retired for years, such players as Satchel Paige, Buck Leonard, Hilton Smith, and Willie Wells were still left out. Aging Negro League stars like Josh Gibson, Cool Papa Bell, Martin Dihigo, and Mule Suttles were past their prime but still active during the war years. Even if they didn't produce the way they did during their prime, they likely would have been better options than many of the players teams turned to. At the very least, they would have created a buzz throughout the league and likely would have drawn fans of all races, eager to see these Negro League legends integrate the sport. There were also many lesser-known Negro League players who would have been better options to fill a lineup. So, while such Hall of Famers as Ted Williams, Joe DiMaggio, Stan Musial, Yogi Berra, and hundreds of other players were absent from the majors, it became evident that owners were ready to try anything to put teams on the field, except integration.

As Major League Baseball navigated the landscape of wartime in the mid-1940s, Kenesaw Mountain Landis's term as commissioner of baseball was waning. Now in his late 70s, years of tireless work had started to take a toll on the elderly Landis. The 1944 World Series was a landmark event, as the sad-sack St. Louis Browns represented the American League as one of the most unlikely pennant winners of all time. The frequently ridiculed Browns were perhaps the team least affected by the exodus of ballplayers into the military, as their roster often featured older players. Their 1944 infield was dubbed the "all-4-F infield," as their main starters all had received 4-F designation from the U.S. military, meaning they were physically unfit for service. The Browns took on the crosstown rival

Cardinals, who still featured Stan Musial, as he didn't join the service until 1945. While the Cardinals dismantled the Browns in six games, Landis was battling an illness and missed his first World Series since taking office in 1920.

Landis never recovered and died about six weeks after the end of the World Series. His obituary hailed him for his "fairness and as a man who always gave the underdog a break." That did not apply to Negro League ballplayers looking to break into the major leagues. Interestingly, the *Pittsburgh Courier*, which frequently covered Landis and his actions as baseball's commissioner, did not report on his death, despite the fact that it was major national news. Landis was mentioned in two articles immediately following his death. An article on December 9, reported that Leslie O'Connor, who was acting as commissioner in the wake of Landis's death, "would not go out of his way to force the issue on Negroes in the majors," saying he would handle the subject diplomatically, the way Landis did.

A second article ran the next week and was an interesting take on Connie Mack's thoughts on integration. Although he's one of the legends of the sport, the iconic manager was often seen as one of the old-guard segregationists who upheld the gentleman's agreement for decades. He was asked about the possible integration of baseball in the aftermath of Landis's death. While Mack acknowledged that the war was causing society to progress quicker, he maintained that integration was up to the owners and thought it would only happen by mutual consent of each owner. Mack's opinions were reflective of the time in which he began in the sport: at the dawn of segregation. Aside from the inferred reference to the gentleman's agreement, Mack also pondered whether Negro League players really wanted to play in the majors. He cited a comment that Satchel Paige made about integrating baseball not being the aim of the race, ignoring the countless other instances of Negro League players saying they would like a chance.

Notable in the article was the mention of a storied African American amateur athlete who made headlines at the University of California, Los Angeles (UCLA) and was returning from the war with the idea of possibly seeking a professional baseball tryout. Jackie Robinson was a multisport star at Pasadena Junior College and UCLA from 1938–1940, with football being his main sport. Robinson pursued a football career immediately after college, but that was put on hold in 1942, when he was drafted into the U.S. Army. Robinson served two years and was discharged on November 28, 1944, three days after Landis died. Mack was asked specifically about Robinson and the possibility of him playing in the majors, three years before he would be the one to integrate the sport. Mack deflected the question, but it was interesting that Robinson was mentioned. At that point, there were already many capable Negro League stars who had much more experience than Robinson. At the time of the article, Robinson hadn't even debuted in the Negro Leagues and was known better as a football player.

Landis's passing did not induce integration or an instant influx of Negro League players, which again points a lot of the blame for segregation at the owners. If Landis was the lone person responsible for segregation, it would be logical to assume that when he was gone, owners would sign the players that could help their teams rather quickly. While Landis's death may not have directly led to immediate integration, at the very least, it was the first domino to fall in the process toward breaking through the color barrier. Kentucky senator A. B. "Happy" Chandler was tabbed as Landis's replacement from a diverse field of candidates that included at least seven other strong candidates, notably National League president Ford Frick and even J. Edgar Hoover. Although Chandler was not known as a baseball man by any means, he supported the continuation of baseball during the war, and his strong political connections were valued by the baseball world as uncertainty remained about the sport's future during the war.

By May 1945, Chandler had been officially on the job for seven months, and the topic of integration remained at the forefront. Chandler did not make his stance on integration public at the onset of his tenure. Instead he handled the topic with a political answer you'd expect from a high-ranking official. Chandler agreed to a roundtable meeting and stated publicly that everyone should have an equal chance, but he was diplomatic in his full comments. In an interview, Chandler addressed the topic, stating the following:

> I am not sure the Negroes know where they favor [integration] into the major leagues, but this is a free country and everybody should have an equal opportunity. It does not follow, however, that by sitting two men down, side by side, that you're giving them equal opportunities. I know nothing, from fact, of any discrimination against Negroes in the big leagues. There is no rule against them. On the other hand, nobody

can guarantee that they can make the grade. That's a matter of their own ability.

Chandler's mixed message was difficult to interpret. He questioned whether African American players were good enough to play in the majors if they even wanted to and toed the tired old position that there was no written rule. He also feigned ignorance about discrimination in the sport; however, it was encouraging that he frequently communicated his stance that everyone should have equal opportunities in the country. His willingness to have formal discussions on integration was also a small step in the right direction. At the same time Chandler made his statement, Yankees president Larry MacPhail addressed rumors that a committee was being formed to explore integration. The committee would potentially consist of a representative from the American League and a representative from the National League, a Major League Baseball writer, a respected figure in the Black baseball community, an African American baseball writer, and a nationally known person to represent the public's interest.

With the suggestion of a committee, coupled with Chandler's promise to hold a roundtable discussion in the future, momentum seemed to be crawling in the right direction. That didn't stop MacPhail from throwing cold water on the situation. MacPhail was strongly against integration, and whether his feelings were based in finance or racism, it didn't matter. As president of the Yankees, MacPhail carried a lot of power among owners, and he made no secret that he was against integration. In a 1945 letter to a committee formed by New York mayor Fiorello LaGuardia to explore integration, MacPhail laid out his thoughts.

MacPhail wrote, "There are few, if any, Negro players who could qualify for play in the major leagues at this time. A major-league player must have something besides natural ability." He continued to belittle Negro League ballplayers and the Negro Leagues in the letter.

They are not even primarily interested in improving the lot of Negro players already employed. They know little about professional baseball—and nothing about the business end of its operation. They have singled out Organized Baseball for attack because it offers a good publicity medium for propaganda. When they charge that Organized Baseball is flying a Jim Crow flag at its masthead and that racial discrimination is the basic reason for failure of major-league clubs to employ Negro players, they are talking through their collective hats.

MacPhail's statement is ignorant on multiple levels. It had already been established that players and managers, the real baseball experts, felt that many Negro League players could already play in the majors and that some of them would be among the best players in the sport. As egregious as MacPhail's claim was, his statement that players knew nothing about the business end of baseball operations was ignorant, and he didn't have to look any further than his own colleagues for proof. The Negro Leagues were one of the most successful African American businesses in the country at the time, rivaled only by the African American insurance industry. Some Negro League teams were also more profitable than major-league teams they shared cities with. For example, while the Washington Senators were a struggling major-league franchise during the 1940s, the Homestead Grays remained successful, easily outdrawing the Senators while playing in their stadium. Senators owner Clark Griffith relied on the success of the Grays and the money he made on rent and concessions to keep his Senators afloat. That wasn't uncommon practice in major-league cities. In fact, in his own letter to LaGuardia, MacPhail cited this principle in a starkly hypocritical paragraph. He wrote,

> Organized Baseball derives substantial revenues from operation of the Negro Leagues and wants these leagues to continue and to prosper. Negro League clubs rent their parks in most cities from clubs in Organized Baseball. The Yankees organization alone nets nearly $100,000 per year from rentals and concessions in connection with Negro League games at Yankee Stadium in New York and at Kansas City, Newark, and Norfolk.

Whether MacPhail's motivation for questioning integration was social or financial, the fact remained that even with a change in the commissioner's office, there were still obstacles to overcome with the owners. In his letter, MacPhail also proposed assisting the Negro Leagues in becoming more organized in a similar fashion to Major League Baseball. While the Negro Leagues drew fans well and featured fantastic players, the league still admittedly needed work on its infrastructure. That was the position the major leagues found themselves in as Happy Chandler took office. They could integrate the majors, which would result in the eventual col-

lapse of the Negro Leagues, ending the cash pipeline major-league owners enjoyed from them renting their stadiums. On the other hand, they
could make the Negro Leagues stronger in the hopes that they would
flourish and ultimately make more money for the stadium owners who
rented their stadiums out for games.

Owners discussed helping the Negro Leagues develop a minor-league
system, formalizing a more structured schedule, putting restrictions on
barnstorming, and developing a better system for umpires who worked
the games. They felt the Negro Leagues should have standard bylaws and
contracts for their players. Essentially, the major-league owners wanted
the Negro Leagues to model their operating procedures to truly flourish.
In the major-league owners' eyes, if the Negro Leagues became more
structured and popular, it might quell the push to integrate the majors and
make it easier for them to uphold the gentleman's agreement.

On September 29, 1945, Wendell Smith wrote a retort to MacPhail's
letter in the *Pittsburgh Courier*, calling out the Yankees president for his
hypocrisy. Smith's column featured the headline, "Larry (The Mouth)
MacPhail Double-Talks," and it exposed the charade that owners were
trying to help the Negro Leagues be more successful. Although Smith
exonerated Clark Griffith of the Senators and Bill Benswanger of the
Pirates, he itemized how the other teams were trying to make every last
dime they could through their rental agreements with Negro League
teams, especially the Yankees, Tigers, and Cardinals owners. Smith mentioned that Negro League teams had to give as much as 40 percent of the
gate to major-league teams when using their stadiums. In addition, they
were charged the costs for policemen, park employees, advertising, seat
dusters, and any other place they could squeeze the Negro League teams
for money. Smith ended the article with a message to his readers: "So,
friends, don't let Larry MacPhail and others of his ilk make you believe
they are giving Negro baseball a real fair shake, because they're not. It's
nothing but MacPhail 'double-talk'!"

While MacPhail probably thought he was making a significant pitch to
keep baseball segregated, the truth was that no matter what he wrote in
his letter to Fiorello LaGuardia's Committee for Unity, it was going to be
completely fruitless. About six weeks earlier, Branch Rickey had held a
secret meeting with Jackie Robinson that resulted in an agreement that
Rickey would sign Robinson as the first African American Major League
Baseball player since Moses Fleetwood Walker. The meeting was the

culmination of a covert operation by Rickey to integrate the Dodgers. Although the meeting was held on August 28, Rickey wanted his intentions to remain a secret until November 1, when they would have a formal signing and press release. Ultimately, the date was moved up, and Robinson signed his deal with the Montreal Royals, a Dodgers minor-league affiliate, on October 25, 1945.

Most of the details of Branch Rickey's secret process for integrating baseball were exposed after the fact, most by Rickey and Robinson themselves; however, in 1987, sports historian John Thorn made an incredible discovery in storage at the Baseball Hall of Fame. Thorn, who would become the official baseball historian for Major League Baseball in 2011, found hundreds of motion-picture frames of Jackie Robinson and two other African American players (Herb Souell and Buster Haywood) working out at Lane Stadium in San Diego on October 7, 1945. The three players wore the uniforms of the Kansas City Royals, the barnstorming team of Negro League players they played for that was in Southern California for games against local all-star teams in the Los Angeles area. The *Pittsburgh Courier* published the results of the games but nothing of the workout in San Diego.

The discovery of the photographs and Thorn's further research filled some holes and provided further insight into what was commonly known about the final stages of Robinson signing with the Dodgers. Rickey claims to have intended to integrate the Dodgers when he was first hired by the club in 1943. Previously, Rickey had been general manager of the St. Louis Cardinals from 1919–1942. He claimed that he was prevented from integrating the Cardinals because St. Louis was considered a Southern baseball city and was perhaps the least ideal place to begin integration. The city was still strictly segregated at the time; the Cardinals still had segregated seating in their park while Rickey was there. Even in Wendell Smith's *Pittsburgh Courier* survey in 1939, members of the Cardinals communicated that while they supported integration, St. Louis was probably not the place to start.

Rickey's plan was intricate when he was finally able to put it in motion. A number of events came together to open the door for Rickey to move forward. Those events included the death of Kenesaw Mountain Landis, the end of World War II, and the signing of the Quinn-Ives Act in March 1945, which banned discrimination in hiring practices in New York. Rickey had maintained that he notified the Dodgers upon his hiring that he intended to integrate, even if the then-commissioner, Landis, was against it. He had kept Robinson on his radar for years, but he wasn't the only one Rickey was considering.

Rickey's larger plan was to have at last three African American players integrate the sport at the same time, assuring that no one person had to deal with all the pressure himself. Rickey was so protective and secretive of his plan that he created an elaborate ruse so that no one would stand in his way. Rickey's support of integration was known, and with the subject of breaking the color barrier a bubbling topic in the postwar baseball world, the staunch supporters of segregation had to dig in their heels if they wanted to keep African Americans out of baseball. If any of them discovered Rickey's plan, he was sure they would step in and delay or stop him. The dilemma was that Rickey needed to scout African American players to make sure he chose the right person or persons for the job. If it was discovered that he was sending scouts to Negro League games, it would raise suspicion.

Rickey claimed he was starting a Negro League franchise called the Brooklyn Brown Dodgers in the newly established United States League to play games at Ebbets Field when the Dodgers were on the road. This would allow him to openly scout African American players without drawing any attention to himself. Rickey kept the secret so close that even the players he was scouting and holding tryouts for believed they were trying out for the Brooklyn Brown Dodgers. Rickey paid scouts thousands of dollars to scout Cuba and Mexico, and even paid a fee to establish the Brown Dodgers. This is tied together with information found by John Thorn in the wake of his discovery of the film of Robinson's workout in San Diego with two teammates.

In preparation for the coverage of Robinson's eventual signing, Rickey collaborated with writer Arthur Mann for a feature to be published in *Look* magazine once it became official. Thorn was able to connect the footage to the article, which provided some unconventional insight. While the article never ran, it did show that the story we know about Robinson was likely incomplete. The most surprising point discovered in the piece was that Rickey intended for at least Don Newcombe and Sam Jethroe to join Robinson. It was likely that he intended for others to join the trio too, most notably Roy Campanella. In early October 1945, with Robinson's announcement looming, Rickey met with Newcombe, Campanella, Roy Partlow, and Johnny Wright. Campanella and Newcombe have both stated that they fully believed they were meeting to be a part of the Brown Dodgers. After those meetings, Rickey reached out to Mann asking to delay the publication of his article. Rickey wrote,

> We just can't go now with the article. The thing isn't dead—not at all. It is more alive than ever, and that is the reason we can't go with any publicity at this time. There is more involved in the situation than I had contemplated. Other players are in it, and it may be that I can't clear these players until after the December meetings, possibly not until after the first of the year. You must simply sit in the boat.

As fascinating as that is, Rickey also brought up additional points in his letter to Mann. He mentioned that Robinson's contract had a November 1 signing date, and he wanted to extend that until January 1, so he could sign other players. He also mentioned that it might not be a good idea to sign Robinson alone with "other and possibly better players unsigned." Rickey expressed a desire to Mann that his article should reflect the integration of baseball accurately, and his article about Robinson alone would not do that. The reason Mann was asked to write the article in the first place was because Rickey wanted to control the narrative about the process and reasons for integrating.

Rickey's expanded plan for integrating with a group of players fell apart quickly, the victim of the New York political scene. With elections looming in November, politicians were beginning to make the integration of baseball a topic in their election. Rickey had been working on integration for years and was now at the precipice of finally doing it. The longer Rickey waited, the more momentum the topic would gain on political platforms, and once the elections were over, the elected politicians could have likely continued the push. When integration finally happened, it would have appeared that baseball caved to political pressure, and Rickey did not want that narrative.

In mid-October, Mayor LaGuardia contacted Rickey to ask for permission to make a statement that as a result of the work he had done with baseball's Committee for Unity, "baseball would shortly be signing Negro players." Rickey asked LaGuardia to delay his comments and then had Robinson report to Montreal to sign his contract shortly thereafter. Robinson signed with the Montreal Royals, a Dodgers minor-league affiliate, that day, as the sole person set to integrate baseball. Rickey's plans to integrate with a group of players fell victim to the rush he made to keep integration out of the political world.

3

BREAKING THROUGH

INTEGRATING MAJOR LEAGUE BASEBALL

On October 23, 1945, less than two weeks after the Detroit Tigers beat the Chicago Cubs to win the World Series, Jackie Robinson signed his contract with the Montreal Royals of the International League. The signing was headline news and widely covered by the media outlets. The *Baltimore Sun* was particularly extensive in covering Robinson's signing. Their coverage began on the front page of the paper with news of the signing and then spilled over to take up much of the front page of the sports section with further insight and feature stories. Rickey tackled the racial issues of signing Robinson in his comments. He acknowledged that he would receive criticism, especially from some sections of the country, but stood by his decision, saying that Robinson was a "fine type of young man, intelligent and college-bred." Robinson was typically soft-spoken and dignified in his comments. Robinson said, "Of course, I can't begin to tell you how happy I am that I am the first member of my race in organized ball. I realize how much it means to me, to my race, and to baseball. I'm very happy over this chance, and I can only say I'll do my very best to come through in every manner."

Initial public reaction from throughout baseball was generally supportive, with the New York Giants declaring that day that they would start scouting the Negro Leagues. Giants team president Horace Stoneham said that signing Robinson was a "really fine way to start the program." He said he would begin scouting the Negro Leagues for younger prospects that year but also expressed concerns about finding places for players returning home from the war to play. Clark Griffith, who had been in baseball since 1891, also brought up a point that had been bandied about in debates about integration. Griffith and others of that time wondered if the major leagues were interfering illegally with players who were under contract in the Negro Leagues.

Upon Robinson's signing, Griffith said,

> The only question that occurs to me is whether organized ball has the right to sign a player from the Negro League. That is a well-established league, and Organized Baseball shouldn't take their players. The Negro League is entitled to full recognition as a full-fledged baseball organization.

This wasn't an attempt to stop or slow Robinson's signing; this was a legitimate concern of people in the Major Leagues and the Negro Leagues.

Somewhat surprisingly, T. Y. Baird, coowner of the Kansas City Monarchs, agreed with Griffith and stated his concerns loudly. Robinson had played the previous season for Baird's Monarchs. He said, "We won't take it lying down. Robinson signed a contract with us last year, and I feel that he is our property. If Chandler lets Montreal and Brooklyn get away with this, he's really starting a mess."

Hall of Famer Eddie Collins, who was the general manager of the Red Sox, was less than enthusiastic with his comments. Collins teamed with his friend, Red Sox owner Tom Yawkey, to strongly oppose integration in the years leading up to Robinson. Even after the Dodgers integrated and other teams followed, the Red Sox were the last team to follow suit. In his comments following the Robinson signing, Collins alluded to a "tryout" that has since become infamous, and his general position on African Americans in the majors always leaned toward segregation. Collins said, "Robinson worked out for us last spring. Very few players can step into the majors from college or sandlot baseball. Of course, they always have a chance to prove themselves in the minors. More power to Robinson if he can make the grade."

The tryout Collins referred to happened in April 1945, and it was a farce from the beginning. Boston city councilman Isadore Muchnick teamed with Wendell Smith to pressure the Sox into holding a tryout for African American players. Muchnick wielded political power and threatened to withhold the Red Sox and Braves permits to play home games on Sundays in Boston unless they held a tryout. The Sox invited Robinson, Sam Jethroe, and Marvin Williams to try out in front of management at Fenway Park to appease Muchnick but with no intent to sign any of them. Robinson said in a 1972 interview, "We knew we were wasting our time. It was April 1945. Nobody was serious then about Black players in the majors, except maybe a few politicians."

The *Montreal Gazette* understandably covered the signing extensively, as Robinson would be playing in their city come the spring. Legendary Canadian sportswriter Dink Carroll addressed some topics that other sportswriters didn't mention in their coverage of Robinson's signing. As integration inched closer, the general chorus was that players and managers would have largely been fine with it and it was the owners who would take issue. Carroll took a different stance. He opined that those "close to professional baseball" said that hostility toward African American players didn't originate with the owners but with the players themselves. While it is true that there were players who were outwardly racist during the era of segregation and spoke out against playing with or against African Americans, the consensus was that it was the owners who were keeping the sport segregated. According to Carroll, owners were worried that white players wouldn't sign with their clubs if they were integrated. Rickey echoed those sentiments in his comments, acknowledging specifically that players from the South may not want to sign with Brooklyn. While he may have been concerned about that, at no point did he consider that a stumbling block for his plan. Rickey also acknowledged that some white players may even quit integrated teams but said they'd come crawling back to the sport after spending a year or two trying to earn a living as a working man.

The Canadian Carroll also tackled the hypocrisy that baseball was viewed as "America's national game" despite the fact that it kept an entire race of its citizens out of the sport for decades. Carroll wrote,

> Many Americans have criticized Organized Baseball for drawing the color line and have argued that it couldn't truly be called America's national game because of this discrimination. They consider it only simple American sporting justice that Negro players be admitted to organized white baseball leagues.

Carroll also touched on Rickey's comments that Japan had used baseball's segregation and overall discrimination as propaganda during World War II to show that Americans were not a united force. Carroll proposed that integrating the sport and ending discrimination at home would motivate and galvanize U.S. forces as they fought overseas. While African American soldiers faced plenty of discrimination during the war, the fact was that they were qualified enough for the government to draft them into war but not qualified enough to play Major League Baseball.

Nearly a year later, sportswriter Sam Maltin described a wild scene that occurred at Delormier Stadium, the home of Robinson's new team, the Montreal Royals. On October 4, 1946, Maltin wrote that Robinson was chased by a crowd, was grabbed at, had clothes torn from his back, and was blocked from packing his gear. Police and stadium ushers were called in to assist but to no avail. The crowd chased him out of the stadium and through the streets. This wasn't, however, a display of petulant racists protesting Robinson's position on the team. These were the actions of a joyous crowd, celebrating a man who had become the city's hero during the baseball season, which had just culminated with the Royals winning the International League championship. Maltin postulated that "it was probably the only day in history that a black man ran from a white mob with love instead of lynching on its mind."

While Robinson's only season in Montreal ended on an incredible athletic high note, its beginning was much different. As Robinson prepared for his first spring training, he and Branch Rickey knew he was about to face the inevitable. The Dodgers held spring training in Daytona Beach, and Robinson's journey from California with his new wife, Rachel, was going to take the couple through the Deep South for the first time. Rachel Robinson described the way they were treated as "horrendous." Among the indignities Robinson suffered were being forced to give up his seat on two separate flights to white men, being forced to sit in the back of buses, and being disallowed to dine with or stay at a hotel with his teammates. Famously, Robinson was selected as the player to integrate the sport because Rickey felt he had the demeanor to incur this racism without the furor inside him exploding. Rickey's assessment was accurate, but holding in his anger took a physical toll on Robinson both in the long and short term.

Robinson endured a long month in Daytona Beach at the Dodgers spring training, but he didn't let it affect his play on the field. Robinson stood out and proved that he was capable of playing at this level, and Branch Rickey was there to witness it all. Rickey wrote extensively during his decades in Major League Baseball, and his work survives to this day. Colloquially known as the Branch Rickey Papers, the collection includes scouting reports, correspondence, and journal entries on his experiences in the sport. In one section, Rickey discusses a spring training interaction he had with Clay Hopper, manager of the Montreal Royals. Paraphrased, Hopper claimed Robinson (and other African Americans) shouldn't even be considered a human being based on his skin color. Hopper was a staunch racist who was born in Mississippi in 1902, and Rickey never made the comments public; however, the story came out in the Branch Rickey Papers.

Although he didn't want any part of managing Robinson, he really had no choice. By the end of the season, after Robinson led the Royals to the title, garnering Hopper a Manager of the Year Award, he changed his tune. Rickey wrote the following of Hopper's turnaround in the course of the six-month season:

> Six months later [Hopper] came into my office after the year at Montreal when he was this boy's manager. He didn't want him to be sent to him. And he said to me, "I want to take back what I said to you last spring." He said, "I'm ashamed of it." "Now," he said, "you may have plans for him to be on your club,"—and he was, "but," he said, "if you don't have plans to have him on the Brooklyn club," he said, "I would like to have him back in Montreal." And then he told me that he was not only a great ballplayer good enough for Brooklyn, but he said that he was a fine gentleman.

When Robinson reported to the Royals for the start of the season, he went north with a talented squad that would end the season with a record of 100–54. Of the 35 men who played for the Royals that season, 22 of them eventually made the major leagues, although none became stars the way Robinson did. Robinson manned second base and led the team with a .349 batting average in 124 games. His double-play partner was Al Campanis, who would go on to build the great Dodgers teams from the 1950s through the 1970s during his career as a scout and general manager. Campanis was a protégé of Branch Rickey and was specifically assigned to Montreal to team with Robinson in the middle of the infield. Campanis's major-league career consisted of seven games in 1943, before he left baseball for the U.S. Navy during World War II. Robinson played short-stop in the Negro Leagues, but the Dodgers already had Pee Wee Reese manning that position. Reese was still in his prime and considered one of the best players in the league, necessitating a shift in positions for Robinson.

Jim Campanis Jr., a third-round draft pick of the Seattle Mariners and member of Team USA in 1988, recalled stories his grandfather told him about teaming with Robinson.

> My grandpa Al used to talk about teaching Jackie how to turn the double play as a second baseman. Jackie had been moved from short-stop to second base by Branch Rickey and offered my grandpa a special assignment—teach Jackie how to play second base in AAA Montreal during the 1946 season. The arrangement with Mr. Rickey also included a job in the front office at the end of the season. My grandpa was thrilled with this opportunity. So thrilled, in fact, he joined Jackie's offseason barnstorming team that toured the U.S. playing against all-white teams like Bob Feller's team prior to the 1946 spring training.

On April 15, 1946, the *Montreal Gazette* began to anticipate Robinson's debut, which would take place three days later at Roosevelt Stadium in Jersey City, New Jersey. Thirty years prior, Luis Padron played the final games of his professional career in the same city. Padron was an outstanding Cuban player whose path to the majors was blocked because it could not be verified if he was a Cuban of Spanish descent or one of African descent. Padron predated Armando Marsans and Rafael Almeida, the first Cubans to play in the majors in the twentieth century, but he never did make it to the majors. At the very least, Padron can be credited as one of the first players who started to blur the color line. The *Gazette* reported that a sellout was expected at Roosevelt Stadium for the opener to see Jackie Robinson's debut. Dink Carroll reported that longtime Jersey City mayor Frank Hague helped sell 50,000 tickets for Opening Day, despite the fact that Roosevelt Stadium only held 35,000 fans.

When the Royals took the field against the Jersey City Little Giants on April 18, Robinson was in the starting lineup, batting second and playing second base. While he was the first African American to take the field in a professional game since Moses Fleetwood Walker, he wasn't the only African American on the Royals. Johnny Wright, a pitcher who Rickey signed away from the Homestead Grays out of the Negro Leagues, also made the Royals Opening Day roster. Wright only appeared in two games for Montreal that season, and it was largely believed that Rickey placed him on the team to be a compatriot for Robinson.

Robinson's debut couldn't have gone any better. The Royals won, 14–1, and after grounding out in his first at-bat, Robinson hit safely in his next four at-bats and displayed the dynamic tools that Rickey hoped to see. His power was on display in the form of a three-run homer for his first professional hit that traveled an estimated 335 feet. He also showed his ability to manufacture a run by himself, dropping a bunt single down the third-base line, stealing second, advancing to third on a ground out, and then inducing a balk when he feigned stealing home. Robinson's debut was a success in every way, and although Montreal was the road team, the fans recognized Robinson's heroics. An Associated Press article said that fans almost pulled the jersey off Robinson's back after the game in celebration as he signed autographs for them.

The Opening Day bludgeoning was a portent of what was to come for Robinson and the Royals that summer. Royals fans embraced Robinson on the field and in the community. Jean Pierre-Roy, a pitcher on the Royals that season, said, "Up in the Royals stands, no one dared insult Jackie. He was black, but in their eyes and hearts, the fans didn't see that."

In May 1946, Wendell Smith wrote a column on Robinson's first two weeks as a professional. He discussed the massive crowd on Opening Day in Jersey City and noted that the crowds followed Robinson for each stop the Royals made on the road. He wrote that Robinson drew well in league cities with large African American populations, like Newark, Jersey City, and Baltimore, but there was also an increase in attendance no matter where they went. The Syracuse Chiefs had 4,500 fans for a game against the Royals early in the season; it was the biggest weekday crowd in Chiefs history. In addition, Smith noted that Robinson hadn't experienced racist "bench jockeying" to that point that some had feared. Smith wrote about an incident where Robinson was hit on the hand with a pitch against Syracuse, but the umpire ruled that Robinson had attempted to swing and refused to award him first. Robinson and his manager argued but to no avail. As Robinson stepped back into the box, a Syracuse player shouted, "All right Robinson, quit trying to hit the ball with your hand," eliciting laughter from Robinson and anyone within earshot. Smith wrote that so far, Robinson was only subject to the same good-natured ribbing every other ballplayer experienced. While every opponent was not that congenial, there wasn't the widespread racism that had been feared.

As Rickey hoped and probably expected, Robinson was a smash hit on the field and respected off it. He faced racial insults in visiting ballparks but nothing to the extent that he experienced in Florida in spring training. In addition to leading the International League with a .349 average, he also stole 40 bases, drove in 66 runs, and scored an incredible 113 runs in 124 games. The Royals won the division by 18.5 games and cruised through the playoffs with an 8–3 record. Interestingly, the first round of the playoffs that season was the first postseason meeting between Robinson and a player he would be involved with in one of the most iconic plays in major-league history. Robinson and the Royals drew the Newark Bears in the first round of the playoffs. The Bears, who were the AAA affiliate of the New York Yankees, were led by a young, 21-year-old catcher named Yogi Berra. Nine years after they faced off in the International League playoffs, Robinson famously stole home in the 1955 World Series with Berra protesting the "safe" call vehemently.

As with any player who dominated AAA the way he did, the stage was set for Robinson to debut with the Dodgers in 1947. He had nothing to prove on the field, and many of the racial concerns Rickey and others had never fully manifested. In an Associated Press article summarizing the 1946 baseball season, Frank Eck briefly mentioned Robinson's success. He wrote that Robinson "is in line to play third base for the Dodgers next season." While that was Rickey's plan, the Dodgers made no formal announcement, and Robinson would attend Dodgers spring training in 1947, as a member of the Montreal Royals, the same as any of his teammates who were trying to make the club.

While Robinson was heaped with attention during his remarkable 1946 season in Montreal, there were two other players enjoying a similar experience for the Class B Nashua Dodgers at the same time. Nashua played in the New England League, and 1946 was their first season of existence. The squad was led by future Hall of Fame manager Walter Alston, who was 34 years old at the time and, aside from one single at-bat in 1936, for the Cardinals, had been a career minor leaguer. The Nashua team had moved from Trenton, New Jersey, and Rickey provided them with two young players who would end up being two of the best players on the team in 1946. So, while Jackie Robinson was tearing up the AAA

International League, Don Newcombe and Roy Campanella were having similar success for Nashua. Their signings were reported on April 4, 1946, and at the time, the 24-year-old Campanella was called the best catcher in the Negro Leagues in his press release. Newcombe was only 20 years old, and while he enjoyed success in the Negro Leagues, he didn't have the established track record of Campanella. The two players would join Robinson in spring training in Havana, Cuba, along with another African American player, Roy Partlow.

On the heels of the racism Robinson endured in Florida during spring training the season before, Rickey searched for a new place to train his team for the upcoming 1947 season. He settled on Havana, Cuba, taking his team out of the country to a place familiar with Negro League stars who had barnstormed their way through the country many times before. Coming into spring training, four of the top five hitters in the International League had already been promoted to their respective affiliated major-league clubs before spring training began, with only Robinson, the league's top player, remaining with his AAA team. In addition, a Dodgers public relations release in early January touted the impact some rookies could have with the team in 1947. That list of rookies included Johnny Van Cuyk, Boris Woyt, and Marvin Rackley, but there was no mention of Robinson. Newspapers took notice and included Robinson in their Hot Stove reporting that winter, regardless of what the press release noted. The press covered Robinson's plight throughout the winter, and his name appeared in newspapers throughout the country on a daily basis that winter. Rickey publicly encouraged fans on multiple occasions not to read anything into the fact that Robinson was still listed as a member of the Royals, saying that was standard operating procedure for the club, and he often cited numerous recent examples of players who were handled similarly.

The Associated Press wrote that the fate of Jackie Robinson was the top question in the baseball world as winter began to turn to spring. The question wasn't only on the minds of fans either, as some players started speaking out against Robinson as the possibility of baseball's color barrier falling started to become more and more of a reality. Veteran catcher Rollie Hemsley, who was entering the final season of a 19-year career that had seen him play for seven different teams, spoke out against Robinson's playing ability, dismissing him as a one-dimensional player. Hemsley said in a February interview, "I played four games against him on a barnstorming trip. He is fast, and when you have said that, you have said it all."

Eddie Dyer, who managed the Cardinals to a World Series championship the year before in his first season as the team's skipper, was even more demonstrative. He declared that if Robinson replaced Eddie Stanky in the Dodgers lineup, it would sabotage their entire season. Dyer's remarks were more praise for Stanky than a detriment to Robinson, but the message was there. Stanky was a solid player for the Dodgers as their second baseman, and it was a common question asked in baseball circles at that time. Robinson was a shortstop in the Negro Leagues and a second baseman in Montreal, and the Dodgers seemed pretty well set at both of those positions. Stanky finished seventh in the Most Valuable Player (MVP) voting in 1946, and his double-play partner, Pee Wee Reese, finished one spot ahead of him in the voting. In an Associated Press article, Dyer said, "I think just as my boys do. If the Dodgers play Jackie Robinson at second base instead of Eddie Stanky, we'll win the pennant easy." He continued, "They say Robinson is at home on second base. Well that's fine because some of my boys are rooting for him over Stanky," intimating that at least some of his players shared the same feeling.

Robinson's detractors weren't limited to his opposition, however. In an article published three days into spring training, writer Herbert Goren surveyed the Dodgers about Robinson potentially joining their team for the 1947 season. Goren's article covered two main points. First, it captured Robinson's feelings on not being placed on the major-league roster, as was common with someone who performed the way he did in AAA the year before. Robinson claimed it didn't bother him one bit, even stating that he could understand it if people wanted proof his fantastic 1946 season wasn't a "flash in the pan." Robinson simply said he would work hard, play whatever position they asked him to, and play at whatever level they wanted him to. Goren wrote that Robinson's clearest path to the Dodgers might be at third base. For his part, Robinson even said that he'd never played first base before, but he was open to doing it if it got him to the majors.

The second part of the article examined the feelings of some of Robinson's teammates. An anonymous player related that he wasn't in agreement that the color barrier should be broken. He hoped that Hall of Famer Arky Vaughan, who was attempting a comeback after a three-year retirement, would make the team instead of Robinson. He even admitted that it wasn't a fact that the great Vaughan could help the team more than Robinson could, he just didn't want the color barrier broken. Two other anonymous Dodgers were also quoted, with one saying he was supportive of Robinson if he would help the club and the other dismissing the question itself and Robinson, saying he hadn't heard much talk about Robinson and it wasn't something worth bringing up.

The teammate most associated with objections to Robinson was Dixie Walker, a veteran outfielder who was still an All-Star late in his career. Hailing from Birmingham, Alabama, Walker's Southern prejudices were on display from the start. Walker's career began as a teammate of Babe Ruth and Lou Gehrig on the 1931 Yankees, and he played a majority of his career in the era of segregation. Some accounts claim Walker started a petition that multiple players signed against Robinson. In an interview in 1997, on the 50th anniversary of Robinson's debut, backup catcher Bobby Bragan disputed that Walker formed a petition. He explained that it wasn't a petition, but a letter that Walker wrote about his own feelings and delivered to Rickey. Bragan also mentioned names of players who were against integration and Robinson. Those players included Walker, Eddie Stanky, Ed Head, and Carl Furillo. Bragan even admitted himself that he was against Robinson at first.

During spring training, manager Leo Durocher claimed that he learned of his team's negative thoughts regarding Robinson and called them into a meeting. In an interview years later, Durocher said, "I told the players that Robinson was going to open the season with us come hell or high water, and if they didn't like it, they could leave now and we'd trade them or get rid of them some other way. Nobody moved." From that point onward, whatever dissention players had was kept to themselves, and the team concluded spring training without any public protest against Robinson.

Robinson did, however, have his supporters. Outfielder Gene Hermanski said, "It was quite obvious he'd end up in Brooklyn. Most guys liked him, especially Pee Wee Reese. I liked the guy, but I'm a little selfish. I was fighting for a job." Even Vaughan, a player who could have been forced into retirement if Robinson made the team, supported him. Vaughan tragically drowned in 1952, and upon his death, Robinson recognized the way he was treated by the Hall of Fame shortstop. In remembering his old teammate, Robinson, then a five-year veteran, said, "He was one of the fellows who went out of his way to be nice to me when I came in as a rookie. Believe me, I needed it. He was a fine fellow."

Aside from Reese, one of Robinson's biggest supporters was pitcher Ralph Branca. Branca grew up in a diverse neighborhood in Mount Vernon, New York, and treated Robinson as if he was just another one of his friends from childhood. Branca ate with Robinson, encouraged him to socialize with his teammates, and famously convinced Robinson that he should shower side by side with his teammates after games instead of waiting until everyone else was finished. Robinson's widow, Rachel, acknowledged what Branca's support meant to Robinson. In an interview in 2014, she said, "There were players who were hostile to Jack and tried to provoke him. Ralph was one of the players who supported him openly. Jack liked and admired him as a friend even after he left the Dodgers."

As March turned to April, and with Opening Day two weeks away, Robinson's status was still unknown. He had been playing both first and second base at times in spring training, and that was starting to cause problems. Branch Rickey decreed that Robinson should exclusively play first base during spring training; however, Montreal manager Clay Hopper frequently played him at second to prepare his own team for the coming season. Finally, less than two weeks before Opening Day, Hopper had experienced enough. Rickey learned that Robinson was playing second base for Montreal again, so he called over to their game and demanded he be moved to first base. Hopper had already submitted his lineup but relented to Rickey's command and made the change. This didn't leave the gruff Hopper pleased.

When asked of Rickey's edict to keep Robinson at first, Hopper bristled, "I have my own problems as manager of the Montreal club. I want to give Ruchser a chance to play first. He's my first baseman. If Robinson stays with me, he plays second. Until I am notified that he has been purchased by Brooklyn, I must assume he is a member of my club." When Robinson was first assigned to Montreal the previous season, Hopper allegedly made some viciously racist comments to Rickey. But by the end of the season, Hopper was one of Robinson's biggest supporters and had been campaigning for Robinson to move up to Brooklyn from the moment he led them to the International League championship the season before. Robinson's limbo status and position uncertainty were starting to become a real controversy in the final weeks of spring training, with some in the media starting to whisper that he wasn't getting a fair chance to make the team. Hopper's frustration may not have been only about the one incident of Rickey interfering, but also an expression of exasperation at the entire situation, which got so far as the media claiming that Rickey's methods were backfiring.

With less than a week left before the season and Robinson's fate still undecided, an unexpected bombshell shocked the baseball world. Dodgers manager Leo Durocher, a strong supporter of Robinson, was suspended for the entire 1947 season for an ongoing pattern of negative behavior. The fiery Durocher had become embroiled in a feud with Yankees president Larry MacPhail that ultimately led to MacPhail filing charges of defamation against Durocher and Rickey. Commissioner Happy Chandler didn't levy any penalty against Rickey but came down hard on Durocher due to his history. As Chandler put it, Durocher "had not measured up to the standards expected or required of managers of our baseball teams." Durocher's suspension left two major questions: Who would be his replacement and what effect would this have on Jackie Robinson?

One of the logical choices for the new managerial position was Montreal's Hopper. He was a respected baseball man and had just managed Robinson and his Royals to one of the greatest seasons in Minor League Baseball history. He also was in the same mindset as Rickey when it came to Robinson's ability as a major leaguer. Ray Blades, Pepper Martin, and even Dixie Walker were rumored to be candidates for the job. Blades, coach Clyde Sukeforth, and even retired former Yankees manager Joe McCarthy turned down the job.

While the Dodgers' managerial situation would take some time to resolve, the question about Robinson only lingered another 24 hours. On April 10, the Dodgers were playing the Royals in an anticipated exhibition at Ebbets Field. Robinson was in the Royals lineup, and Sukeforth was helming the Dodgers until Durocher's replacement could be found. In the top of the fifth inning, the Royals led the Dodgers, 4–2, on the strength of two-run homers by Al Campanis and Don Lund when a short bulletin was given to members of the press on hand covering the game. It simply said, "The Brooklyn Dodgers today purchased the contract of Jackie Roosevelt Robinson from the Montreal Royals." With that terse 15-word statement, baseball's unwritten color barrier, which had stood for 60 years, was set to fall five days later, on Opening Day.

On April 15, the 1947 Major League Baseball season began with more anticipation than any season in recent memory. There was a feeling that it was a time of change throughout the majors, and it wasn't just propelled by Robinson. Hall of Famer Hank Greenberg shockingly switched teams in the offseason, and his debut as a Pittsburgh Pirate garnered headlines as newspapers heralded the start of the season. Durocher's suspension was still being digested, and this was also the day that Rickey admitted to the press that Babe Ruth's old manager, Joe McCarthy, had turned down the Dodgers gig. Yogi Berra, another heralded rookie, began his first full season for the Yankees, while Joe DiMaggio started the season on the disabled list as he recovered from surgery. Three Hall of Famers started on the mound that day, one of whom was Cleveland Indians legend Bob Feller. With the scars of World War II starting to fade, things were about to change, and Ebbets Field was going to be at the epicenter for a 2:00 p.m. game. As sportswriter Davis Walsh wrote, "Some [Opening Day baseball events] will kick tradition's pearly teeth in—notably the official Ebbets Field debut of Jackie Robinson at first base for the Brooklyn Dodgers."

Robinson was set to bat second in the Dodgers lineup and was stationed at first base on defense. The Dodgers played three scrimmage games against the Yankees the previous three days, and Robinson played first in all three to prepare for the season. The Dodgers were up against the Boston Braves, who would finish in third place in the eight-team National League that season. On the mound for the Braves was Johnny Sain, who won 20 games in 1946, his first year back from military service. Sain was 29, but he was only in his second full season as a major-league starter. In 1948, writer Gerald Hearn would write the famed poem "Spahn & Sain," after the righty won 20 games for the third-straight season. Sain was not going to be an easy test for Robinson in his first game.

Opening Day brought the usual fanfare, and as the first pitch drew closer, the teams took to the grass for the national anthem. Robinson's friend Ralph Branca took the field alongside Robinson, and the two men stood together facing the flag. Later, Branca's brother confronted him about standing next to Robinson. But his concerns weren't racially motivated.

Branca remembered, "When I got home, John [Branca] asked if I was crazy. I said, 'What are you talking about?' He said, 'You stood next to

Jackie. Suppose the guy was a lousy shot and missed by three feet.'" Branca responded to this concern about an assassination attempt gone awry by saying, "I would have died a hero."

There were rumors that the game was a sellout, but 26,623 fans showed up, about 6,000 less than capacity. Dodgers starter Joe Hatten pitched through trouble in the first, with Robinson recording the first putout of the season on a ground ball to third. After Dodgers leadoff man Eddie Stanky grounded out leading off the bottom of the first, Robinson took his first turn at bat in the majors. While the at-bat was a huge historical milestone, it was otherwise uneventful, as Robinson grounded out to third. He flew out and hit into a double play his next two times up, and then flashed his athleticism in his final at-bat of the game. With the Dodgers down, 3–2, in the seventh, Stanky drew a leadoff walk, and Robinson came up in a clear bunt situation. Robinson squared, his feet touching the chalk lines of the batter's box. Sain's pitch sailed low and inside, but Robinson pivoted his back foot and dropped his bat head to lay down a perfect bunt up the first-base line. Sain and first baseman Earl Torgeson converged on the ball as Robinson sped by them toward first. Torgeson fielded, and his throw was rushed due to Robinson's speed. His throw sailed and hit Robinson in the back, caroming into foul territory up the right-field line. Right fielder Mike McCormick was backing up the play, but that didn't stop Stanky from motoring to third as Robinson went to second. Pete Reiser then doubled both of them home to give the Dodgers a 4–3 lead on the way to a 5–3 win.

Robinson was held hitless in his first game, but that didn't last long. He went 9 for his next 23, and the Dodgers won 8 of their first 10 games. The Dodgers never dipped below .500 at any point in the season in a competitive National League and finished the season in first place, five games clear of Stan Musial and the St. Louis Cardinals. Robinson won over his teammates quickly, including Dixie Walker, who had been outspoken in spring training against Robinson.

While he faced frequent racial taunts throughout the season, the most notorious incident came against the Philadelphia Phillies. Manager Ben Chapman, a rough-around-the-edges Southerner from Nashville, was identified by Robinson later in life as the most savage with his racist comments. In an interview on the *Dick Cavett Show* that aired on January 26, 1972, Robinson reported that Chapman was particularly vicious during an early series season at Ebbets Field, and many Phillies players

followed his lead. Robinson mentioned two things about that series, however, that helped him and the Dodgers. First, he recalled what happened
when Phillies first baseman Lee Handley reached first base, where Robinson was playing that day. Robinson remembered,

> [Handley] came down to first base when I was there and apologized
> for the Phillies. He just says, "I just want you to know all of us don't
> feel that way, but it's been led by the manager, and many of the guys
> are doing it simply by instructions, I would have to imagine." But it
> did give me a good feeling to know that in spite of what's coming out
> of the Phillies dugout, one guy would come down and say he's awfully
> sorry. And actually what they did was to sort of solidify the Brooklyn
> ballclub because Mr. Rickey told me, one of the things he said early
> was that when your ballclub starts to take up for you in certain situa-
> tions, our battle is most of the way won. I think that Phillie incident
> started the Dodgers to kind of mold as a unit.

In addition to the controversy with the Phillies, there were also rumors
that the Cardinals were organizing a boycott. In an Associated Press
article published on May 8, 1947, with remarks from National League
president Ford Frick, who can be credited with taking a stand against not
only the Cardinals, but also Ben Chapman and the Phillies. Frick said in
the article that he received a phone call the day of the game asking what
he thought of a potential boycott. Frick responded that anyone who participated in a boycott against Jackie Robinson would be suspended indefi-
nitely. He communicated that with Cardinals owner Sam Breadon, who
then addressed the team and quelled the situation. Likewise, Frick told
Chapman that his behavior was "not becoming from any National League
bench" and would not be tolerated. Chapman and the Phillies abided by
Frick's edict.

While Robinson and the Dodgers were enjoying a fantastic season, a
23-year-old Larry Doby was having his own success on the diamond for
the Newark Eagles in the Negro Leagues. Four years earlier, Doby was
serving in the U.S. Navy during World War II and was stationed in Uthili,
an island east of the Philippines in the Pacific Ocean. While serving there,
Doby experienced two life-changing events. First, he befriended Mickey
Vernon, who was a star first baseman for the Washington Senators, and
he also learned on an Armed Forces Radio broadcast that Branch Rickey
had signed Jackie Robinson to play for the Montreal Royals. Doby was a

physically gifted athlete and had played on some military baseball teams. Vernon was so impressed with Doby that he sent a letter to Senators owner Clark Griffith recommending Doby for the Senators if Major League Baseball integrated. The signing of Robinson gave Doby hope that he could eventually pursue a career in Major League Baseball.

Doby was able to realize that dream less than three months after Robinson debuted when he became the first African American ballplayer in the American League. He was signed by eccentric Cleveland Indians owner Bill Veeck, and the process was in stark contrast to the meticulous methods followed by Branch Rickey with Jackie Robinson. As the 1947 season barreled toward the "Dog Days" in late June, Veeck contacted the Newark Eagles about the possibility of signing Doby, who teamed with Monte Irvin to form a popular tandem for the Negro League club. Effa Manley, the team's pioneering owner, reacted much differently than Kansas City Monarchs owner T. Y. Baird did when the Dodgers signed Robinson; she wholeheartedly supported Doby as a possible major leaguer.

The Indians announced on July 2, that they had purchased Doby from the Eagles and that he would be reporting to Chicago for the Indians series against the White Sox. Doby would not have a year to ply his trade in the minors, as the Indians did not have a minor-league system in place the way the Dodgers did. While Robinson was 28 years old at the time of his debut with a year of physical and mental preparation in professional ball under his belt, Doby was being asked to go from the Negro Leagues to the major leagues in the span of a week at 23 years old. And the atmosphere in Cleveland wasn't as welcoming as it was in Brooklyn.

"Larry was just 23 years old; he was just a baby thrown into a powder keg. He may have even gone through more than Jackie did," said Bob Kendrick, president of the Negro Leagues Baseball Museum in Kansas City.

> Sometimes I think of Larry as the forgotten man. It's typical of how we are in society. We always remember who came first but not necessarily who came second. It's been in the last couple of decades that we're really starting to appreciate what Doby meant and went through. That's one of the purposes of the [Negro Leagues Baseball] Museum, to make sure guys like Doby are not forgotten.

Doby debuted on July 5, just three days after the Indians announced his signing. He was introduced to his Indians teammates on the day of the game, and although the Associated Press reported that he was greeted "cordially" by his team, Doby told a slightly different story.

"[The situation] was very tough," said the soft-spoken Doby in an interview years after his career ended. "I'd never faced any circumstances like that. Teammates were lined up, and some would greet you and some wouldn't. You could deal with it, but it was hard."

Even though Doby struck out in his only at-bat, a pinch-hitting appearance in the seventh inning, newspapers covered his debut as an important event. The *New York Daily News* ran a photo of Doby with Veeck, each flashing a big smile, along with a caption that read, "And Then There Were Two." Doby also grabbed headlines and a full article about his debut. The article touched on his pregame work in the infield with fellow Hall of Famer Joe Gordon and Doby being assigned number 14, which would be retired by the Indians 47 years later. Doby would play a part-time role in 1947 for the Indians, who finished in fourth place in the American League that season. He finished with a .156 batting average that season, with 5 hits in 32 at-bats.

As the first hints of fall started to drift into the summer of 1947, the Dodgers were beginning to separate themselves from the pack in the National League. The Yankees were already running away in the American League, and if the Dodgers were planning on facing them in the World Series, Branch Rickey figured he needed to shore up his team's starting pitching, which had been a weakness. By his own account, Rickey scoured the country for weeks in search of a pitcher who could help him. Ralph Branca was having a good season as their ace, but aside from him, most of the other pitchers were unreliable at best. Rickey ended up turning to the place where his last big experiment was born: the Negro Leagues.

After extensive scouting, Rickey settled on Dan Bankhead, a 27-year-old righty who was pitching for the Memphis Red Sox. Bankhead, who was also a strong hitter, was signed by Rickey on August 25. Unlike other Negro League players Rickey had signed, he could not afford patience with his new pitcher. There was such a need on the major-league club that instead of sending him to the minors to develop, Rickey had him report right to Brooklyn, where Bankhead would become the first African American pitcher in major-league history. Burt Shotton, the Dodgers manager who took over for Clyde Sukeforth in the season's third game, remarked that he might use Bankhead the first day he reported to the team. Rickey compared his potential to Dizzy Dean, if only he could command his pitches a little better. The Dodgers seemed optimistically excited about their new pitcher.

Shotton was true to his word and sent Bankhead to the mound in his first game as a Dodger. His duty came in relief of Hal Gregg, who lasted just one inning against the Pittsburgh Pirates. Gregg gave up four runs in the first, and after starting the second with a single and walk, Shotton pulled Gregg for Bankhead. Coming into a tough spot with the heart of the Pirates lineup due up, Bankhead wasn't effective his first time in action. He gave up four runs of his own as the Pirates built an 8–0 lead through two innings. The highlight of the day for Bankhead came in the bottom of the second, when he blasted a home run in his first at-bat.

Bankhead pitched 3.1 innings in his debut, giving up 10 hits and 8 runs in a 16–3 loss. While the Dodgers were disappointed with the loss, they weren't going to judge him on his first appearance. Shotton was complimentary of Bankhead after the game, saying, "He has speed, a good curve, and control." Anonymous Dodgers teammates urged the sportswriters to give him time. Shotton also provided additional insight into Bankhead's struggles. Shotton commented that Bankhead was tipping his pitches, and the Pirates were calling them out before they came. He also said Bankhead's delivery was too slow with runners on base, but he would get another chance. Bankhead didn't get much more of a chance in 1947, but he pitched well when called on. After his tough debut, Bankhead pitched 6.2 innings in three more games while only allowing two runs. He didn't appear in the postseason as a pitcher, but he did have one appearance as a pinch-runner, scoring a run in game six. He spent the next two seasons in the minor leagues.

The St. Louis Browns were another team that integrated quickly. The Browns were in a different situation than the Dodgers, however. The moribund franchise was back in last place, where they spent most of their time, and just looking for some talent to avoid finishing in the basement again. They signed Willard "Home Run" Brown and Hank Thompson, two position players, for a trial with the team. Brown's signing was big news, as he was one of the most powerful hitters in Negro League history, but he was also aloof and undisciplined. Thompson was a World War II hero who fought in the Battle of the Bulge. Neither Brown nor Thompson produced in the short opportunity they were given, and they were removed from the roster before the end of August. Although they were only in the majors for a short time, their names are etched in the record books multiple times. When they appeared in a game on July 20, it marked the first time two African American teammates had played together since Fleetwood and Weldy Walker in the 1880s. When the Browns faced off against the Indians, Thompson and Larry Doby became the first African Americans to play against one another in the majors. Brown also made history when he became the first African American player to homer in the American League when he connected for an inside-the-park home run against future Hall of Famer Hal Newhouser.

With Robinson's success coupled with the presence of Doby and Bankhead, it would have made sense for teams other than the Dodgers and Indians to quickly integrate. Teammates and fans largely accepted the three players, and Robinson was quickly becoming one of the top attractions in the league, while Don Newcombe and Roy Campanella were doing well in the minors. An entire pool of talented players was open, and there should have been nothing holding back teams from signing them. The infusion of talent could have changed the fate of entire franchises and saturated the league with exciting talent; however, things didn't happen that way.

There wasn't a single new team to integrate during the 1948 season, as the only African American ballplayers to make their debuts that season were Don Newcombe with the Dodgers and Satchel Paige with the Indians, two teams that had already integrated. Although overall the league was slow to integrate, Major League Baseball was ahead of its time when it came to civil rights in the United States. When Jackie Robinson debuted the U.S. military was still segregated; Martin Luther King was just 18 years old; *Brown v. the Topeka Board of Education*, banning segregation in public schools, was still seven years away from being heard in the Supreme Court; and it would be eight years before Rosa Parks would refuse to sit in the back of a bus.

Bob Kendrick noted the significance of Major League Baseball's 1947 season in the scope of American history.

> Players in the Negro Leagues had to love the sport in order to endure the things that they had to endure just to play baseball in this country. And yet they would never allow the social adversity to kill their love of the game. So, if I got to sleep on the bus and eat my peanut butter and crackers, I'm gonna keep playing ball. You're not gonna rob me of this joy of playing ball. And it was that prevailing spirit that drove them,

and ultimately it was that prevailing spirit that not only changed the game of baseball, but changed this country. Baseball was at the forefront of the civil rights movement. I think sports in general have united us in ways that few other things in society ever have. The [Negro Leagues Baseball] Museum makes the bold assertion that Jackie Robinson's breaking of the color barrier was not just a part of the civil rights movement, it was the beginning of the civil rights movement in this country. For all intents and purposes, this is what started the ball rolling for social progress in our country.

The Dodgers won the National League pennant in 1947, and Robinson was one of the team's top players. He batted .297 and led the league with 29 stolen bases and 28 sacrifice hits, and led the Dodgers with 12 home runs. Robinson's performance was strong enough to win the Rookie of the Year Award the first year it was presented. For the first two seasons, the award was given to the top rookie in all of baseball, and Robinson easily outdistanced New York Giants pitcher Larry Jansen and Yankees pitcher Spec Shea. In addition, Robinson finished fifth in the National League MVP voting, placing one spot ahead of Ralph Kiner, who hit 51 home runs that year. Robinson battled through the racist insults and segregated hotels to have a fantastic season and was recognized for it by the baseball writers who voted on awards. Branch Rickey's grand experiment was a wild success.

THE NEXT STEPS

Jackie Robinson's 1948 season was statistically similar to his rookie year, but the Dodgers were a team in flux, as the seeds of the "Boys of Summer" teams of the 1950s were just starting to be sown. Leo Durocher returned as manager but was fired mid-season. A young Gil Hodges was the team's Opening Day catcher before making the move to first base when Roy Campanella emerged. Eddie Stanky was traded so Robinson could slide over to second base. Duke Snider was called up mid-season while Don Newcombe progressed through the minor leagues leading up to his 1949 call-up. The Dodgers finished third in the National League. The Cleveland Indians won the World Series over the Boston Braves and were buoyed by the play of Larry Doby, who had a breakout season after being a part-timer the year before. While Doby, Bob Feller, Bob Lemon, and Lou Boudreau were some of the top players in the game, it was another bold signing by eccentric owner Bill Veeck that may have put the Indians over the top.

On July 7, 1948, the Indians were tied with the Philadelphia A's for first place in the American League with the Yankees just 3.5 games behind. Looking for extra pitching, Veeck seized on an opportunity to create one of the most appropriate pairings of the time. Veeck is one of the great showmen in the game's history; he was somewhat of a folk hero. He also had long wanted to integrate the sport, and although he was beaten to the punch by Branch Rickey, he was at least able to integrate the American League three months after Jackie Robinson's debut.

When given the opportunity to help his club and bring in the top showman of the Negro Leagues, Veeck took advantage and signed Satchel Paige for $40,000, for the remaining three months of the season. At the time, Paige claimed he was 39, but records suggest he was 42. Never one to put an age on himself, Paige famously said, "If someone asked how old you were and you didn't know your age, how old would you think you were?"

Paige was long established as the top Negro League pitcher of his era, if not of all time. Although he was somewhere in the neighborhood of 40 years old, he was still effective. Paige was a flamethrower as a youngster, but with his advanced age, he adjusted his game to try to "out-cute" batters. Paige had hoped to be the first to integrate the sport at various times in his career, but he later admitted it was best that Robinson was the one to break the color barrier. Paige believed it was beneficial for everyone that Robinson played a full season in the minors before making the jump to the Dodgers, and he thought if he was signed and asked to go to the minors, it would have been considered insulting.

Newspaper coverage of Paige's signing was extensive, and writers lauded the Indians and Veeck for their move. The *Chicago Tribune* ran an extensive feature and called Paige one of the all-time greats. The *Tribune* referenced a 1–0 barnstorming win against Dizzy Dean's team, a game that went 13 innings and was declared one of the best he'd ever seen by Veeck. It also mentioned a game he pitched against Bob Feller's All-Stars in which Paige won, 8–0, with 16 strikeouts. Paige had struck out as many as 18 batters in a game and was reported to have thrown a "hatful" of no-hitters. Paige was recommended to Veeck by Feller, and the Indians owner was happy to oblige, as they needed righty help in their bullpen.

Paige made his debut on July 9, 1948, in relief of fellow Hall of Famer Bob Lemon, against the St. Louis Browns. He gave up a single to Chuck Stevens, the first batter he faced in the majors, but retired the next three batters. The next inning, he faced the minimum with the help of a double play before being lifted for pinch-hitter Larry Doby when his spot in the lineup came up.

Paige's debut was highly anticipated, as would be expected. Before his debut in that night's game, the morning papers documented the build-up. The headline in the *Sandusky Register* on July 9, didn't as much laud the Indians for a 14–1 rout of the Chicago White Sox as it noted that another game passed without Paige making his debut. He had only been on the roster for two days, but according to the article, "fans in Cleveland have been dying to see the famed Satchel Paige, the immortal Negro League pitching star, perform." But the Indians' bats had been hot, and Paige wasn't needed in either game. The *Sandusky Register* gave Paige equal billing the next day after his two-inning debut. His stint was mentioned in the headline, and Paige's smiling headshot ran with the article.

Paige was fantastic in his swingman role in 1948. He appeared in 21 regular-season games, starting seven of them. He finished the season with a 2.48 ERA and a 5–1 record. Paige's first start came against the Washington Senators and Hall of Famer Early Wynn. He outpitched Wynn, allowing three runs in seven innings, and even recorded his first career hit, an infield single to short. Starting with that game, Paige reeled off an incredible 26.1 scoreless innings in the month of August, including two straight shutouts, as the Indians were locked in a heated pennant race with the Red Sox and A's. During that month, the Indians went 21–12, and Paige was a huge reason why. Paige appeared in one-third of those 21 wins, starting five games and appearing in relief twice. As August turned to September, the Indians were 1.5 games ahead of the Red Sox for first and continued to battle through the end of the season, winning the American League in a one-game playoff against the Red Sox after they ended the season tied.

The Indians would go on to beat the Boston Braves in a historical World Series in six games. The World Series was the first to have an expanded television broadcast. The previous year had a live broadcast only in the New York City area, while this Series had an increased broadcast range in each team's home city. Major League Baseball didn't start naming World Series MVPs until 1955, but Larry Doby would have been the leading candidate for that honor in 1948. Doby led the Tribe with a .318 batting average in the Series, including a home run and double. When Paige appeared in Game 5, he became the first African American to pitch in a World Series. Paige got the final two outs of the seventh inning in mop-up duty with the Indians down big. It would be his only appearance in the World Series.

While Paige and Doby were leading the Indians to a World Series title, Roy Campanella and Jackie Robinson were thriving for the Dodgers. Robinson's statistics were nearly identical to his rookie season, as he led the Dodgers in runs, hits, extra-base hits, and wins above replacement. Campanella made his debut in April but only played in three games. He returned in July and supplanted Bruce Edwards as the team's everyday catcher. Edwards had been an All-Star the previous season and finished fourth in the MVP voting in 1947. While Campanella and Edwards had almost identical offensive seasons in 1948, Campanella was far superior defensively. Campanella's defensive prowess and the Dodgers' need for extra help in the infield forced Edwards into a utility role as the 1948 season progressed.

Campanella ended up catching 83 games for the Dodgers in 1948, and was remarkably impactful for essentially playing in half of the team's games. He led National League catchers with 12 double plays turned and threw out two-thirds of the baserunners who tried to steal on him, a mark that also led the league. Campanella also led the National League in fielding percentage at catcher and topped the circuit in such advanced defensive metrics as total zone runs and range factor. Campanella finished in the top five in the National League in putouts, assists, and caught stealing for catchers, a notable accomplishment considering he only played half the season. It was clear Campanella was on a path to stardom, and as his offensive performance caught up to his defensive excellence throughout the years, he quickly established himself as one of the top players in baseball.

Despite the success of Paige, Robinson, Doby, and Campanella, 1948 wasn't exactly a year of progress for integration in Major League Baseball. The Dodgers and Indians were the only teams who were integrated. The Browns, who had given short trials to Hank Thompson and Willard Brown the season before, did not sign any African American players in 1948, despite finishing 60–93. Other African American stars of the era, for instance, Monte Irvin, Minnie Minoso, and Luke Easter, played out the season in the Negro Leagues and continued to thrive. Don Newcombe and Sam Jethroe spent the season in AAA for the Montreal Royals, who were still managed by Jackie Robinson's old manager, Clay Hopper. Newcombe went 17–6, with a 3.14 ERA, and Jethroe batted .322, but neither garnered a call-up during the season. As the idea of integration gained momentum in the mid-1940s, there were thoughts that once a team integrated a wave of Negro League stars would assimilate throughout the major leagues on each team, especially if the first players were as successful as Robinson, Doby, Paige, and Campanella; however, that wasn't the case. The Dodgers and Indians were the only two teams to embrace integration, and it took until July 1949, for the New York Giants to join them.

THE 1949 MAJOR LEAGUE BASEBALL ALL-STAR GAME

When cataloging the seminal moments of the integration of Major League Baseball, the 1949 All-Star Game is not generally an event that garners much attention. The debuts of Jackie Robinson, Larry Doby, and Satchel Paige are always at the forefront—and rightfully so. The significance of the Boston Red Sox and New York Yankees finally integrating with Pumpsie Green and Elston Howard, respectively, is also usually mentioned. The Red Sox were the last team to integrate, and the Yankees were the preeminent franchise in baseball at the time. Some may even point to the second wave of African American stars. Players like Hank Aaron, Ernie Banks, Willie Mays, and Frank Robinson are clearly pioneers, even if they weren't among the first to integrate the sport. With so many impactful events happening in the first decade of integration, it is easy to see why the 1949 All-Star Game gets lost in the shuffle, but that doesn't mean it's any less significant.

The first All-Star Game Jackie Robinson was eligible for was in 1947, his rookie season. While Robinson was having a solid season, his competition at first base was strong. Johnny Mize was in the midst of his famous 51-home run season, and Stan Musial was in the early stages of appearing in 24 straight All-Star Games. The 1947 season was the first time voting returned to the fans through newspaper ballots after that practice had been shelved in prior years. Blank ballots appeared in newspapers daily, and fans simply wrote in their candidates and mailed their ballot to the *Chica-*

go Tribune to be tallied. Robinson finished third in the voting, as Mize was a runaway winner. National League manager Eddie Dyer, who was manager of the Cardinals at the time, understandably picked Musial as the backup. In addition to being a revered star on his own team, he also finished second on the ballot. In 1947, one backup per position was the general practice. So, while baseball was integrated in 1947, the All-Star Game had to wait for integration.

The 1948 season seemed like it could be a good opportunity for the first African American All-Star. Robinson was an established star in just his second season, and Larry Doby was performing well for the Indians. Moreover, Dodgers manager Leo Durocher was the National League skipper and had the opportunity to select Robinson as a backup if he didn't get voted in; however, Robinson was hurt in the voting by playing multiple positions. Again, fans were given blank ballots, and Robinson could have been listed at any of the three positions in the infield he was playing in the first half. As it turned out, Robinson finished fifth in the voting at first base. While managers still had the right to pick backups in 1948, they typically selected the runner-up in the public voting. Durocher was a big supporter of Robinson throughout his career, but choosing the person who finished fifth in the balloting would have been a real stretch at the time. Doby finished fifth on the ballot for American League center fielders as well, so another season passed without an African American All-Star.

The 1949 season presented an even better chance to integrate the All-Star Game, as the contest was slated to be held at Ebbets Field. New York's baseball-crazed fans were sure to support Robinson, as well as his Dodgers teammates. On July 3, 1949, the final All-Star voting was announced, and the results were historic. Jackie Robinson received not only the most votes at second base, but also the most votes of any National League player. He was second overall in voting, outdistanced by only Ted Williams. The significance of this was not lost on the media; a column written by the Newspaper Enterprise Association declared, "The runaway vote achieved by Robinson is a tremendous tribute to the ideal condition of racial relationships in baseball."

The breakthroughs didn't stop with Robinson, however. Teammate Roy Campanella finished second in the voting and was named as a reserve. Likewise, Doby finished fifth in voting for outfielders and was named a reserve. The 1949 voting combined all three outfield positions into one category, which was different from previous years, when each outfield position had been voted on separately. Rookie pitcher Don Newcombe was one of three Dodgers pitchers selected to the team as well. The selection of those four players meant that every full-time African American player playing in the major leagues at that time had been selected as an All-Star. Minnie Minoso had debuted for the Cleveland Indians early in the season but only played in nine games before the break. Luke Easter, another African American player on the Cleveland Indians, didn't make his major-league debut until after the All-Star Game.

The Dodgers and Cardinals dominated the National League All-Star roster, as the two teams combined for 17 of the 25 players on the roster. In addition to Robinson, Newcombe, and Campanella, there was Gil Hodges, Pee Wee Reese, Preacher Roe, and Ralph Branca. Hodges's appearance in the game was the first of his eight appearances and came in abnormal circumstances.

Hodges finished a distant third in the voting, behind starter Johnny Mize and Eddie Waitkus of the Phillies. Normally, Waitkus would have been selected as the backup, with Hodges likely missing out; however, just weeks before the final voting was announced, Waitkus was shot in a hotel room by a teenage female stalker and almost lost his life. The incident loosely inspired the scene in *The Natural* in which Roy Hobbs is shot. In the following days, newspapers warned that Waitkus might die, but luckily he survived and was named an honorary member of the All-Star Team.

The All-Star Game was still relatively new in 1949, and the American League had won 11 of the 15 contests to date. There were grumblings that the once-popular exhibition was losing its appeal, as the National League didn't take too well to their annual beating. But the game was still popular with fans, and profits from the gate were put into a fund to help players when they retired. The game took place on July 12, a Tuesday afternoon. The National League starting lineup featured six future Hall of Famers, while the American League's only Hall of Famer starters were Ted Williams, Joe DiMaggio, and George Kell. The National League even trotted out Warren Spahn against Mel Parnell, but despite the perceived talent mismatch, newspapers tabbed the American League the favorite.

The American League didn't waste time establishing its dominance, as the team scored four unearned runs in the top of the first. After Pee Wee

Reese led off the bottom of the first by grounding back to the pitcher, Robinson came to bat as the first African American player to step into a batter's box in an All-Star Game. He promptly doubled to left off Parnell and then scored when Stan Musial followed him with a two-run homer. Spahn struggled again in the second, and after putting Kell and Williams on base, National League manager Billy Southworth turned to the rookie Newcombe with DiMaggio coming to the plate. An African American took the mound for the first time in an All-Star Game in about as tight a spot as can be imagined. Newcombe got DiMaggio on a fly out to left, however, and then escaped the inning by inducing a popup to second by Eddie Joost.

If Newcombe's great escape wasn't enough, he almost hit a three-run homer in his plate appearance in the bottom of the inning. Instead, Newcombe, who is considered one of the best hitting pitchers of all time, settled for a sacrifice fly to draw the National League one run closer. Throughout his career, Newcombe established many firsts for African American pitchers, but in this case, he became the first African American player to drive in a run in the All-Star Game. Newcombe pitched a scoreless third, and the National League scored two runs in the bottom of the inning, including a run by Robinson, to take a 5–4 lead.

By rule at the time, All-Star starters had to play three innings, so Southworth gave the hometown fans a treat. He installed Campanella and Hodges into the lineup but left the other Dodgers in and let all four Dodgers position players finish out the game. Unfortunately for Newcombe, he stayed in long enough to surrender the lead and was saddled with the loss in an 11–7 American League win.

Robinson played the entire game and went 1-for-4 with three runs and a walk. Campanella went 0-for-2 with an intentional walk, and Newcombe finished with 2.2 innings pitched while allowing two runs. Doby entered the game in the sixth inning as a pinch-runner for Joe DiMaggio to become the first African American All-Star in the American League. Doby grounded out to first in his only at-bat.

During this era, the All-Star Game was much more than an exhibition, as players took a tremendous amount of pride in their leagues. Player movement was much less prevalent then, and most players, especially the stars, typically stayed with one team, in one league for their entire career. The next day, the *Brooklyn Daily Eagle* ran five separate articles about the game, and the significance of the African American All-Stars was not lost on the host city's paper. The *Eagle* ran a large photo of Robinson, Doby, Newcombe, and Campanella in the Ebbets Field dugout above a caption that read, "Negro Foursome in All-Star Game." The caption went on to recognize the significance of these four players in the game.

Columnist Tommy Holmes dug deeper into Newcombe's performance. He wrote that the two-run single Newcombe gave up to Joost was more of a matter of bad luck than a bad pitch. Newcombe had fooled Joost on the pitch, and he hit a cue-shot down off Hodges's hand at first. The spinning ball eluded Hodges so badly it went as a hit instead of an error and allowed the decisive runs to score. Holmes also provided more detail about Newcombe's batting.

Newcombe came up with the bases loaded and no outs, and noticed left fielder Ted Williams shaded toward center field. Newcombe lined a shot down the left-field line, and off the bat it looked like it could go for a bases-clearing double; however, Williams ranged far to his right to make a fantastic leaping catch. The importance of the game was reflected in Newcombe's comments.

The rookie righty said, "Boy, I thought I had that one. I never hit a ball any harder, and I'd caught Williams over in left-center. But he got it anyway. It was the biggest day of my life, and I sure wanted to win."

Despite the historical significance of the game, the narrative that followed was that the game had run its course. Interestingly, many of the complaints were similar to ones that have been lobbed at modern-day All-Star Games in every sport. The *Daily Eagle* ran a column calling for owners to put an end to the game. The 1949 game was particularly sloppy, as the teams combined for 6 errors, 25 hits, and 8 walks. In addition, the column complained that some players didn't take the game seriously enough, that the fans were bored, and that aside from a few of the game's superstars, not many players hustled on the field. This came on the heels of a growing narrative that players had been using minor injuries as an excuse to skip out on the game.

The 1950 All-Star Game went on as planned but not without continued controversy. There were the typical arguments that persist today. Columnists and fans cried out at American League manager Casey Stengel for favoring his own players when filling out his roster after the fan vote. Such lesser-known players as Dale Mitchell, Johnny Groth, Bob Miller, and Max Lanier were passed over for more popular players like Joe DiMaggio and Ewell Blackwell, drawing the ire of fans and columnists who believed a spot on the roster should be based solely that season's performance rather than name recognition. The final straw came when Dodgers manager Burt Shotton requested that Hank Sauer be removed from the starting lineup because he didn't have a natural center fielder that was voted in. National League president Ford Frick approved the move and allowed Shotton to slot Duke Snider into a starting role.

After all the controversy, however, the game went on, and for the first time, there were multiple African American starters. Robinson again garnered the start at second base, the second of his six straight All-Star berths. Roy Campanella joined him in the National League starting lineup in what would be his second of eight straight appearances. On the American League side, Larry Doby drew the start in center field and played all 14 innings of the game. Doby would go on to appear in seven consecutive All-Star Games. If the 1949 game was the first time that fans and personnel showed they truly recognized the impact African American players were having on the sport, the 1950 game verified it. From the 1949 All-Star Game onward, there would never be another Major League Baseball All-Star Game lacking an African American player.

THE '56 IMMORTALS

By the mid-1950s, almost every Major League Baseball team had integrated. When Yankees rookie Elston Howard entered the second game of an Opening Day doubleheader against the Red Sox in the sixth inning as a left fielder, he became the first African American player to take the field for the Yankees. They were the 13th of 16 teams to integrate, leaving only the Phillies, Tigers, and Red Sox. During the first five years of the 1950s, a steady stream of teams began to integrate, albeit much slower than they should have. That isn't the only reason the 1955 season is considered a watershed year, however.

When looking back at the different eras in baseball history, it's easy to point at two particular spans that helped revive the sport. The transformative "Liveball Era" of the 1920s is credited with modernizing baseball while thriving behind Babe Ruth and is vitally important. Baseball experienced a similar revival in the 1950s. The Great Depression, World War II, and the Korean War of the early 1950s provided major hurdles in the development of the sport, and the specter of segregation hung over the sport that entire time. In the mid-1950s, baseball experienced its second great era.

By 1955, Major League Baseball was ready to put the previous 25 years and the bad times that had accompanied them behind it. The impact of the Korean War had faded from the sport, and by then the icons from the previous era—for instance, Joe DiMaggio, Mel Ott, and Jimmie Foxx—had been out of the game for years. Even though there were still three teams yet to integrate, many of the first wave of African American players were already past their prime or gone. Jackie Robinson was still productive, but he was a 36-year-old third baseman who batted in the bottom of the order by 1955. Monte Irvin, who didn't come into the league until he was 30, only played 51 games that year for the Giants and retired the next season. Larry Doby was still an All-Star in 1955, but he began a slow fade after that. Satchel Paige was allegedly 49 years old in 1955, and although he had now been out of the league for two seasons, it wouldn't be the last fans saw of him. Looking back with the benefit of hindsight, Major League Baseball was in a clear transition.

Leading the transition into the second half of the twentieth century was an influx of thrilling young players who had fans imitating their styles of play on sandlots throughout the United States. Mickey Mantle came into the game in 1951, and was a player the likes of which the sport had never seen. Al Kaline emerged as a teenage superstar for the Detroit Tigers, full of the promise that had been robbed from a young Hank Greenberg. Eddie Mathews, another young slugger whose raw power was rivaled by only Mantle's, was hitting home runs at a historic pace for the Milwaukee Braves; however, it was a trio of young African American superstars who were bringing the game to life. Between 1951–1954, Hank Aaron, Willie Mays, and Ernie Banks made their debuts.

April 19 was the eve of Opening Day for the 1948 Major League Baseball season. It was a little more than a year to the day of Jackie Robinson's debut, and the Dodgers again had uncertainty surrounding their star player. The big talk in Brooklyn was who was going to play first base in place of Robinson, who had recently shifted to second base, a more natural position. While Leo Durocher was trying to sort that out, a young, 16-year-old phenom was playing inspiring ball in Macon, Georgia, in a league in which he should have been in well over his head. That young player was Willie Mays.

Mays grew up in Westfield, Alabama, the son of a star baseball player who was his namesake. Mays learned the game from his dad at an early age. Mays's father taught him to hit as a toddler by handing young Willie a small broomstick and tossing rubber balls to him. Willie's father, known as Cat, would mentor him throughout his developmental years, with Willie even playing alongside Cat in the outfield as a youngster in the competitive Birmingham Industrial League, one of the top outlets for African Americans to play baseball in the South before integration. On April 19, as Major League Baseball was readying for Opening Day, Mays was playing his usual position in center field for the Chattanooga Choo Choos of the Negro Southern League against the Newark Eagles. The Eagles had won the 1947 Negro National League and featured Hall of Famers Larry Doby, Monte Irvin, and Biz Mackey. The game that day ended in a 12-inning, 1–1 tie, which was a great showing for the Choo Choos. The next day, the *Chattanooga Daily Times* lauded Mays as the hitting and fielding star of the game for the Choo Choos.

The next season, Mays made the jump from the Choo Choos to the Birmingham Black Barons, a revered team in the Negro American League. Three of his teammates would eventually go on to have cups of coffee in the major leagues. Mays was a full 20 years younger than the team's oldest player, Lloyd Bassett, and was the youngest regular player on the team by seven years. He played 73 games that season, batting .262, while flashing his brilliance on the basepaths and in the outfield. His play caught the eye of New York Giants scout Eddie Montague, a former infielder for the Cleveland Indians who played against Ty Cobb and Babe Ruth. Montague was scouting Alonzo Perry, a first baseman for the Black Barons, when he spotted Mays. He would label Mays the "greatest young player I had ever seen in my life or my scouting career." Montague later signed Mays to the Giants for a $4,000 signing bonus and a salary of $250 a month.

Mays is so synonymous with the Giants and New York baseball that it's hard to picture him in another uniform; however, he was almost a Boston Brave, a Brooklyn Dodger, and, in a less likely scenario, a Boston Red Sock. The Braves scouted Mays extensively and petitioned Major League Baseball commissioner Happy Chandler to offer him a contract, even though he was a minor. Boston was prepared to offer him $7,500, but the team got cold feet when a different scout convinced Braves ownership that Mays couldn't hit a curveball. The scout wasn't wrong; Mays had trouble with the curve early in his career, and even Buck Leonard had the same assessment of Mays as a youngster. But Mays could hit a fastball, and overall his skills were otherworldly. Foolishly, the Braves passed on Mays, robbing fans of an outfield made up of Hank Aaron and Mays—one that likely would have been the best in baseball history.

The Braves weren't the only team to blow a chance at Mays. The Boston Red Sox sent scout George Digby to research Mays with the Black Barons, and he returned with the same assessment as Montague, calling Mays the greatest prospect he had ever seen. Although Red Sox owner Tom Yawkey was staunchly against African Americans in Major League Baseball, the team's general manager, Joe Cronin, sent a second scout to see Mays. Regardless of that scout's assessment, however, Cronin and Yawkey were in lockstep to keep the Red Sox segregated. An outfield of Ted Williams in left and Willie Mays in center was blocked from happening by the stubborn racism of Yawkey.

With the Red Sox and Braves out of the picture, Mays almost became a teammate of Robinson in Brooklyn. In 1949, Mays played against Roy Campanella and other major leaguers in a barnstorming tour. In a game between the Black Barons and Campanella's Stars, Mays threw out Larry Doby at the plate from the center-field wall. Campanella alerted the Dodgers to Mays, and they sent one of their most trusted scouts, Wid Matthews, to have a look at him. Matthews returned with the same concern of others before him: Mays couldn't handle a curveball. While Matthews whiffed on that moment in history, he did play an important role not long thereafter. Remarkably, Mays was passed over by three teams before he landed on the Giants.

Despite his gaffe with Mays, Matthews was hired by the Chicago Cubs as their director of player personnel in 1950. He quickly signed shortstop Gene Baker from the Kansas City Monarchs. While Baker's name tends to be lost in public sentiment among such players as Mays, Aaron, and Robinson, he would go on to become a good player and a trailblazer in many respects. Baker slowly ascended in the minors during the course of six seasons, with some even suggesting he was intentionally being brought along little by little as the Cubs debated integrating. Six years after Robinson's debut in Brooklyn, Baker became the first African American player to appear on a Cubs roster when he was a September call-up in 1953; however, an injury kept him from being the first African American player to take the field for the Cubs. Baker first appeared for the Cubs as a pinch-hitter for pitcher Don Elston in the seventh inning of a game against the Cardinals. In that same game, the Cubs' new rookie shortstop went 3-for-4 with the first of his 512 career home runs. That player was another Wid Matthews signee, Ernie Banks.

On September 8, 1953, in an Associated Press article, it was announced that the Cubs had purchased Banks from the Kansas City Monarchs for an undisclosed sum of money. Banks was 22 years old, and the article estimated that he would beat Gene Baker in a "plane race" to be the first African American to report to the Cubs. At the time of the signing, Banks was leading the Negro Leagues with 22 home runs, batting .388. The signing of Banks and Baker, and the integration of the Cubs, didn't draw much more than a passing mention in the media, as there were now more than 30 African American players playing in the major leagues.

The bigger story about the integration era was how slow teams were to integrate once Jackie Robinson debuted. Many African American players had become some of the top players in the game, and the Dodgers, Indians, and Giants were thriving as integrated teams. Between 1947–1953, the historic Yankees won six of seven World Series titles. Although they remained segregated during that period, they were stocked with Hall of Famers the likes of Joe DiMaggio, Yogi Berra, Whitey Ford, Phil Rizzuto, and Mickey Mantle. The only year they lost the World Series in that span was 1948, when they fell to Satchel Paige, Larry Doby, and the Indians. During the great Yankees run, they faced integrated teams five out of seven times. Despite a track record of respect and acceptance, teams were still painfully slow to integrate. Although the number of African American players was increasing, the Cubs were only the eighth team to integrate out of 16. Banks was the 37th African American to play in the majors, so the previous 36 were spread out on seven teams.

When the Cubs integrated in 1953, they were the first National League team to do so in three seasons, the previous one being the Braves in 1950. Although it took three years for the Braves to integrate after Robinson, they soon became one of the most progressive teams as more African American players debuted in the majors. Sam Jethroe and Luis Marquez were the first African Americans to play for the Braves, but the most impactful figure came three years after that pair debuted, with Hank Aaron. Aaron started with the Braves as a 20-year-old outfielder in 1954, and began one of the most remarkable careers in Major League Baseball history.

Aaron was a baseball star at a young age growing up in Alabama. He began his semipro career with the Pritchett Athletics as a 14-year-old in 1947, and by the time he was 16, he had signed a contract with the Negro American League Indianapolis Clowns for $200 a month. He had a fantastic year for the Clowns in 1952, leading them to the Negro League World Series championship and drawing the attention of major-league scouts along the way. As with Mays and the Giants, Aaron almost didn't end up with the franchise he's most synonymous with. The Dodgers, a team he tried out for unsuccessfully as a 15-year-old, were one of the first teams back on his trail. They sent Jackie Robinson's old minor-league teammate, Al Campanis, to scout Aaron with the Clowns. Al's grandson, Jim, who played in the Seattle Mariners system, recalled a story about his grandfather regarding Aaron.

> He (Campanis) was sent to Indianapolis to see a shortstop. The current Brooklyn Dodgers shortstop, Pee Wee Reese, was nearing retirement, so the Dodgers sent my grandpa specifically to see if this shortstop from Indy could transition into the majors. My grandpa wrote a scouting report touting this player as one of the best hitters he'd ever seen. He went on to write that he recommended the Dodgers sign him immediately and put him in AAA. But when it came to scouting defensive— he mentioned this player should be moved to the outfield. Because the Dodgers needed a shortstop, they passed on signing this player. Too bad for them—that player was Hank Aaron.

The Dodgers weren't the only ones to miss out on Aaron. After the Clowns won the championship, Aaron received two contract offers from major-league teams. The Braves and Giants both bid for his services, forcing him to choose between joining Monte Irvin and Willie Mays in New York and a Braves team that was struggling through another difficult season. While the Giants' situation was much more desirable, the Braves offered Aaron an extra $50 a month for his services, so that's where he went. One of baseball's great opportunities, having Willie Mays and Hank Aaron playing in the same outfield, was dashed by a mere $50, as lore would have it. Aaron's signing was lauded by the *Alabama Tribune*, which noted that he was leading the Negro Leagues in every offensive category. Aaron's talent was evident, even if he may have offered an inaccurate scouting report of himself. At the time of his signing, Aaron said, "I'm not a long-ball hitter, but I managed to turn plenty of ordinary singles into doubles."

Aaron played the remainder of the 1952 season and continued his torrid hitting. Playing for the Eau Claire Bears in the Northern League, he batted .336 in 87 games, running away with Rookie of the Year honors. Prior to the 1953 season, legendary Braves general manager John Quinn offered a recollection of Aaron's previous season in the *Boston Globe*. Quinn said,

> He's 18 years old, and he never had played a game of minor-league ball. Yet, two weeks after he joined the club, he made the league's All-Star Team. His name is Henry Aaron, and one of our scouts spotted him playing with the Indianapolis Clowns of the Negro League. We found he'd only been with the Clowns a few weeks, and until last May, he never had played anything but sandlot ball. He's a shortstop, and he looks as though he may be a beauty. We started him with a Class C team, Eau Claire, Wisconsin, in the Northern League. And he went to town there right away—as shown by his making the All-Star Team when he'd only been there a couple of weeks.

The article gave a short scouting report on the young phenom as well. Writer Roger Birtwell noted that Aaron is a "slender youth—about 5′10″ and 165 pounds." Aaron was reported to be an excellent hitter and fielder, and, according to Birtwell, "Like most Negro ballplayers, Aaron is fast on his feet." Aaron would be training with the Braves the coming spring at shortstop, along with Felix Mantilla, who would go on to have a solid major-league career. Aaron was signed by the Jacksonville Braves, an A-ball affiliate of the Braves in the Southern Atlantic League, on March 30, 1953, and promptly moved to second base, with Mantilla signing on to play short. Just two days later, Jacksonville played an exhibition game against the Boston Red Sox and, to no one's surprise, was trounced, 14–1. The only run of the game for Jacksonville came on a solo home run by Aaron off Red Sox righty Ike Delock. Aaron would hit two home runs in three exhibition games for Jacksonville, both described as line drives that went almost 400 feet, an incredible accomplishment for someone who was listed as a slight 160-pound middle infielder. The *Alabama Journal* touted the start of the 1953 minor-league season by previewing Jacksonville's team and new situation. The club was previously known as the

Jacksonville Tars, a despondent team that had not won a championship since 1912.

Prior to the 1953 season, the Tars changed owners and were rebranded as the Braves. As part of their transformation, the newly formed ownership group signed their first three African American players, and it made headline news in the South. The "Sally" League had remained segregated up to that point, but the Braves had three players ready to break the color barrier that season, along with two other players on the Savannah Indians.

On April 10, the *Alabama Journal* ran an article previewing the team with the headline "Three Negroes to Open for Jacksonville." The lede introduced the changes coming to the team by saying that the "Jacksonville club has shattered precedent to smithereens," noting that Aaron, Horace Gardner, and Mantilla would be in the starting lineup on Opening Day. Aaron led the club with 22 home runs, while Gardner, a career minor leaguer, finished second on the team with 15. Mantilla, who was born in Puerto Rico, was considered African American due to his father's African heritage. He manned the shortstop position throughout the season and was one of the team's top players as well.

The three men led Jacksonville to a 93–44 record, with Aaron capturing the league's MVP Award. Speaking of Aaron's accomplishments, league president Dick Butler said, "The color barrier (in Southern baseball) has been broken, there's no doubt about that." Butler was supportive of Aaron and his African American colleagues, often following the team closely as they faced the expected hateful treatment by opposing fans. Manager Ben Geraghty, who played 70 games in the majors in the 1930s and 1940s during the era of segregation, also took extra care to help Aaron, Mantilla, and Gardner adjust. He was known to eat dinner and socialize with the three players, who still had to abide by rules of segregation in the South. In August 1953, it was reported that Aaron had started working out in left field to prepare for what seemed to be a guaranteed leap to the majors for the youngster. Both Butler and Geraghty labeled Aaron a tremendous all-around prospect and someone who was clearly on the path to the major leagues.

As early as January, Aaron was being touted as a top prospect for the Braves as a second baseman in 1954. An Associated Press article by Joe Reichler that ran nationally on January 21, declared Aaron and pitcher Gene Conley can't-miss prospects. The article ran through the litany of Aaron's offensive accomplishments from the previous season while emphasizing that he was still only 19, and had played just two years of Organized Baseball. Writer Ken Blanchard raised the bar a month later, writing that according to baseball people, Aaron had the potential to be an all-time great.

Aaron was a daily story line in the Milwaukee newspapers leading up to spring training, and once workouts started, all eyes were on the future immortal. For perhaps the first time as a baseball player, however, Aaron disappointed. He started the spring just 2-for-9, and made two errors in right field. Within the first 10 days of spring training, Aaron was replaced by Andy Pafko in right field, and he was discussed in the press as someone who needed more seasoning, likely to start the season in the minors. Aaron steadied throughout the spring, but the sentiment was that he would begin the season in Toledo.

The Braves were coming off a good 1953 season and had added veteran power hitter Bobby Thomson, three years removed from his "Shot Heard 'Round the World," in the offseason. When Thomson was acquired in early February, the team's general manager, Charlie Grimm, declared that Thomson was going to be his left fielder and cleanup hitter. With Andy Pafko in right and Aaron permanently moved off the infield, there simply would be no room for him in the starting lineup; however, Thomson broke his ankle halfway through spring training, and on March 20, with Opening Day 10 days away, Aaron was named as Thomson's replacement in the starting lineup.

An article in the *La Crosse Tribune* announcing Aaron's elevation to the starting lineup painted the young man as the legend he would become. It was reported that Aaron wasn't just going to be a six-week injury replacement. He had a chance to prove he belonged and would be given an opportunity to earn a full-time position. Mickey Owen, who had been in baseball since the 1930s and managed Aaron in winter ball, said he indeed was a can't-miss prospect. Veteran Braves first basemen Joe Adcock heaped more hype on Aaron.

Adcock said, "Everything this kid hits is a line drive, and he hits more line drives through the box than anybody I ever saw. He's already come close to flattening a couple of pitchers with his screamers through the middle of the diamond. Those fellows better watch out or he'll unpeel 'em." Aaron was then described in the article as having heavy, sloping shoulders, like Mickey Mantle, and thick, powerful wrists that allowed him to drive the ball to all fields. A common theme of Aaron's early scouting reports was the power he showed in his wrists. Like just about everything else that was predicted for Aaron, these high compliments bore out in the success of his 23-year career.

While Aaron was impressing in Milwaukee, another African American teenager was debuting in the Southern Atlantic League, which Aaron just left. Frank Robinson was just 18 years old but would bludgeon the Sally League the way Aaron had the year before. Robinson was named an All-Star after belting 25 home runs while batting .336 for the season. He returned to Columbia of the Sally League in 1955, and while his power remained, his average fell, and Robinson never received a call to the majors. The following spring, however, he left no doubt that he was ready for the major leagues.

On April 17, 1956, Frank Robinson made his major-league debut. He went 2-for-3 while batting seventh and playing left field for the Reds in a 4–2 loss to the Cardinals. On the same day in Milwaukee, the Cubs and Braves faced off in front of 39,000 fans. Hank Aaron started in right field and went 2-for-3 with a home run while batting cleanup. His Braves beat Ernie Banks, Monte Irvin, and the Cubs, 6–0. The Cleveland Indians played the White Sox on Opening Day 1956, in a game that featured two of the game's premiere pitchers at the time: Billy Pierce of the White Sox outdueled Hall of Famer Bob Lemon as Chicago topped Cleveland, 2–1. Larry Doby played center field and batted third for the White Sox but went 0-for-3 against his former team. At the Polo Grounds, Willie Mays scored the go-ahead run in the eighth inning of a 4–3 win for the Giants against the Pittsburgh Pirates. Not far from the Polo Grounds, the Dodgers were in an Opening Day tussle with the Phillies. Don Newcombe was on the mound for the Dodgers, but the Phillies touched him for five runs in the third to knock him out of the game. Roy Campanella went 2-for-5 with a home run off Hall of Famer Robin Roberts, but it wasn't enough, as the Dodgers lost, 8–6. Jackie Robinson went 0-for-3 in the game while starting at third base.

On Opening Day of the 1956 season, eight future African American Hall of Famers took the field together, albeit at different ballparks. There were eight games played that day, and each game featured at least one integrated team—the first time that had ever happened on Opening Day. April 17, 1956, can be pointed to as the exact marker where the first generation of African American stars intersected with the second generation. Jackie Robinson and Irvin would retire following the year, making the 1956 season the only time all eight of these legends played together. Their performances took decidedly different paths throughout the season.

With a solid rookie year under his belt, Aaron became an All-Star for the first time as a 21-year-old in 1956. He batted .314, with 27 home runs and 106 RBI, while leading the National League with 37 doubles. The next time Aaron would miss the All-Star Game was as a 42-year-old man playing in his final season. Banks continued to blossom in his third full season as one of the best shortstops in the game. He made the second of 14 All-Star appearances and was the lone bright spot on a Cubs team that lost 94 games. Mays had one of his iconic seasons in 1956, when he reached 40 stolen bases for the only time in his career. He smashed 36 home runs, almost becoming the game's first 40–40 player, while establishing himself as the best center fielder in the game. Frank Robinson was not to be outdone. The fearsome righty won Rookie of the Year honors for the Reds, tying Wally Berger's major-league rookie home record, at 38, which had stood for 26 years. He batted .290, while finishing seventh in the MVP voting, ahead of eight Hall of Famers. Each young icon in this collection of icons was 25 years old or younger and clearly ready to take over the sport.

On the other hand, the group of four veterans were all in their mid-30s and on the tail end of careers that bridged the major leagues and Negro Leagues. Jackie Robinson helped the Dodgers to the World Series for the second year in a row as a veteran leader. Coming off the incredible 1955 World Series win against the Yankees, Robinson batted .275 during the regular season and went 6-for-24 in the World Series, with an important home run off Whitey Ford in Game 1; however, the Dodgers lost a deciding game seven, 9–0. Robinson struck out for the last out of the World Series. In December of that offseason, Robinson was traded across town to the New York Giants but decided to retire instead. In a classy move, he penned a letter to Giants owner Horace Stoneham explaining that his retirement had nothing to do with the trade, as he had previously decided to pursue other business opportunities. He wished his longtime rival well and bid adieu to Major League Baseball.

Doby was the youngest of the first-generation players, at just 32, but he was already past his prime. The 1956 season would be the last time Doby would play more than 120 games, and for the first time as a full-time player, he failed to make the All-Star Team. Doby still knocked 26 home runs and drove in 105 for the White Sox. The man who integrated the American League would retire in 1959, after combining to play 39 games for the Tigers and White Sox at the age of 35. Irvin didn't debut until he was 30, and he was 37 years old by 1956. He completed his eight-year career with his only season in Chicago as Banks's teammate. Irvin hit .271 in 111 games while playing center field at Wrigley.

Campanella's story was decidedly more tragic than his pioneering counterparts. He was an All-Star for the eighth and final time in 1956, despite batting .219 for the season. He hit 20 home runs while catching 120 games for the National League champions and batted just .182 in the World Series. Despite his visibly eroding skills, Campanella returned for 1957. Now 35 years old, Campy was productive while catching 107 games. He raised his average to .242, but continued to slide in most other offensive categories. He was planning on returning for the 1958 season but never had the chance.

Campanella operated a liquor store as his offseason job, and while returning home on January 28, 1957, his car hit a patch of ice and skidded off the road. Campanella broke two vertebrae in his neck and was paralyzed from the neck down. He would go on to become a great ambassador for the sport and continued to maintain his reputation as one of the game's most beloved figures. On May 7, 1959, the Yankees famously traveled to Los Angeles to play an exhibition at the Coliseum to honor Campanella. The game, dubbed "Roy Campanella Night," drew 93,103 fans, setting the record for attendance at a single major-league game.

The 1956 All-Star Game featured eight African American players. The young icons Mays, Aaron, Banks, and Frank Robinson were joined by Campanella and his Dodgers teammate, Jim Gilliam, and Harry Simpson and Vic Power of the Kansas City A's. The World Series featured the Dodgers, pioneers of integration, against the Yankees, who had only integrated the season before with Elston Howard and were slow to continue from there. The Dodgers featured their "big three" African American stars, Robinson, Newcombe, and Campanella. They also had the solid Gilliam at second and Charlie Neal as a utility infielder. Sandy Amoros was a strong outfielder as well. Amoros, a Cuban of African descent, had been signed by Al Campanis after playing for the New York Cubans in 1950.

Jerry Reuss broke into the majors in 1969, as a teammate of Bob Gibson, Curt Flood, and Lou Brock, and spoke about what it was like to play among the greatest of African American stars.

"I played with so many of the great superstars of the era, and they were just incredibly talented players," said Reuss.

> I pitched against Hank Aaron, Willie Mays, Roberto Clemente, Frank Robinson, Ernie Banks, Billy Williams, and Joe Morgan, among others. As a pitcher, I always thought my job was to make the perfect pitch, each pitch. You have to have that kind of focus to be successful on that level. I always tried to throw my best pitch, every pitch. I would throw a perfect pitch to players of that nature and they would foul it off, while it would get most anyone else out. Those guys would foul it off though. What do you do when you throw your perfect pitch and you still can't get them out with it? How do you improve on a perfect pitch? That's what it was like facing them. That's why they're in the Hall of Fame. It was incredible to pitch against them. Just years before I was collecting their likeness on baseball cards, and now I was playing with and against them. There's no words to describe that feeling.

By the end of the 1956 season, 75 African American players had played in the major leagues. Future National League president and labor pioneer Curt Flood also debuted in 1956. The year was a crossroads, and it seemed like every team had an African American pioneer or budding superstar. Jackie Robinson came into the sport alone as the first African American ballplayer in 1947, and as he was leaving it, there were plenty of immortals ready to continue his legacy. Robinson debuted in celebrated yet controversial circumstances, and by the time he left the sport, the presence of African American talent was bustling. But despite the all-around steady growth, abundance of stars, and social acceptance of African American baseball players, three teams remained segregated—the Phillies, Red Sox, and Tigers.

THE FINAL TEAMS TO INTEGRATE

On July 22, 1959, *Boston Globe* columnist Robert McLean interviewed Judge Herbert Tucker Jr., a civil rights leader who was also president of the Boston chapter of the National Association for the Advancement of Colored People (NAACP). McLean was interested in getting Tucker's opinion on the latest rookie to be called up to the struggling Boston Red

Sox. In his comments, Tucker declared, "I think that now there will be more emphasis on an athlete's ability rather than the accident of his birth." His quote was in reference to the Red Sox signing Pumpsie Green from the Minneapolis Millers, their AAA affiliate. Green would be the first African American to play for the Red Sox, the final team to integrate.

There had been a push for Green to make the Red Sox out of spring training in 1959. On March 7, the Red Sox were preparing to play reigning MVP Ernie Banks and the Chicago Cubs in their spring training opener, and the headlines that day focused on two items. First, Ted Williams would not be playing in the game. Manager Mike Higgins afforded the aging legend the right to ease into the spring. The other was that Green was set to start the game at shortstop. By the time Green took the field for the Red Sox in July, 115 African American players had played in the majors. When a new African American player arrived, it didn't draw the headlines as it had in the past. Teams and fans were becoming accustomed to integration, and the mere color of someone's skin generally didn't draw attention the way it did a decade earlier.

The Red Sox, however, with the leadership of owner Tom Yawkey, Eddie Collins (prior to his death in 1951), and GM Pinky Higgins, remained steadfast in their desire to remain segregated. Civil rights leader Walter Carrington, who would later become Bill Clinton's ambassador to Nigeria, conducted an investigation into the Red Sox organization in 1959, and found that the Red Sox had not only chosen to remain segregated on the diamond, but also never hired an African American in any capacity, "even in the most menial position," as Carrington put it.

Columnist Harold Kaese profiled Green's spring training experience in the *Boston Globe* on March 15. The story painted a picture of a likable player who got along well with his teammates. In the Red Sox clubhouse, Green could be seen as just another teammate, laughing with other players and personnel, sharing stories, and talking baseball; however, once the players left the park, Green was anything but just another player. The town of Scottsdale, Arizona, banned him as a resident, so the Red Sox put him up in a motel on the outskirts of Phoenix. Each day, a young local boy who worked as a groundskeeper shuttled Green to and from the training complex. His living conditions at the motel were said to be satisfactory, but Green was left there in isolation. He was without a car, without his wife and son, and without any teammates or friends with whom to socialize. Green passed the time by reading, listening to music, and writing letters while the rest of his teammates stayed at the team hotel in Scottsdale. Green eventually was allowed to move to the Adams Hotel in Phoenix, where African American players from the San Francisco Giants were staying.

There was another underlying question in the Red Sox spring training in 1959. What if Green was beat out for his roster spot fair and square? The Red Sox were deep with middle infielders, and it was possible that the incumbents would hold on to their spots. Green could be beaten out for a job and sent to the minors, but fans and writers were likely to point to his race as the reason for a possible demotion. There was tremendous pressure on the Sox to have Green on their Opening Day roster, and if he wasn't, the Sox didn't have much of a leg to stand on against the claim of racism. It was a paradox of their own making, and Kaese addressed it in his article. He mentioned that Ted Lepcio and Billy Consolo were good utility infielders with power, and Don Buddin was the returning shortstop and a switch-hitter. Green rated as the best fielder of the group but possibly the weakest hitter. Green was a switch-hitter as well, and his former manager, Hall of Famer Joe Gordon, endorsed him as a player. Gordon said, "He saved us. He's a good fielder and can play anywhere. He strikes out a lot left-handed but meets the ball better right-handed. He's a good baserunner and a good fellow. He'll help you." Green's teams won minor-league championships the two previous seasons, and he was one of the big reasons why.

With less than three weeks left in spring training, Green looked like he had a great shot at making the Opening Day roster. The *Boston Globe* ran an article on March 25, with the headline "Pumpsie's Chances Good of Staying Up with Sox." The lede even went as far as to declare, "Pumpsie Green's performance this spring will earn him a spot on the Red Sox varsity." The article addressed the overstock of middle infielders, saying the Sox would likely try to trade Consolo. Green's batting average hovered at about .400 throughout the spring, and Lepcio was hitting the ball well, too. With Buddin locked in as a stalwart, Consolo looked to be the odd man out and, reading the writing on the wall, even asked to be traded somewhere he could play.

With Opening Day less than a week away, Green received word that he would be sent back to Minneapolis instead of breaking camp with the big club. Green faltered late in spring training, ending the exhibition season with a 2-for-19 slump. He committed two errors as well, and Red

Sox management claimed they wanted Green to play regularly in the minors to continue to improve, rather than sit on the bench in the majors. Overall, Green had a good spring, batting .327, but objectively, it was the right move to make. Even the reporters who had been stumping for Green conceded that this was the right baseball move. Nonetheless, because of the long history of racism in the Red Sox organization, fans and social groups were outraged that Green was sent to AAA.

The *Boston Globe* ran multiple articles on Green's demotion and sought reactions from fans, scholars, and social activists. The comments published were almost all in favor of Green staying with the Red Sox. Some even remarked that Green should have replaced Buddin, who started 250 games the previous two seasons. Harold Kaese, a supporter of Green throughout the spring and someone who recognized the baseball sense of the move, contended that Green wasn't given a fair shot from the start. While he was given ample playing time and a fair chance on the field, he had no support off the field. Kaese mentioned the willingness of the Red Sox to let Green stay 10 miles from the stadium by himself because of segregation laws in Scottsdale. He suggested that the Red Sox could have stayed at a place where everyone was welcome.

Kaese wrote that if the Red Sox had stood up to the racial policies of the city of Scottsdale by moving spring training elsewhere, they would have been "admired by 99 percent of the nation." He also should have suggested that the Red Sox invite another African American to camp, mentioning Earl Wilson, a big right-hander who was on the precipice of breaking into the majors. Kaese had offered the most evenhanded characterization of Green's spring training all along, and he was correct again. Green could have been treated better, but it would benefit him to play every day in the minors rather than sit on the bench at a time when subs were used much more sparsely than they are today. Even Ted Williams, long a champion of integration, agreed on this point.

Through all of this, Green handled the situation with as much class as Jackie Robinson, without all the fanfare. He was a great teammate in spring training and did nothing but work hard and give an honest effort to make the team. Any questions he received about racism were brushed aside by Green, saying he was just here to work hard and play ball. He never complained about staying alone and graciously accepted the offer to join the Giants at the Adams Hotel. Even weeks later, while the Red Sox were embroiled in an investigation on racial discrimination amid a wave of public embarrassment, Green simply reported to Minneapolis and performed great. After a game on April 21, a young Gene Mauch, who was Green's manager in Minneapolis, remarked on Green's disposition. Mauch said,

> He's done some fantastic things. He's made impossible plays. He had one of the greatest doubleheaders in Fort Worth the other night that I ever saw. The fans in Houston and Fort Worth got on him pretty hard about [being sent down]. When he finally made an out in Fort Worth in the last inning, they hollered that I'd probably have to write a letter to the NAACP explaining it. But Green has never changed expression, never acted like he heard them. He came to us with a good attitude. He wants to play ball. He never mentions that other stuff.

On April 13, formal hearings about discrimination in the Red Sox organization were held by the Commission against Discrimination. During these proceedings, groups alleged that Green's demotion was an example of racial discrimination. The NAACP, the Ministerial Alliance (made up of 41 Boston clergymen), and Thomas Sullivan (the state chairman of the American Veterans Committee) expressed claims that Green's demotion was based on discrimination. Herbert Tucker of the NAACP alleged that "Green's transfer was unwarranted and is purely symbolic of the employment policy of the Boston club." Sullivan's letter was more diplomatic but made the point clear. Sullivan said in his note, "I am loathe to lay charges against the Boston Red Sox management, but it has aroused suspicion in our minds. While the cutting of Green makes sense, we are disturbed by the publicity on the matter." Sullivan also decried Green's housing situation in spring training. The Red Sox did not have a representative at the hearings, but GM Bucky Harris sent a statement that said Green was given a fair opportunity but was returned to Minneapolis to develop for the future by playing regularly. The end result of the hearings was that Boston gave its word that Green would be given a fair shot with the Red Sox at some point during the season if he deserved it and the Sox needed him—not that many people believed that.

In mid-July, the Red Sox found themselves in last place in the American League. Almost everyone in the infield was battling injury, and when Don Buddin jammed his thumb sliding into second base, the Red Sox were in dire need of help. Buddin tried to play through the injury, but it was making it worse. Eventually, the Red Sox dipped down to Minneapolis and gave Green his chance. On July 21, the Red Sox were hooked in a 2–1 pitchers' duel against the White Sox at Comiskey Park. In the eighth inning, Red Sox manager Billy Jurgess sent Vic Wertz to pinch hit for Buddin. Five years earlier, it was Wertz who had hit a long fly ball to center field in the 1954 World Series, which Willie Mays improbably ran down for what has become known as "The Catch." He played a secondary role in this bit of history as well. Wertz singled to center leading off the eighth. Representing the tying run, Jurgess made another strategic move by sending the adept baserunner Green to pinch run. It was at that point that Major League Baseball became fully integrated. Green was stranded at second and played the ninth without a defensive chance at shortstop, but history had been made either way. The Boston Red Sox became the 16th team in the majors to integrate, 12 years after Jackie Robinson did so for the Brooklyn Dodgers.

The stubborn racism of the Red Sox is the most glaring example of the painfully slow integration Major League Baseball faced throughout the 1950s. Had the Red Sox been as progressive as the Dodgers or Indians, their history would be much different. The team would have not only avoided their plight as the last holdout of integration, but also been more successful on the field. Despite wasting the final 15 seasons of Ted Williams's career by remaining segregated, the Red Sox were typically a middle-of-the-pack team in the American League. If they would have approached integration the way the Dodgers did, they could have built an incredible supporting cast around Williams. Baseball implications aside, the Red Sox earned their shameful place in baseball history.

If it wasn't for the Red Sox, the Detroit Tigers and Philadelphia Phillies would be held in much worse regard than they typically are. The Phillies earned the most disdain in baseball's racial history for the way they treated Jackie Robinson. Manager Ben Chapman ordered his players to shout racial epithets at Robinson during his first game in Philadelphia and happily joined in this behavior. Their conduct was so bad that a Phillies player apologized to Robinson on the field, saying that not everyone felt the same way and that they were following orders from their manager. If their shameful treatment of Robinson wasn't enough to brand their franchise racist, the decade it took for them to integrate surely did.

Entering the 1957 season, the Phillies were the only National League team that hadn't integrated. In the offseason, they purchased John Kennedy, a somewhat mysterious shortstop from the Kansas City Monarchs.

Kennedy surely made himself known in 1956, when he dominated the Negro League for the Monarchs, but before that, he played little Organized Baseball. Coming into spring training, Kennedy himself admitted that he just wanted to make a minor-league team. Considering his lack of experience, it wasn't a surprising plight; however, he quickly changed opinions by swinging a hot bat from the start of the spring. In less than two weeks, Kennedy went from an obscure player to someone who looked like a starting shortstop.

Kennedy's batting average was hovering at about .400 for most of the spring, before settling in the .330s. News coverage of the possible integration of the Phillies wasn't as intense as it was when the Red Sox integrated. In fact, Kennedy allegedly had no idea the Phillies were segregated until a reporter asked him about it. He seemingly nailed down the starting shortstop role and drew rave reviews from almost everyone who saw him play. He went from being an unknown to being compared to Ernie Banks in a little more than a month. So, when the Phillies traded for shortstop Chico Fernandez 10 days before Opening Day, fans were disgruntled to say the least.

When the Phillies went out of their way to bring in a shortstop despite Kennedy's play, skepticism was rightly raised. Kennedy had seemingly erased all doubts about his ability in the spring and at least earned a chance to prove himself, and it made no sense for the Phillies to purchase Fernandez from the Dodgers. Most people jumped to the conclusion that the Phillies were not ready to integrate. But years later it became known that Kennedy had lied about his age at some point early in his baseball career. By spring of 1959, he was 32 years old but had claimed to be 23. It is not known if the Fernandez trade was spurred by this discovery, but it could be an explanation. At the time, Fernandez himself was also considered by some to be African American. He was Cuban but had African descent. In fact, when Kennedy and Fernandez both made the Opening Day roster, the *Philadelphia Tribune* ran a headline that read, "City Hails Negro Players."

The Phillies played the Dodgers on Opening Day 1957. It was the first Opening Day the Dodgers spent without Jackie Robinson since 1946. Fernandez batted second and played short while Kennedy remained on the bench. Interestingly, while the *Tribune* had labeled Fernandez as a "Negro player" the day before, there was no mention of Fernandez as the one to integrate the Phillies. Kennedy made his debut on April 22, in the

Phillies' sixth game of the season. They faced off against the Dodgers in the eighth major-league game ever played at Roosevelt Stadium in Jersey City, New Jersey. This was the same stadium where Jackie Robinson made his professional debut with the Montreal Royals and the same city where Luis Padron, denied his chance at the major leagues 50 years earlier, ended his playing days. The Dodgers played a handful of games at Roosevelt Stadium instead of Ebbets Field as a negotiation ploy between the Dodgers and the city of Brooklyn.

Kennedy pinch ran in the eighth inning to integrate the Phillies. It was historic yet anticlimactic. There wasn't even a mention of it in the *Philadelphia Tribune* the next day. Kennedy only registered two hitless at-bats in five games for the Phillies before being sent to the minors, never to appear in the majors again. While there were some accusations that race played a role in Kennedy's departure, it wasn't anything like the uproar that would follow two years later when Pumpsie Green was sent to the minors by the Red Sox. The *Pittsburgh Courier* ran a column two weeks after Kennedy's demotion broaching the subject of racism with Kennedy's departure. While reporter Bob Queen raised questions of racial bias, he stopped short of flatly accusing the Phillies of discriminatory practices. He speculated that Kennedy may not have been ready, but the Phillies rushed him to appease the growing public pressure to integrate.

4

THRIVING IN A DIVERSE GAME

THE RISE TO THE PEAK

In the latter half of the 1950s, the first influx of young African American superstars reached the major leagues. By 1960, players like Willie Mays, Hank Aaron, and Ernie Banks were solidly established as some of the best players in the game. Along with young white stars Mickey Mantle, Stan Musial, and Yogi Berra, and Latino standouts Luis Aparicio, Orlando Cepeda, and Roberto Clemente, there was a diverse group of young dynamic stars for the first time in major-league history. The sport had fully recovered from the World War II era and was on a path toward the prosperous and colorful era of the 1970s.

In 1960, 8.9 percent of Major League Baseball players were African American. This was more than double the 3.7 percent that populated the sport just seven years earlier. Every major-league team was now integrated. Moreover, for the first time since 1950, Latino participation was equal to that of African American involvement. Approximately 18 percent of Major League Baseball was made up of underrepresented populations, which continued a slow but steady trend diversifying the sport.

The numbers were important, and the growth was encouraging. But what mattered most was the impact those groups were having on the game. They weren't just participating, they were dominating. They weren't just filling roles, their playing style brought creativity to the sport. They weren't just winning fans, they were drawing in a generation of young fanatics who wanted to be just like them.

The Giants and Dodgers were starting their third year in California at the start of the decade, and the game was careening into a new era, right along with American culture. Not even a month after Bill Mazeroski hit the first Game 7 walk-off home run to win a World Series, John F. Kennedy was elected president. The highlight of the baseball world on May 6, 1960, was that Willie Mays and a young budding star named Willie McCovey hit home runs to lead the Giants over the Pirates at Candlestick Park. The highlight in that day's news was the enactment of the Civil Rights Act of 1960, which expanded on the landmark 1957 act. The Vietnam War was underway and about to escalate, while Kennedy turned his attention to the Cold War. Fidel Castro and Che Guevara rose to power in Cuba, and the Cuban Missile Crisis was just two years away. It was a time of change and revolution throughout the world, and Major League Baseball was a part of it in its own way.

The African American stars of the early 1960s carried the torch for Jackie Robinson in more ways than one. They not only played with the class and dignity of Robinson, but also brought the same flair and personality, and some even expanded on it. This was not limited to immortals like Mays and Aaron either. Many African American stars of the 1960s had huge personalities and distinct traits that left a lasting impact on fans and motivated young fans to pretend they were their idols in stickball games and on sandlots throughout the country.

With Mays already an established star by 1960, Giants fans were blessed with a second Hall of Famer to pair with the immortal. The name McCovey is conjoined with Mays when discussing 1960s baseball in San Francisco, but that historical pairing almost never came to pass. McCovey got his start in professional ball playing for the Class D Sandersville Giants as a 17-year-old in Georgia. Early media coverage of McCovey described him as lanky and a "string bean." That may have been true in 1955, but by the time he became an established star he was a strapping, fearsome slugger. At spring training in 1959, McCovey was a big prospect, but he was stuck in a logjam at first base behind Bill White and fellow Hall of Famer Orlando Cepeda, who was coming off a 1958 Rookie of the Year season. White was the veteran of the group at 25 years old.

White had a tremendous rookie season in 1956, but he was drafted into the U.S. Army and missed the entire 1957 season and most of 1958. It was White's stint in the military that prompted the Giants to trade for

Jackie Robinson, who retired instead. Robinson's retirement opened the door for Cepeda. With Cepeda one of the brightest young stars in the game and McCovey knocking on the door, the Giants put their faith in Cepeda and traded White to the Cardinals late in spring training. White, who was the second African American to play in the Carolina League in 1953, would go on to have a fantastic career as a seven-time Gold Glove first baseman and make eight All-Star Game rosters.

With White gone, it was speculated that McCovey would make the Opening Day roster, albeit in a "bench splintering" role; however, a week after the White trade, McCovey was sent to AAA despite a strong spring. McCovey tore the Pacific Coast League to pieces in the 95 games he played by the end of July. He was leading the league in all three Triple Crown categories (.372 average, 29 home runs, and 92 RBI) and had nothing else to prove in the minors. With the Giants in a tight race for the National League pennant with the Dodgers and Braves, they finally called up McCovey on July 29. Cepeda, at 21 years of age, had just been the starting first baseman in the All-Star Game three weeks prior, but he was shuffled to third to make room for the highly touted McCovey. In an interview on July 29, manager Bill Rigney lamented the Giants lack of hitting when they slipped into second place. Their pitching had kept them at the top of the National League to that point, but they needed offensive reinforcements to battle the Dodgers and Braves, two of the better-hitting teams in the league. Rigney said in the interview, "We're not going to stay like this. We've got some ideas. We're going to talk about McCovey and some of the others tonight." When pressed for further explanation, Rigney was tight-lipped.

The next day, the Giants made their move. They called up the Phoenix Giants' top two hitters, McCovey and Jose Pagan, and sent Felipe Alou and Andre Rodgers to the minors.

McCovey was scouted as a strong fielding first baseman, but he lacked the versatility to play anywhere else at the major-league level. Rigney had no reservations about McCovey whatsoever. He immediately slotted the big lefty into the starting lineup and batted him third, giving the Giants a fearsome trio of Mays, McCovey, and Cepeda. The Giants would need all the support they could get on July 30, 1959, as they were slated to face Hall of Famer Robin Roberts and the Phillies.

Rigney could have eased McCovey into the lineup by giving him a pinch-hitting role in the first few games, but instead he sent McCovey up against one of the toughest pitchers in the game. McCovey responded with a sensational debut, blistering Roberts for four hits in four at-bats, including two triples, to lead the Giants to a 7–2 win. He missed a chance to go 5-for-5 when Mays flied out to end the game. Rigney, who had been downright morose just the day before, lamenting the team's offensive woes, was understandably giddy after watching McCovey's performance. Postgame, Rigney chuckled and simply said, "I've never seen anyone break into the big leagues and hit the ball like that." He also declared that McCovey would now be the everyday first baseman, squelching the belief that he might platoon with the righty Cepeda.

Rigney looked like a genius for having such confidence in McCovey from the start. He didn't stop hitting the rest of the season, and with just eight games left, the Giants had a two-game lead in the National League standings. But the Giants lost seven of those games to finish in third place behind the Braves and Dodgers. The collapse wasn't the fault of McCovey or Mays, who hit .370 and .464, respectively, in the final stretch. After the season, despite playing in just 52 games, McCovey was named Rookie of the Year unanimously after hitting .354, with 13 home runs. Rigney heaped praise on his young slugger.

Rigney said, "Watch him go in 1960. He could be baseball's next .400 hitter. How many home runs will he hit? I'll put it conservatively at 30." Despite his performance and Rigney's accolades, there were rumors of a blockbuster trade involving McCovey that offseason, which would allow Cepeda to shift back to first. Rigney squashed that idea, saying, "We'll never deal him off as long as I'm the manager of the Giants and still breathing."

After McCovey won Rookie of the Year, the *Pittsburgh Courier*, one of the leading African American newspaper publications in the United States, noted a trend in National League Rookie of the Year voting since Jackie Robinson had won the initial award in 1947. Of the award's first 13 winners, nine were African American. Five of those nine would go on to become Hall of Famers, and that doesn't include Ernie Banks or Hank Aaron, who weren't Rookie of the Year winners. McCovey never did hit .400 in the majors, as was projected at the time. He only hit over .300 once in his career as he developed physically and became a feared slugger, capable of hitting some of the most towering home runs and vicious line drives of anyone in the game.

McCovey manned first base for the Giants until he was traded to the Padres after the 1973 season. He returned to San Francisco in 1977, and stayed until he retired in July 1980. In May 1980, McCovey hit his 521st and final home run. It was his only home run of the season, but with it came a major accomplishment. He became just the second player to homer in four different decades. Going into the 2020 season, only four players had accomplished the feat, with Ted Williams, Rickey Henderson, and Omar Vizquel being the others. Fans will have to wait until at least 2030 to see if anyone else can join the club, as there weren't any active players from the 1990s playing in the 2020 season.

While McCovey and Mays were dominating the 1960s in San Francisco, 400 miles to the south another revolution was going on in Los Angeles. As baseball came out of the Deadball Era, the stolen base became passé. What was once the weapon of choice for the most valuable and adept players had become a lost craft. Managers started to believe the risk of being thrown out outweighed the reward of an extra base. As home run totals exploded, managers began to rely more on the big hit, rather than manufacturing runs. Thus, the number of stolen bases plummeted for decades. As late as 1956, teams barely used the stolen base as a weapon. Luis Aparicio led the American League that year with 21 steals and was one of just four players in the majors to top 20 steals. The Pirates as a team stole just 24 bases, with half the total coming from two players. That began to change in 1950, thanks to Maury Wills. The speedy Dodger swiped 50 bags in his first season in the majors, becoming the first National League player to reach that total since Max Carey did in preintegration 1923.

While Aparicio had topped 50 the year before in the American League, it was Wills who truly popularized the stolen base. Wills's Dodgers teams were generally more successful than Aparicio's White Sox, so Wills was more visible. While his total dipped to 35 in 1961, Wills rebounded incredibly the next season. In 1962, Wills won the National League Most Valuable Player (MVP) Award after he robbed 104 bases while getting caught only 13 times. He was the first person in the modern era to top 100 steals in a season. The last man to do it was Sliding Billy Hamilton, who stole 111 bases during the game's infancy in 1891. Wills was a thrilling player in his prime, but he didn't reach the majors until he was 26. He led the league in steals his first six full years in the bigs, including 94 in 1965, but by the age of 32, his physical style of play had begun to take a toll on his slight body. Wills began to get caught much more frequently, and his all-around play slowed. He retired in 1972, with 586 steals, 10th overall in major-league history, but he was the only modern player in the top 10.

When Wills became the first modern player to reach 50 steals in 1960, Vada Pinson finished second in the National League, with 32, a total that would have led the league in each of the previous two seasons. The fact that Pinson's top stolen-base season was overshadowed by Wills's record-breaking season is on par with the general sentiment of his entire career. Ask any Reds fan who watched Pinson glide around the outfield at Crosley Field in the 1960s and they'll swear by his abilities. Outside of Cincinnati, however, the national narrative was more about Mays and Mantle. Even in his own outfield, Pinson played next to the immortal Frank Robinson in his prime. There were many other huge names in the outfield during Pinson's prime. Such players as Hank Aaron, Roberto Clemente, and Al Kaline are counted among the greatest to ever play the sport. It was arguably the greatest era for outfielders in major-league history, so it is easy to see why Pinson would be overshadowed. To fans in Cincinnati, however, that wouldn't happen.

At the start of the 1960s, Pinson emerged as one of the great young stars to break into the game in years. In his first spring training, Pinson was brough to camp after a strong season at the low-level Class C Seattle Rainiers. He made the Reds Opening Day roster in 1958, as a 19-year-old, and singled against Hall of Famer Robin Roberts for his first hit. His youth and inexperience made him a longshot to break camp with the Reds, but in the final weeks of spring training, it looked like he might do it. Pinson turned heads throughout the spring with his defensive prowess, strong arm, and adept bat.

A syndicated article that ran less than two weeks before Opening Day featured Pinson and the optimistic headline, "Just Like Frankie Robinson." The article featured comments from veteran manager Birdie Tebbetts, who tried to calm fans by saying that Pinson was "not superman" but then fanned the excitement that had grown for his young star. Tebbetts spoke of Pinson's great minor-league numbers and said that he was brought into camp just for a look but had far surpassed expectations. Tebbetts stopped short of declaring him the Opening Day starter, but the writer continued to heap high praise on him. The article intimated that

Pinson had the speed of Mickey Mantle and played the outfield like Willie Mays, all at the age of 19.

By the age of 26, Pinson had played seven full seasons and established himself as a young superstar who was about to enter his prime. At age 26, Pinson already had 1,381 hits, more than Pete Rose, Hank Aaron, Rod Carew, and many other Hall of Famers at the same age. He had some pop, too. Pinson led the league in doubles twice and hit 20 homers in six of his first seven seasons. He was a Gold Glove outfielder and a weapon on the bases. There was nothing Pinson couldn't do, and fans in Cincinnati loved him for it. He had his best season in 1961, when he led the Reds to the World Series and finished third in MVP voting. The start of Pinson's career rivaled that of just about any player of the era.

In the final 10 years of his career, Pinson's seemingly clear path to the Hall of Fame took a detour. Slowed by injuries, he managed to perform well but didn't continue the trajectory that most anticipated. He played for five teams in his final eight seasons and finished his career with 2,757 hits, placing him sixth in the postsegregation era upon his retirement. The only three eligible non-Hall of Famers who had more hits than Pinson going into the 2020 season were Barry Bonds, Omar Vizquel, and Johnny Damon. Yet, once again the quiet and classy Pinson was overlooked when it came time for Hall of Fame voting. Pinson was first listed on the Hall of Fame ballot at about the same time as Mays, Aaron, Brooks Robinson, and Bob Gibson, creating a crowded field. He received only 4.1 percent of the vote in the first year he was eligible for the Hall and topped 15 percent only once in his 15 years on the ballot. As of 2020, Pinson's candidacy remains in limbo, but it maintains support among Reds fans who saw him play and people who want to remember the legacy of the great underrated star of the 1960s.

The stolen-base revival may have been started by Aparicio, Wills, and Pinson, but it was taken to levels the game had never seen before by Lou Brock. Brock played just one year in the minors before making his debut for the Cubs in late 1961. He played two full seasons for the Cubs but didn't develop as quickly as management would have liked, so he was traded to the Cardinals in the middle of the 1964 season. Encouraged to run more in his first full season in St. Louis, Brock found his niche in the sport. He topped 50 steals in each of his first 12 seasons with the Cardinals, including his historic 1974 season, when he swiped 118 bases, a major-league record. He finished his career with a record 938 stolen bases, topping Ty Cobb for the major-league career lead, a record that many believed would never be beat.

Young African American stars weren't just lighting up the basepaths and blasting home runs in the 1960s. Brock had a teammate in St. Louis who was battling Sandy Koufax as the best pitcher of the decade. Bob Gibson, the fearsome righty from Nebraska, came to professional baseball in 1957, after spending a year playing basketball with the Harlem Globetrotters. He didn't make his first All-Star Game until 1962, when he was 26, but from that point onward, Gibson went on to establish himself as one of the toughest pitchers to ever take the mound. Gibson menacingly glared at batters and hurled dangerous fastballs past them to send many different messages.

Through 1967, Gibson was very good. He had a career record of 125–88, and was coming off his second World Series title; each one featured a World Series MVP for Gibson as well. In 1967, he won three World Series games, including one of the most dominant Game 7 pitching performances in major-league history. With the Series on the line and the Red Sox having won Game 6, Gibson gave up just one hit through the first seven innings on the way to a complete-game, 10-strikeout performance. He was set to appear on *The Tonight Show Starring Johnny Carson* and *The Ed Sullivan Show* the following week, and rightfully hailed as a hero. Upon returning home to Omaha, Gibson found a throng of fans outside his house. They had decorated his home with balloons, signs, and streamers. Local cheerleaders were even on hand, and Gibson was named honorary mayor of Omaha for a day. To imagine that he would only get better from there was inconceivable.

Gibson did get better, however, turning in perhaps the best season for a pitcher in the game's history in 1968. He went 22–9, with a historic ERA of 1.12, still a record for the modern game. Gibson's stretch of dominance in June and July is arguably the best performance during a two-month span for anyone who has ever played the game, pitcher or otherwise. Gibson went into June having lost his last three starts to fall to 3–5 early in the season; however, from June 2 to July 30, he was superhuman. He started 12 games and finished each one. He not only completed each game, but also won them all. Gibson pitched 108 innings during that stretch and allowed just six earned runs. By August 1, Gibson's ERA had plummeted to 0.96. With the help of Brock, Gibson, and Curt Flood, the Cardinals ran away in the National League standings.

Gibson understandably started Game 1 of the World Series and continued his dominance. He struck out 17 batters in a 4–0 shutout and followed that up four days later with another complete-game win. Gibson found himself on the mound in a deciding Game 7 for the second year in a row, this time against Mickey Lolich and the Detroit Tigers. Gibson again cruised into the seventh without giving up a run, but after getting the first two outs, the Tigers struck for three runs. They would go on to win, 4–1, to capture the World Series. Gibson topped 20 wins in each of the next two seasons and captured his second Cy Young Award in 1970. He never returned to the World Series but retired with 251 wins and a reputation best summed up by Hank Aaron. Aaron said,

> Don't dig in against Bob Gibson, he'll knock you down. He'd knock down his own grandmother if she dared to challenge him. Don't stare at him, don't smile at him, don't talk to him. He doesn't like it. If you happen to hit a home run, don't run too slow, don't run too fast. If you happen to want to celebrate, get to the tunnel first. And if he hits you, don't charge the mound because he's a Gold Glove boxer.

Gibson wasn't the only star African American pitcher of the decade. Just as he was reaching his peak in the late 1960s, Ferguson Jenkins emerged as a star when the Cubs moved the tall righty into the starting rotation. Considered the best major-league pitcher to come out of Canada, Jenkins won 20 games in his first season in the Cubs rotation. It would be the first of six straight 20-win seasons for the Cubs. He won the 1971 Cy Young Award and finished in the top three in the voting four other times. By the time he retired, Jenkins had won 284 games and was sixth all-time in strikeouts, with 3,192. Often overshadowed by contemporaries like Gibson, Tom Seaver, Nolan Ryan, and Steve Carlton, Jenkins was elected to the National Baseball Hall of Fame on his third try in 1991. He remains the leader among African American pitchers in wins and strikeouts.

While all this was happening, the son of a legendary pitcher from the Cuban Leagues and Negro National League was introducing himself to the majors in a big way. On July 19, 1964, a 23-year-old right-hander made his debut on the mound at Yankee Stadium opposite an aging but still-dominant Whitey Ford. After going 15–1 in 17 minor-league games that season, the Cleveland Indians practically had no choice but to call up Luis Tiant. Tiant shut down the Yankees, striking out 11 in a four-hit shutout that served as a warning for what was to come for the American League for the next decade and a half.

Tiant's debut came just two days after the White Sox released Minnie Minoso, ending the career of the Cuban legend aside from two publicity-stunt appearances in his 50s. Minoso's career is a link between two generations of Tiants, and all three Cubans experienced different levels of acceptance of Cuban-born players. Luis Tiant Sr. used a legendary screwball as a star lefty for the New York Cubans in the Negro National League during the segregated era of Major League Baseball. As Jackie Robinson was breaking the color barrier in 1947, Tiant Sr. authored a 10–0 record as a 40-year-old in his final Negro League season. Minoso debuted two years later as just the eighth African American ballplayer in major-league history. The man who came to be known as El Tiante, Luis Jr. pitched 19 seasons in the majors and remains perhaps the best Cuban ballplayer to have graced the majors, regardless of position.

While Gibson, Tiant, and Jenkins were in the early throes of careers that would land them in Cooperstown, another African American pitcher was trying to realize his limitless potential in Cleveland. Jim "Mudcat" Grant debuted for the Indians a year before Gibson broke in with the Cardinals, and it seemed that Grant would be the heir apparent to Don Newcombe as the game's top African American pitcher. Grant was discovered by Indians scout Fred Merkle as a 17-year-old while he was scouting the State Negro Baseball Tournament in Florida in 1952. Merkle, who is better known for committing one of the game's great blunders in 1908, thought highly of Grant but could not sign him, as he was just 17 at the time. Grant ultimately attended Florida A&M but dropped out to go to work in carpentry; however, once Merkle heard that Grant had left school and was now of age, he sought out the soft-spoken, lanky pitcher and brought him to the attention of the Indians.

After going 70–28 in four minor-league seasons, Grant was given a shot to make it into the Indians rotation out of spring training in 1958. At just 22 years old, Grant debuted in the Indians' third game of the season and pitched a complete game in a 3–2 win against the Kansas City A's. It took only four starts before Grant had Indians fans abuzz. After a win against the Orioles, Grant was 3–0, with a 1.85 ERA, with all three wins coming as complete games. On a team with Larry Doby, Minnie Minoso, and Vic Power, it was the tall, thin righty with the funny nickname who was stealing headlines.

Grant gained his nickname at an Indians minor-league camp years earlier during a tryout. He struck out a batter named Leroy Irby on three pitches, and as Irby returned to the dugout, he uttered something along the lines of, "That mudcat sure is tough." The nickname stuck, although Grant didn't know it at the time, as he was on the mound and didn't hear the remark. Grant later said that Hall of Famer Red Ruffing, who was working with Indians pitchers, was calling out field assignments in spring training and called the name "Mudcat Grant." Thinking he was referring to someone else, Grant stood patiently waiting to hear "Jim Grant." Once the confusion was settled, Grant ambled off to his assigned field with a nickname that has stood ever since.

After his fast start, Indians fans dreamed that Grant would be their savior on the mound. In early May, baseball columnist Bob McCarthy wrote that Grant looked like he was going to continue a long tradition of pitching excellence in Cleveland. McCarthy rattled off the names of such Hall of Famers as Cy Young, Addie Joss, Bob Feller, and other legendary hurlers who pitched for the tribe in the first half of the twentieth century. He ended his column by saying that the Indians "now seem to have another bright young pitching star in James 'Mudcat' Grant."

Grant's career never did pan out like that of Gibson, Jenkins, or Newcombe, as he struggled to find consistency. He had seven solid seasons in Cleveland, making the All-Star Game in 1963. Grant's best season came in 1965, when he went 21–7 for the Twins, while leading the American League with six shutouts. He made his second All-Star Game that year, and when he took the mound in the second inning, he faced a parade of some of the biggest names in the sport. He faced eight batters in two innings, including Hank Aaron, Willie Stargell, Willie Mays, Pete Rose, and Ernie Banks. Grant should be given credit for allowing only a two-run homer to Stargell in that span. Maury Wills was also in the starting lineup that day for the National League All-Stars, meaning that six of the eight position players in the starting lineup were African American.

While Grant never reached the heights projected for him, he stayed in the majors until 1972, pitching for seven teams in 17 seasons. He was always a popular player and became an effective reliever in the second half of his career. Grant's legacy lies in the 1965 season. When he hurled a one-hitter on September 25, against the Washington Senators, he became just the third African American pitcher to win 20 games in a season. Bob Gibson would join him two weeks later as an exclusive club began to form. The club would later become known as the "Black Aces," a name coined by Grant in a book he wrote in 2006.

The Black Aces consists of African American pitchers who won 20 games in the major leagues. Before Grant and Gibson joined the club in 1965, only Don Newcombe and Sam Jones had accomplished the feat. Through the 2020 season, there have been only 13 African American pitchers to have won 20 games. While Jenkins and Gibson combined for 12 seasons of 20 wins throughout much of the 1960s and 1970s, other members were slowly joining the club. Earl Wilson, who became the first African American pitcher in Red Sox history in 1959, won 22 games for the Tigers in 1967, and Al Downing, who famously gave up Hank Aaron's 715th home run, became a "Black Ace" in 1971, when he won 22 games in his first season with the Dodgers.

Downing's 1971 season was the peak of a solid career that saw him win 123 games. He went 20–9, with a 2.68 ERA, and finished third in the Cy Young Award voting and 10th in MVP voting. In the National League in 1971, four of the top five finishers for the Cy Young Award were African Americans. Fergie Jenkins took home the award that season, while Downing, Dock Ellis, and Gibson finished third, fourth, and fifth, respectively; however, the fantastic seasons by African American pitchers in the National League were overshadowed by the newest pitching dynamo in the American League. As early as January 1971, Hall of Fame A's manager Dick Williams was singing the praises of a young Vida Blue, who was just 20 years old at the time.

One can't fault Williams for being excited about Blue. In 1970, Blue was called up for a September tryout in the A's rotation, and he quickly showed he was more than capable despite his youth. In just his second start, Blue carried a no-hitter into the eighth inning against the Royals before giving up a lone single to Pat Kelly. Blue would have to settle for a one-hit shutout.

Incredibly, he would top that game two starts later when he faced the Minnesota Twins, who needed to beat the young Blue to clinch the American League West. But Blue had other ideas and fired a no-hitter against the powerful Twins, missing a perfect game when he delivered a pitch-around walk to Harmon Killebrew. The fireballing Blue flipped a 3–1 curve to Killebrew in the fourth inning that the Hall of Famer took for a walk. After the game, Killebrew said he was just lucky to get on base.

Blue's September audition was enough for Williams to pencil the young lefty into the starting rotation the following season, especially with Blue Moon Odom struggling through arm problems. Blue was set to join Catfish Hunter, Chuck Dobson, and possibly Diego Segui, the 1970 ERA champion, in the rotation as the A's were about to embark on a five-year dynasty that would include three straight World Series titles. A syndicated article written on February 22, 1970, announcing the signing of Blue, came with an understated compliment of Blue, simply saying, "He could find stardom this year." In the history of players who blew through expectations, few have "found stardom" the way Blue did in 1971.

Blue earned the Opening Day start for the A's as they took on the Senators in Washington to start the season. The Senators were managed by Ted Williams, and Opening Day in Washington was a big stage. Traditionally, the sitting U.S. president started the season in Washington by throwing the first pitch, and Blue was looking forward to meeting Richard Nixon, who would have been assigned that duty. But Nixon relinquished his honor to a returning Vietnam War prisoner and wasn't on hand. The cool Blue wouldn't admit to Opening Day jitters, but that logical conclusion could be drawn when looking at his pitching line. Blue didn't make it out of the second inning. He walked four batters and allowed four runs, and was hurt by two errors by shortstop Bert Campaneris. Blue was saddled with the loss, but that bad start would not define him. His next 10 starts introduced him to those in the baseball world who hadn't heard about him yet.

Blue's next start came against the Kansas City Royals, and he threw a game that was more representative of his talent. The lefty dynamo seemed to be on his way to setting the American League record for strikeouts in a game as he fanned 13 batters through six innings before the game was called due to rain. Blue was credited with the third shutout win in his young career, even if the weather robbed him of a chance to make history. After the game, Dick Williams wasn't shy with accolades for his young starter. Williams said, "I've faced Bob Feller, Sandy Koufax, Herb Score, Don Newcombe, and Sam McDowell, and Blue can throw as hard as any of them." Catcher Dave Duncan also said that Blue was the fastest pitcher he'd ever caught.

The praise lapped upon Blue as a youngster may have seemed like hyperbole, but each time he took the mound in the first half of the year, he outdid himself. Blue threw complete games in each of his remaining five starts in April and finished the month with a 6–1 record. He continued to roll through the first half of the season and, by the All-Star break, had put up numbers that any pitcher would be proud to compile in a full season. After firing another complete game on the Fourth of July against the Angels, Blue's record stood at 17–3, with a 1.51 ERA. In his final start before the All-Star break, Blue squared off against Rudy May, another promising young African American lefty, for an epic pitching duel in Oakland. Blue pitched 11 shutout innings with 17 strikeouts against the Angels, but May matched him pitch for pitch. May hurled 12 shutout innings in a game that wouldn't be decided until the 20th inning, when the A's pushed across a run for a 1–0 win.

To no one's surprise, Blue started the 1971 All-Star Game in Detroit. The 1971 All-Star Game is considered one of the most historic Midsummer Classics in the sport's history. When Blue took the mound in the top of the first, he became the first African American pitcher to start an All-Star Game. His counterpart in the National League was African American righty Dock Ellis, who was amid a great season for the Pirates. The American League won the game, 6–4, with all 10 runs scored as a result of six home runs, all hit by Hall of Famers. All 10 runs were scored by Hall of Famers as well. Blue picked up the win in the game, hurling three innings while allowing home runs to Johnny Bench and Hank Aaron.

Blue had a strong second half in 1971, even if he didn't match his historic first half. He went 7–5, with a 2.40 ERA, in the season's final two months to finish with a 24–8 record and a league-leading 1.82 ERA. He also led the league in shutouts while capturing the Cy Young and MVP awards. Blue became the youngest player to ever win an MVP Award and was just the fifth pitcher to claim the Cy Young and MVP awards in the same season. That group already consisted of pitchers he was being compared to: Bob Gibson and Don Newcombe.

During the season, even the game's greats were in awe of Blue. Sandy Koufax said in an interview, "I couldn't get the ball over the way he does at age 22. He's not only ahead of me, he's ahead of the world. He's already made me look pretty tame." All-Star outfielder Paul Blair described what it was like to hit against Blue. The Orioles center fielder said, "He doesn't give you a single thing. He strips you naked right there in public. Trying to hit the thing he throws is like trying to hit dead weight." At different times that season, Blue found himself on the cover of *Sports Illustrated* and *Time* magazine.

Blue never again reached the heights of 1971 in his 17-year career. He missed time the next season due to a contract dispute with mercurial A's owner Charlie Finley but returned and stayed with the team until 1977. Finley attempted to trade him twice in his career, to the Yankees and Reds, but both trades were vetoed by Commissioner Bowie Kuhn. Finley was ultimately successful in shipping Blue out of Oakland in 1978, when he was traded to the Giants. Blue became embroiled in the drug scandal that tarnished baseball in the mid-1980s, and he was effectively finished as a successful pitcher by the age of 32. He made five more All-Star appearances after his incredible 1971 season and won 20 games two more times, but he was never able to recapture that '71 magic.

THE 1971 PITTSBURGH PIRATES

Even though most baseball fans are immersed in the stats and tradition of the game, sometimes history is made and few people take immediate notice. That scenario played out on September 1, 1971, when the Pittsburgh Pirates took on the Philadelphia Phillies at Three Rivers Stadium. As the season entered the final month of the regular season, all four division races were just about wrapped up. The Pirates had the slimmest lead of the four division leaders, at 5.5 games ahead of the Cardinals.

The Cards featured five Hall of Famers, but the Pirates had kept a hold on first place since early June and seemed to be a team of destiny. They were led by Willie Stargell, Roberto Clemente, and Manny Sanguillen, all of whom finished in the top eight in the MVP voting that season. So, when manager Danny Murtaugh filled out his lineup card and the Pirates took the field that night, no one had an inclination that anything special was happening for a few innings. According to Pirates first baseman Al Oliver, third baseman Dave Cash approached him in the early stages of the game and said, "Hey Scoop, we've got all brothers out there." As Oliver reviewed the lineup, he realized that all nine players in the starting lineup that night were African American—the first time in major-league history that had been the case. The lineup featured Clemente, Sanguillen, Stargell, Oliver, Cash, Jackie Hernandez, Rennie Stennett, and Gene Clines. Dock Ellis started the historic game just two months after he paired with Vida Blue to become the first two African American pitchers to start the All-Star Game.

A United Press International article captured the scene in the locker room after the Pirates won. Clines asked Cash, "Hey Dave, we've started nine brothers before, haven't we?" Before Cash could answer, Stargell interjected that this was the first time it had ever happened. According to the article, Stargell pointed out that the Pirates started eight African American and Hispanic position players on June 17, 1967, against the Phillies, with the only white player in the starting lineup being pitcher Dennis Ribant. That game was the only game in 1967 that Bill Mazeroski didn't start at second, giving way to backup Andre Rodgers, an African American veteran from the Bahamas.

Murtaugh made no special mention of the occurrence to his team on September 1, 1971, and after the game he simply said he was putting his best lineup on the field. Murtaugh said,

> When it comes to making out the lineup, I am color blind, and my athletes know it. They don't know it because I told them, they know it because they're familiar with the way I operate. The best men in our organization are the ones who are here. And the ones that are here all play, depending on when the circumstances present themselves.

The game itself was slugfest, as the Pirates held a 9–6 lead after three innings. Luke Walker, a white relief pitcher, came on to pitch the final six innings for the Pirates, picking up the win in relief. After the game, Walker also said he hadn't noticed the lineup rarity, and he too supported Murtaugh's statement that they simply put the players on the field each game who give the Pirates the best chance to win.

"All I know is that St. Louis has been putting the heat on us, and we've got to go out there and win this thing," said Walker. "All I saw in the field were eight men and myself, and I think the guys on the team feel the same way." It was noted in the article that the Pirates were the most diverse team in the majors at that time. Their roster was comprised of 14 whites, 6 African Americans, and 7 Hispanics, some of whom were of African descent.

The Cardinals may have been putting heat on the Pirates, but the Pirates ended up winning the National League East by seven games. The Pirates got past Willie Mays and the Giants in the National League Championship Series in four games to advance to the World Series against a powerful Orioles team that had won the American League East by 12 games. The Orioles had their own group of African American stars featuring Frank Robinson, Paul Blair, Don Buford, and Elrod Hendricks. The World Series looked like it would be a classic matchup of two powerful teams featuring some of the game's true legends, and it didn't disappoint.

The Orioles won the first two games, but the Pirates bounced back and won the next two. The teams split Game 5 and Game 6, setting up a decisive Game 7. The first six games were won by the home team, so if the Pirates wanted to win, they had to break the pattern in Baltimore. The Orioles used three pitchers in the game, all of whom were members of their vaunted starting rotation. The Pirates started Steve Blass, a solid veteran who was coming off one of his best seasons. Orioles starter Mike Cuellar was cruising early, retiring the first 11 batters who faced him, until Clemente ended that streak in dramatic fashion. The immortal Clemente jumped on a first-pitch hanging curveball from lefty Cuellar and blasted it over the left-center field fence to give the Pirates a 1–0 lead.

The Pirates tacked on an important insurance run in the eighth, which proved to be the difference in the game. Hendricks and Mark Belanger led off the bottom of the eighth with singles for the Orioles and were bunted to second and third; however, Blass induced Buford and Davey Johnson to ground out with only one run scoring. Blass made the slim lead stand by retiring the Orioles in order in the ninth to give the Pirates their fourth World Series title in team history. It was the first since Mazeroski's famous walk-off homer to beat the Yankees in 1960. Through 2020, the Pirates only won one other World Series, a 1979 rematch with the Orioles.

The 1971 Pirates represented a change in baseball, and their franchise mirrored American culture in the 1970s. Their first World Series came during the advent of the disco era and ended with a World Series title in 1979, when the maligned music genre was dying. They were led into the decade by Clemente and ushered into the 1980s by Stargell. They overcame Clemente's death in 1972, by winning the National League East three of the next seven years, while finishing second three other times. Stargell finished in the top 10 in MVP voting seven years in that decade, including a 1979 win.

Jerry Reuss pitched 22 seasons in the majors and was teammates with Stargell for six seasons in Pittsburgh. He recalled the impact Stargell had on the Pirates as follows:

Willie was the leader of the Pirates when I was there. He assumed that role after Clemente's death, and that wasn't easy to do. Willie never got cheated, and that was the example he set for everyone. He worked hard, played hard, and swung hard. He was also a model of consistency, and his teammates saw that. He didn't get too high or too low and was a steadying presence that everyone respected. Nobody ever questioned Willie's leadership. When he hit a home run, he came back to the dugout, put his helmet in the rack, and sat down. He did the same thing when he struck out. He was better than anyone I ever played with when it came to staying calm and focused.

Stargell was seven years old when Jackie Robinson debuted in 1947. He represents the first generation of players who had African American superstars to admire during their childhood as they developed a love for the game. Stargell was 15 years old when Robinson led the Dodgers to their first World Series. His youth and career bridged the racial unrest of the 1940s through the civil rights era, the turbulent 1960s, the colorful 1970s, and into the early 1980s. When Stargell was in the minor leagues, he still had to stay in separate hotels from his white teammates, and by the time he was done as a player, that concept was unheard-of. He began his career just three years after Larry Doby retired and played against a rookie named Tony Gwynn in one of his final games. The span from the start of Doby's career to the end of Gwynn's stretches from 1947–2001, and Stargell came close to connecting them both. He was a father figure who awarded "Stargell Stars" to teammates after they made great plays and was an affable person who never had a bad word for anyone. The Pittsburgh Pirates were one of the most progressive, diverse, and successful National League teams of the Stargell era. They were led by Clemente, a hero to baseball lovers everywhere, and Stargell, who represented one of the most visible and colorful stars of the decade.

GENERATION THREE

By the 1970s, African American participation in Major League Baseball had about reached its peak. Steady growth in the two decades after Jackie Robinson's debut had brought African American participation in Major League Baseball to 15.4 percent by 1968, and aside from a slight dip the following year when Major League Baseball expanded by four teams, the number stayed above 15 percent until 1998. In addition, the late 1960s saw participation among Latino players top 10 percent for the first time. The 1968 baseball season is commonly referred to as the "Year of the Pitcher," but it was also the first time African American and Latino players combined to make up more than 25 percent of the league. That number of white Major League Baseball players would never rise above 75 percent again.

The 1970s weren't just about the number of African Americans playing Major League Baseball, however. Those years were about what they brought to the table and the way they played the game. The pioneers of the 1940s made up the first generation, and wave two was defined by the superstars of the 1950s and 1960s, for example, Willie Mays, Frank Robinson, Hank Aaron, and Bob Gibson. The third generation surely had its superstars. Hall of Famers like Reggie Jackson, Joe Morgan, and Dave Winfield established themselves as some of the top players in the game, and there were many great players and personalities of differing accomplishments who played alongside them. The visibility and personalities of the African American players during the 1970s helped to bring on one of the most colorful and entertaining decades of baseball in the game's history.

The dominant teams of the decade were the Oakland A's, Cincinnati Reds, Pittsburgh Pirates, and New York Yankees. They combined to win nine World Series in the 1970s, and each of those teams had many African American stars. The Pirates were one of the first teams to fully embrace diversity on their roster, and their brand of baseball was thrilling to watch. While Stargell led the team through the decade, their teams also featured such African American stars as Willie Randolph, Bill Robinson, and Al Oliver. But the biggest character to play on that team, or any team for that matter, was Dock Ellis.

Ellis was flamboyant and fearless. He had the intimidation factor of Bob Gibson but was perhaps more dangerous because of his unpredictability. Players knew what they were going to get with Gibson. They came to the plate already knowing Gibson owned the inside corner, and if they did anything to show him up or try to gain an upper hand, they were getting knocked down. With Ellis, no one knew what to expect before, during, or after a game. He was immensely talented and labeled a can't-miss prospect, but drug use hindered his development. Ellis claimed that he never pitched a game without the use of amphetamines, that he started using cocaine in the late 1960s, and that he frequently used acid on his off days. As a youngster, Ellis was mentored and encouraged to sign with the Pirates by Chet Brewer, a former Negro League star who pitched on the same Kansas City Monarchs staff as Satchel Paige and Bullet Joe Rogan.

Ellis's turbulent career with the Pirates lasted from 1968 to 1975, and wasn't short on excitement. He wore hair curlers in the bullpen while warming up for games instead of a hat and was an infamous practical joker. He also once took extensive means to send a message to the Reds, their chief rivals of the decade. Ellis declared before the game that he would go out to the mound and just start hitting batters until he was ejected. True to his word, Ellis hit Pete Rose, Joe Morgan, and Dan Driessen, the first three batters, on six pitches. After walking Tony Perez, Ellis then threw two pitches that sent Johnny Bench scrambling. He was removed from the game by Danny Murtaugh. Speaking to the media after the game, Murtaugh and catcher Manny Sanguillen brushed it off as unexpected wildness, and Ellis wasn't around for comment, as he had left the park not long after being removed. Ellis hadn't hit a batter all season prior to that and had hit just one batter the entire season before.

Shockingly, the incident with the Reds wasn't Ellis's most outlandish game. The no-hitter he pitched while high on LSD is most often associated with him and rates as one of the wildest stories in baseball history. Ellis overindulged partying on Wednesday, June 10, 1970, and when the partying stopped, he crashed. On what he thought was Thursday, he woke up and took some acid. His girlfriend was flipping through the newspaper and noticed that he was supposed to pitch that day. Ellis brushed her off, saying he was pitching Friday. His girlfriend responded with, "This is Friday, you slept through Thursday."

Ellis had only hours to get from Los Angeles to San Diego to prepare to pitch the first game of a doubleheader against the Padres, while completely high on acid. He doesn't remember exactly how, but he did make it to the stadium. Ellis was uncharacteristically wild, walking eight and hitting a batter, but that was to be expected. As he described it, sometimes the ball felt like it was a balloon, sometimes it felt like it was a golf ball. Sometimes he couldn't see the catcher, sometimes he couldn't see the batter. He thought Richard Nixon was the home plate umpire and Jimi Hendrix was up at bat, swinging a guitar; however, he worked his way through, and sometime in the middle innings, teammate Dave Cash pointed out the no-hitter to Ellis, breaking the tradition of not mentioning a word to a pitcher while he is working on a no-hitter. Ellis and Cash continued to acknowledge the no-hitter throughout the game, and when Ed Spiezio struck out looking to end the game, Ellis completed his infamous no-hitter on LSD.

While Ellis never fully harnessed his seemingly otherworldly talent, the man who played right field behind him did before also having his career curtailed by injury and drug use. The 6-foot-5, 230-pound physical specimen who patrolled right field for the Pirates after Clemente was Dave Parker, and during his peak, he was on the short list of players considered to be the best in the game.

Opening Day of the 1973 season was the first time the Pirates had started the season without Roberto Clemente since 1954. Clemente's close friend, Manny Sanguillen, originally switched from catcher to take over in right, but that experiment only lasted until mid-June. By July, the Pirates had installed the rookie Parker in right field, and he remained there for a decade. Parker was one of those players known for feats that are part reality and part Paul Bunyan. During a game in 1979, he literally knocked the cover off the ball, belting a hit into right field so hard that the leather and seams of the baseball burst. In the 1979 All-Star Game, he uncorked a throw from right field, nailing Brian Downing at home. It was so impressive it's still talked about regularly four decades later. He also has a claim to the "longest" home run ever hit in professional baseball history. Playing in a minor-league game in Charleston, West Virginia, Parker blasted a long home run that landed in a moving coal train beyond the outfield fence. The train stopped 150 miles later in Columbus, Ohio. It may not have officially counted as the longest homer ever hit, but it's a story befitting Parker's exploits and personality.

Parker was a true five-tool player. It's a term that's used more liberally than it should be at times, but proof of Parker's overall ability lies in his accomplishments. He wasn't a big-time power hitter, but he still belted 339 career home runs, topping 30 three times. When he retired, he ranked in the top 25 in major-league history in doubles and had won two batting titles. He had some speed on the bases early in his career and won three Gold Gloves before injuries started taking their toll. Parker is always in the discussion of the best outfield arms of all-time as well. Jerry Reuss, an All-Star pitcher who played 19 seasons in the majors, was Parker's teammate in Pittsburgh and had a front-row seat to his exploits.

"I played with Dave for five seasons, and for the two-year period from 1977–1978, he was the best player in baseball by far," said Reuss. "He did things in an extraordinary fashion and could really do it all on the baseball field."

Nicknamed "The Cobra," Parker was the antithesis of teammate Willie Stargell, even if they both swung a sledgehammer in the on-deck circle. Stargell was the father figure, intense but jolly and universally respected. Parker was more gifted physically and played the game with a violent flair. He swung hard, threw hard, and played the game like a middle linebacker.

The Pirates were the second winningest team of the 1970s, topped by only the Cincinnati Reds, who finished the decade almost 300 games over .500. The Big Red Machine is a team for all time and was bursting at the seams with Hall of Famers and superstars, each one with a bigger personality than the next. The sparkplugs that ran the Big Red Machine were Pete Rose and Joe Morgan. Morgan began his career as a 19-year-old in 1963, with the Houston Colt .45s, and was a solid player there for a decade before moving on to the Reds, the team he is most associated with. Morgan went from star to icon after the trade to Cincinnati.

Hindsight offers that this trade was a home run for the Reds, but at the time reaction was mixed at best. The news of the day in Cincinnati wasn't centered on the acquisition of the future Hall of Famer; the narrative was more about the Reds including popular leader Lee May as part of the eight-man trade in return. May claimed at the time that he was dealt away for disobeying requests from Reds management to stop playing basketball in the offseason, but manager Sparky Anderson claimed it was a philosophical shift to tighten up the team's defense and speed. Morgan, a solid fielder and dangerous basestealer, would be installed at second; Tony Perez would be shifted from third to first; and Dennis Menke, who also came over in the trade, would play third. At the time of the trade, Morgan was happy to be going to a contender. He said, "I think maybe I'll get to play in a World Series now." That was an understatement for sure.

Morgan batted second in the lineup behind Pete Rose and immediately raised his level of production. Previously, Morgan had made two All-Star Games as a reserve in Houston, but in his first season in Cincinnati, he quickly became one of the best all-around players in the game as he entered his prime. He stole 58 bases and led the National League in runs, on-base percentage, and walks. It wasn't just his production that made him a quick fan favorite. Morgan's diminutive stature (he stood just 5-foot-7 and 160 pounds) and hustling style of play endeared him to blue-collar fans in Cincinnati. His trademark "elbow flap" was imitated in sandlots throughout the country and remains one of the most iconic idiosyncrasies in baseball history. Morgan would take his stance in the lefty batter's box and hold his bat straight vertical with his back elbow extended and level. He then would flap the elbow down quickly multiple times as the pitcher readied to deliver. Morgan developed the habit when he played with Hall of Famer Nellie Fox in Houston. Fox, who was in the final years of his career, offered the tip to Morgan, who was having trouble with his swing. It stuck with Morgan for the entirety of his 22-year career.

Morgan played eight years in Cincinnati and was the starting second baseman in the All-Star Game in each of his first seven seasons. He finished in the top 10 in MVP voting in each of his first five seasons in Cincinnati, winning the award in both 1975 and 1976. When he comfortably beat out teammate George Foster for the award in 1976, he became just the second National League player to win the award in back-to-back seasons, joining Ernie Banks, who did so for the Cubs two decades earlier. At the time, Morgan recognized the honor of winning two MVPs consecutively.

"It's a real honor. I think of it as being unique. Ernie was one of a kind, and I think maybe this award is the same thing," said Morgan. Foster, whose numbers were similar to Morgan's, wasn't happy he was passed over, however, and suggested the players take over MVP voting from the baseball writers.

Foster said, "No knock against Joe, but I felt I had the credentials to win it. Writers have a tendency to be influenced by other writers. Players know more about what things should be considered and know more about the game. A lot of politics and other things [are involved]." Foster would leave no doubt about who should get the award the following season, when he belted 52 home runs and drove in 149 RBI to easily take the honor. Foster was the first National Leaguer to top 50 home runs since Willie Mays had done so 12 years prior, and no one would do it again in a full National League season until Greg Vaughn in 1998, for the Padres.

When Foster won the award, he recalled how much it meant to him to be the first National League player to reach 50 home runs since Willie

Mays. Like Willie Stargell, Foster was among the first group of African American stars who were able to look up to other African American players while developing a love of the sport as a child. Upon winning the award, Foster said, "Going back to high school, Willie [Mays] was my hero. The big reason is, as a kid, you relate to someone—a black—who does something well. That's where it started for me." Foster would end up playing in the same outfield as Mays and Bobby Bonds in San Francisco as a minor-league call-up in the early 1970s, but he never received a chance to prove himself and was traded away to the Reds, where he flourished.

Foster and Morgan weren't the only minority stars on the Big Red Machine. The Reds followed the Pirates' model of fully embracing diversity on their roster. The starting eight position players for the 1976 Reds included three Hispanic players (Tony Perez, Cesar Geronimo, and Dave Concepcion), two white players (Pete Rose and Johnny Bench), and three African American players (Morgan, Foster, and Ken Griffey). Their top player off the bench, Dan Driessen, was African American as well.

Griffey played 12 seasons for the Reds and 19 overall in the majors. While he didn't reach the levels of his son or Hall of Fame teammates, he was a key player on the Big Red Machine. He batted .303 during his time in Cincinnati and was a leader in the clubhouse. Griffey was a talented baseball player growing up, but the gifted athlete lists football and track as his best sports. Griffey attended Donora High School in Pennsylvania, the same high school that his father, Buddy, attended a generation earlier. Buddy was high school teammates with Stan Musial, who incidentally shares a birthday with Ken Griffey Jr.

What the Big Red Machine and the Pirates were to the National League in the 1970s, the Yankees and A's were to the American League during that era. The two teams combined for six World Series appearances and five titles in the decade, and like the Reds and Pirates, they were led by a diverse group of players. Although the ingredients of both teams consisted of many All-Stars and Hall of Famers, there was one common straw that stirred the drink: Reggie Jackson. He was the star of the A's in three consecutive World Series, and after a short respite with the Orioles in 1976, he joined the Yankees and led them to back-to-back World Series titles in 1977 and 1978.

Jackson was a historic postseason performer, earning the nickname "Mr. October," which has followed him for decades. He was a stalwart in the All-Star Game and appeared on MVP ballots throughout the decade. Jackson grew up outside of Philadelphia, and sports were a huge part of his childhood. His father, Martinez Jackson, played some second base for the Newark Eagles, most likely in 1935, and passed on his love of sports to his son. A tremendous athlete, Reggie was recruited by some of the top football schools in the country as a running back. He attended Arizona State as a football player and asked to try out with the baseball team as well. The coaches worked it out, and it took Jackson one short batting session to show how dangerous of a baseball player he could be. Jackson was one of the football team's leading tacklers as a defensive back as a sophomore and intercepted three passes on the year; however, he switched permanently to baseball and went on to set home run records at Arizona State while playing center field. The Kansas City A's made him the second pick in the 1966 Major League Draft after the Mets drafted 17-year-old catcher Steve Chilcott, allegedly due to a need at the position in the organization. Chilcott never made the major leagues.

Jackson's brashness was on display from the time after he was drafted. Upon being drafted by the A's, he was asked about his potential signing bonus. Jackson said he wasn't sure how much it would be, but he added that it would be "high up there, where the air is rare." He went on to explain his frugal spending habits, saying, "Everybody's been telling me how much money I'll be getting, but you know, I'm going to wait and see. When I left school [two weeks ago] I had $100, and I still have most of it. Everybody seems to think I should be throwing money away—everybody but me." Jackson was described as "articulate and intelligent, good-looking, unassuming, and modest" by sportswriter James Jackson. The unassuming and modest might fly in the face of the way he is remembered by baseball fans, but his bravado is part of what made him great.

Jackson was also described as having the speed of a sprinter and the shoulders and biceps of a weightlifter. James Jackson wrote that these features enabled him to lead the NCAA in home runs the previous year. Incredibly, he increased that production in the minor leagues, putting him on a fast track to the majors. Jackson crushed an improbable 23 home runs in just 68 minor-league games in 1966, a pace that would have put him at more than 50 home runs in the course of a major-league season. He was called up in June 1967, after continuing to produce in the minors the following season. An Associated Press article announcing his call-up said that Jackson had already become known for tape-measure home runs, blasting one in Birmingham that had been surpassed by only Stan Musial and Babe Ruth. He struggled in his initial 35-game trial with the A's in 1967, but was in the starting lineup batting second on Opening Day of the 1968 season. Jackson hit the first of his 563 home runs that day, and the legend of Reggie Jackson began to form.

By his second full season in 1969, Jackson was already one of the top players in the league. He started in center field in the All-Star Game that year next to Frank Robinson in right and batted second, sandwiched between Hall of Famers Rod Carew and Robinson. By the time he was 23, Jackson was already one of the best players in baseball and led the moribund A's to one of the most improbable rises to prominence of the twentieth century. The A's hadn't finished higher than third place in the American League since 1932, and since integration, the team had only finished as high as fourth twice. In the six years before Jackson arrived, the A's finished more than 40 games out of first place three times. But with Jackson now established as a star, the A's finished second in the American League in 1969 and 1970, before winning five straight American League West division titles.

In 1972, the A's won their first World Series since 1930, and it is quite possible they wouldn't have been there if it wasn't for Jackson's heroics in Game 7 of the American League Championship Series. Jackson is known as one of the great October players for his clutch hitting and historic home runs, but this time it was his legs that carried his team to postseason glory. Down 1–0 to the Tigers early in Game 7, Jackson walked leading off the second. He stole second and advanced to third on a sacrifice fly. With two outs, Jackson executed a daring delayed steal of home to tie the game; however, he tore a hamstring on the play, and the injury kept him out of the World Series. Johnny "Blue Moon" Odom and Vida Blue held the Tigers to just one run on five singles to secure the 2–1 win.

Jackson returned to have one of his best seasons in 1973, capturing his only MVP Award. He led the A's back to the World Series and won series MVP honors on the strength of his clutch postseason home runs. Jackson's two-run home run in Game 6 extended an early A's lead to 4–0, and in a series dominated by pitching, that lead would prove insurmountable. Jackson played nine full seasons in Oakland and averaged 32 home runs. He made seven All-Star Games and finished in the top five in

MVP voting four times. His on-field production might only have been topped by his brashness.

While Reggie Jackson couldn't play in the 1972 World Series, he still made headlines. When Game 3 was rained out, Jackson, still hobbled and on crutches, limped into the Reds clubhouse. During that era, even shaking hands with an opponent or talking to them on the field was strictly taboo. The "no fraternizing" rule was woven deep into the fibers of the game, and the clubhouse was a sacred team space. It was beyond the realm of imagination that a bitter rival would venture into an opposing team's clubhouse at the World Series, but that was Reggie Jackson. Heads turned when Jackson arrived, and Johnny Bench spotted him across the room. The amiable Bench moved toward Jackson and asked him how he was feeling. Reds teammates looked on as the two young superstars converged in a place and time when this shouldn't have happened. Jackson was there to invite Bench out for dinner, again something that was strictly forbidden by baseball's unwritten rules.

Jackson didn't know Bench that well, but it was in character for Jackson to do something like this, seemingly out of the blue. Jackson said, "I don't know, I just know him from All-Star Games and things like that, but I feel like I've known him forever. It's hard to explain this, I've read about him, he probably read about me, and we've shared a lot of experience even though we've never played for the same team." Jackson said he and Bench ate dinner at an Italian restaurant, shared wine, and spent five hours talking.

This wasn't the only unwritten baseball rule Jackson decided he would break. In 1972, he showed up to spring training with a mustache. As benign as that may seem today, he was one of the few baseball players in the twentieth century to have done so. Up to that point, it was fully expected that Major League Baseball players be clean shaven. Wally Schang wore a mustache in 1914, and after that having facial hair was understood to be forbidden. In 1936, practical joker Frenchy Bordagaray showed up to Dodgers spring training with a mustache, but manager Casey Stengel ordered that he shave it off. In 1970, Dick Allen had varying facial hair, some of which included a mustache, and Felipe Alou was known to go unshaven at times; however, when Jackson marched into spring training in 1972, with a full mustache, and threatening to grow a full beard, it raised more than a few eyebrows.

At first, owner Charlie Finley ordered manager Dick Williams to tell Jackson to shave it, but Jackson refused. Not wanting to start an internal war, Finley decided to go the other way. What irked Finley about Jackson's mustache, aside from his flouting of major-league traditions, was that it made him an individual rather than part of a team. He knew Jackson wouldn't shave, so he suggested that everyone on the team grow mustaches. At first this was allegedly to anger Jackson, but it was embraced by the team and eventually ownership, and it became a rallying point. Known as the "Mustache Gang," the A's became the first team to break out of staid baseball tradition to bring color and excitement to the diamond. In an instant, it went from players not wearing mustaches for decades to the A's having a full team of mustachioed players. This also included Rollie Fingers and the birth of his trademark handlebar mustache. Manager Dick Williams even joined in.

In addition to the mustaches and long hair, the A's had also broken from uniform tradition. The A's were the first team to brush aside traditional white uniforms at home and grey uniforms on the road, much to the chagrin of baseball brass. They used any number of combinations that included gold, green, white, or grey and wore different styles of hats as well. When the mustaches were added to the garish uniform combinations, the A's had broken through a wall and were baseball's fun renegades. It all started with Jackson showing up to spring training in 1972, wearing a mustache with a beard on deck.

In 1975, Jackson had his typical All-Star season, leading the American League in home runs while finishing fifth in the MVP voting. He also led the A's to the postseason, where he batted .417 in the American League Championship Series. The Red Sox overmatched them, however, and swept the A's in three games, ending their quest for a fourth straight World Series title. A's fans expected that Jackson and the club would be back in 1976, to make another run, and when spring training rolled around, it looked like they were right; however, things took a dramatic turn on April 2, at the start of spring training.

Jackson and A's owner Charlie Finley were in contract negotiations, and when an arbitrator ruled in Finley's favor, it looked like the conclusion of the issue. Jackson's salary was set to be slashed by 20 percent, from $140,000 to $112,000; however, despite winning the case, Finley traded Jackson to the Orioles, along with star pitcher Ken Holtzman, in return for Don Baylor, Mike Torrez, and Paul Mitchell. Finley insisted the move had nothing to do with salary, even though the A's saved an estimated $100,000 in the deal. He said he had no ill will toward Jackson and wished him well. Jackson had requested trades in the past, but he would have preferred to stay on the West Coast. Finley also thought Baylor, three years younger than Jackson, was a player on the rise.

Jackson didn't comment at the time, and his agent reported that he was considering not reporting to the Orioles, as he had many business ventures in Oakland and Arizona, and didn't want to relocate to the East Coast. His businesses were successful, and Jackson didn't need to play baseball for income, so he considered sitting out the 1976 season. Jackson's teammate, Bill North, made comments reflecting the typical feelings of most of Jackson's teammates throughout the years. North said, "Reggie and I had our differences, that's true, but that's in the past. I really hate to see him go. If I was Reggie Jackson, I would get a cabin in Lake Tahoe and sit and think about this for a couple of days." Jackson's outspoken and flamboyant nature helped make him the player he was, but sometimes it rubbed teammates the wrong way. Nonetheless, his teammates generally respected Jackson. He was among the best players in the sport, and the fact that his teams made the postseason in 10 of his 20 full seasons was no coincidence. Jackson made his teams and the players around him better.

In the days after the trade, Jackson said through his agent that he had decided not to report and that by sitting out, he would be a free agent after the season. Labor leader Marvin Miller confirmed this, and that appeared to be Jackson's plan. The Orioles gave Jackson until Opening Day to report, and when he didn't, they requested he be placed on Major League Baseball's disqualified list. After a four-week holdout, Jackson reported to the Orioles on May 1, 16 games into the season. Jackson was inserted into the lineup for the second game of a doubleheader against the A's team he had just been traded from and went 0-for-2 with an RBI groundout that tied the game in the sixth inning, a game the Orioles won, 4–3.

Jackson had a good season in Baltimore, leading the American League in slugging percentage while also setting a career high in stolen bases with 28. It was his only season in the majors that he topped 25 home runs and stolen bases. The Orioles missed the postseason, but Jackson didn't. He served as a color commentator during the 1976 American League playoffs and spoke glowingly of the Yankees and George Steinbrenner. The Yanks advanced to the World Series when Chris Chambliss belted a leadoff home run in the bottom of the ninth of the decisive Game 5, but they were swept by the Big Red Machine in the Series. Steinbrenner would not let that happen again in 1977.

With Jackson hitting free agency on November 1, many teams clamored for his services. The Expos offered him the most money, but Montreal was not a place Jackson wanted to go. The franchise had only existed for eight seasons at that point and had finished below .500 each time. In 1976, they were the worst team in baseball by 17 games, and their cold, outdoor stadium was a place where not many wanted to play, especially Jackson, who had his pick of any team in the majors. The Padres gave Jackson a shot to move back to the West Coast, offering him the second-highest sum of money of any team, but the Padres were also a young team in their eighth season and had actually performed worse than the Expos during that time. Jackson wanted and needed the big stage.

When Jackson visited New York to meet with Steinbrenner, the man known as "The Boss" took him on a walking tour of the city he would own. Steinbrenner and Jackson walked through the East Side of Manhattan while they got to know one another. He walked him past the high-end shops on Madison Avenue and through the everyday people who brought the city to life. In the 1970s, New York had a dangerous edge and excitement to it, and it seemed like the center of the universe. Some kids spotted Jackson on their walk and asked him for an autograph. Jackson knew the city was starved for a World Series, as the Yankees hadn't won a championship in 14 years. Their longest streak before that was three years. They had come close two months before his visit and needed a star like Jackson to topple the Big Red Machine. They needed one another, they got one another, and it went exactly as everyone expected.

Jackson's tenure in the Bronx got off to a tumultuous start, thanks largely to an article that appeared in the June 1977 issue of *Sport* magazine. The article is infamous for Jackson's "I'm the straw that stirs the drink" remark, which angered Jackson's teammates and sent the New York media ablaze; however, the article itself painted a broader picture of the slugger's first days as a Yankee. According to Jackson's comments, Thurman Munson wasn't keen on Jackson's arrival, as he felt it put his spot as the team leader in question. Lou Piniella was standoffish, and even the respected Chris Chambliss didn't welcome him with open arms. Chambliss and Jackson's lockers were next to one another in spring training, and at the time of the interview, Jackson said that Chambliss hadn't even said hello to him yet. Sparky Lyle said the Yankees should have gone after a right-handed power hitter instead. The players interviewed conceded that Jackson was a good player who would help the team win ballgames, but that was it.

The article's author, Robert Ward, even said he felt bad for Jackson in a follow-up article. He hadn't done anything wrong, and Jackson was an open and honest interview subject. The article also paints a picture of Jackson wanting to be much more than a baseball player. Jackson was always a highly intelligent person, and to him, it was just as important to be known as an intellect as it was to be a baseball star. In a separate spring training interview, Jackson expounded on that idea.

"I am not merely a baseball player," he said. "I am a black man who has done what he wants, gotten what he wanted, and will continue to get it. Now what I want to do is develop my intellect." When Ward conducted his interview for his *Sport* magazine article, Jackson continued on that path. He said proudly,

> I've got this big name that comes before me, and I've got to adjust to it. Or what it has been projected to be. That's not really me, but I've got to deal with it. Also, I used to just be known as a black athlete, now I'm respected as a tremendous intellect. That now people talk to me as if I were a person of substance. That's important to me.

That was the paradox of Jackson, and it fed into his larger-than-life personality. He was certainly brash and confident, but he was also someone who prioritized team success ahead of anything else, and he did have a humble side to him. Jackson had his typical season in 1977. He belted home runs consistently and was an RBI machine. He also battled with manager Billy Martin, teammates, and the media throughout the season.

The tension finally boiled over in the heat of early summer in Fenway Park. Martin wasn't happy with Jackson's effort on a single to right that allowed Fred Lynn to go from first to third when Martin felt Jackson could have held him at second. Martin removed Jackson from the game, and by the time he got to the dugout from his right-field position, he went right at Martin. The two nearly came to blows, but Jimmy Wynn, an ally of Jackson's from the start, and Elston Howard, a coach on the team, were quick to jump between them.

The Yankees went 42–18 in the season's final 60 games to win the American League East by 2.5 games and faced the Royals in the

American League Championship Series. Jackson struggled mightily in the hotly contested series, and Martin benched him for the decisive game five. With the Yankees down, 3–1, in the eighth, Martin sent Jackson up with two runners on. He stroked a pinch-hit RBI single to bring the Yankees to within one run. The Yanks rallied for three runs in the ninth, sending them to their second straight World Series. Jackson's hit went a long way to ease the tension in the game. Even in a series that saw him bat .125, he still had a meaningful impact.

Jackson was back in the starting lineup for the World Series against the Dodgers, and his play ensured that Martin wouldn't consider removing him again. Jackson's performance was punctuated by one of the most historic postseason games any athlete has ever played in any sport. As Dodgers first baseman Steve Garvey put it, "I think he was able to release all his emotional tension of the entire season in this one game." Jackson went 3-for-3 with 3 runs, 5 RBI, and 3 home runs to lead the Yankees to an 8–4 win in Game 6, to lead the Yankees to the World Series title, just like he was brought there to do. He had also homered in his final at-bat in Game 5, so that made four official at-bats in a row in which Jackson homered.

Even more incredible, the three home runs in Game 6 came on Jackson's only three swings of the game, each coming on the first pitch of the at-bat. Considering his home run in his final at-bat the game before, Jackson hit four home runs on the last four swings he took in the 1977 World Series. He hit .450 with five home runs in the series and was the easiest selection for World Series MVP since they established the award. Jackson put on such an incredible display that the *Los Angeles Times* ran four articles and two full-size pictures of the slugger the next day. *Times* reporter Charles Maher put it best in the lede of his article covering the game when he wrote, "There's no today, it's been canceled on account of Reggie Jackson, who had a game few, if any have matched in the 74-year history of the World Series." Jackson's Mr. October nickname was already in use prior to the 1977 season, but his performance cemented the moniker in the lexicon of baseball history.

After the World Series, Jackson and Martin filmed a segment to air on *Good Morning America*. More relaxed, they were predictably entertaining. The appearance showed a different side of both men. They had the same goal at the start of the season and accomplished it, even if they fought the entire way there. Jackson's humble exchanges with Martin flew in the face of someone who was so competitive throughout the season. Jackson was quick to credit Martin, Thurman Munson, and George Steinbrenner, saying, "The four of us have been humiliated and embarrassed, and put on the sport to test our humility and our manhood." Jackson also addressed his record World Series. Martin pointed out that Jackson had broken his own record for most total bases in a World Series. Jackson's response was, "Aw, what's the difference? We won." Winning was always the most important thing to him. He was just going to put on a show doing it.

The Yankees beat the Dodgers again in the 1978 World Series, and Jackson was spectacular. He batted .391 with two home runs as the Yankees won in six games for the second year in a row. For as great as Jackson was, and he was indeed the straw that stirred the drink, the Yankees teams of the late 1970s were full of African American stars whose play matched their personalities. In center field, they had Mickey Rivers, who was as eccentric and quotable as he was fast. "Mick the Quick" had a number of famous quotes, for instance, "Me, George [Steinbrenner], and Billy [Martin], we're two of a kind." When a reporter informed him that Reggie Jackson had an IQ of 160, Rivers retorted, "Out of what? A thousand?" He was known to go right from the ballpark to the racetrack on payday. Considering the impact Rivers has had on Yankees lore, it's hard to believe he spent just three full seasons in the Bronx. He received MVP votes in each of those three seasons, finishing third in 1976.

Roy White and Chris Chambliss were quiet veteran leaders. Chambliss was intense and known for his clutch hitting and excellent defense at first base. White was a classy left fielder from Compton whose quiet confidence and athleticism made it seem like he was gliding around the outfield, much the way Vada Pinson did for the Reds throughout the 1960s. A young Willie Randolph manned second base on those teams and was a stalwart with the Yankees for 13 years. Randolph was an All-Star for the first time at age 21 in 1976, with the Yankees, and repeated the feat the next season. He was a tough player from Brooklyn who combined the classiness of White with the intensity of Chambliss.

The Yankees bench was also dotted with African American players who filled important roles on the championship teams. Paul Blair was an eight-time Gold Glove Award winner with the Orioles and came to the Yankees in an offseason trade in 1977. Blair struggled his final two seasons as a full-time player in Baltimore but found a new role as a valued pinch-hitter and extra outfielder on both World Series teams. Cliff Johnson, Carlos May, Jimmy Wynn, and Elrod Hendricks also circulated on and off the team during that time, each player a veteran leader with a history of success.

The Yankees were one of the slowest teams to integrate, but they had finally embraced diversity during the George Steinbrenner era. At the start of the decade, the Yankees had only two full-time African American players on their roster, Roy White and Horace Clark. It took them almost three decades to have a team that reflected the diversity of their Bronx home, and when they finally did, they found the same success that the Big Red Machine and Pittsburgh Pirates had earlier in the decade.

Team photo of the Toledo Blue Stockings from 1884, their only season in existence. Moses Fleetwood Walker (top row, center) played 42 games in 1884, for the Toledo Blue Stockings in the American Association. He was the last African American player to appear in a game until Jackie Robinson in 1947. *Wikimedia Commons*

Team photo from the 1936 East–West All-Star Game featuring the best Negro League players of the time. Satchel Paige (top row, seventh from left) was the main attraction as the East topped the West, 10–2. The game also featured Major League Baseball Hall of Famers Josh Gibson (top row, seventh from right) and Cool Papa Bell (seated, third from left) among other Negro League legends. *Courtesy of Heritage Auctions*

Satchel Paige talks with Cleveland Indians manager Lou Boudreau during his two-year stint with the club. Paige pitched in 52 games for the Indians from 1948–1949, going 10–8, with a 2.78 ERA. *Courtesy of the Boston Public Library, Leslie Jones Collection; Leslie Jones photographer*

Members of the 1951 Boston Braves (from left, Luis Marquez, Earl Torgeson, Sam Jethroe, and Roy Hartsfield) on the steps of the dugout at Braves Field. Nicknamed "The Jet" for his blazing speed, Jethroe became the first African American player to suit up for the Braves in 1950. He won the Rookie of the Year Award in 1950, after he hit .273, with 18 home runs, while leading the National League with 35 stolen bases. *Courtesy of the Boston Public Library, Leslie Jones Collection; Leslie Jones photographer*

Sam Hairston (left) and Don Lenhardt of the Chicago White Sox on the dugout steps at Fenway Park in July 1951. Hairston was a star in the Negro Leagues for the Birmingham Black Barons and Indianapolis Clowns before a short four-game stint with the White Sox, and was one of the first 20 African American players to appear in the majors. *Courtesy of the Boston Public Library, Leslie Jones Collection; Leslie Jones photographer*

From left, Al Rosen, Bobby Avila, Joe Gordon, and Luke Easter on the field before the Indians played the Red Sox in a game at Fenway Park in 1950. That year was Easter's first full season in the majors, and the strapping first baseman belted 28 homers with 107 RBI for the Tribe. *Courtesy of the Boston Public Library, Leslie Jones Collection; Leslie Jones photographer*

From left, Monte Irvin, Artie Wilson, Hank Thompson, and Ray Noble pose on the dugout steps of Braves Field in 1951. Irvin was the first African American to play for the Giants when he debuted on July 8, 1949. Thompson was the third African American player to play in the major leagues, making his debut 12 days after Larry Doby integrated the American League in 1947. *Courtesy of the Boston Public Library, Leslie Jones Collection; Leslie Jones photographer*

From left, Red Sox infielders Frank Malzone, Don Buddin, Pumpsie Green, and Pete Runnels take a knee at Fenway Park in 1959. The Red Sox became the final team to integrate after facing intense public pressure when Green debuted on July 21, 1959. *Courtesy of the Boston Public Library, Leslie Jones Collection; Leslie Jones photographer*

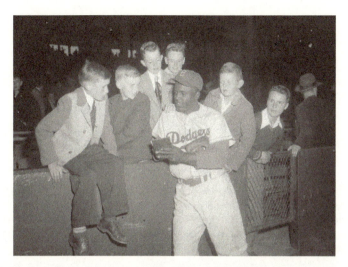

Jackie Robinson poses for a photo before his Brooklyn Dodgers took on the Boston Braves at Braves Field. Robinson won the first Rookie of the Year Award in the major leagues in 1947, when he integrated the sport. Robinson was an All-Star in six of his 10 seasons for the Brooklyn Dodgers. *Courtesy of the Boston Public Library, Leslie Jones Collection; Leslie Jones photographer*

Yankees catchers Yogi Berra and Elston Howard pose for a photo during Howard's rookie year in 1955. Howard was the first African American player to play for the Yankees, one of the final teams to integrate. *Courtesy of the Boston Public Library, Leslie Jones Collection; Leslie Jones photographer*

Reggie Jackson takes one of his trademark big swings in a game at Yankee Stadium in 1979. Jackson debuted with the Kansas City A's in 1967. Known as "Mr. October," Jackson won five World Series titles in his 21-year Hall of Fame career. When he retired, his 563 home runs ranked sixth all-time. *Photo by Jim Accordino*

Hank Aaron sits in the Oval Office with President Jimmy Carter in 1978, two years after his retirement from baseball. Aaron entered the majors at 20 years old in 1954, before the league was fully integrated, and retired as one of the best to ever play the game. *Courtesy of the National Archives and Records Administration*

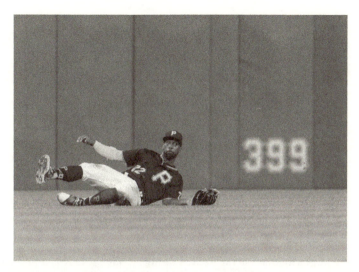

Andrew McCutchen makes a sliding catch in the outfield for the Pirates in 2017. McCutchen was one of the top players in the sport at the start of the 2010s and the National League MVP in 2013. *Gene Wang*

Curtis Granderson signs autographs for fans as a member of the New York Mets. Granderson was one of the young African American stars to usher the sport into the new millennium. Considered among the most charitable and respected players of his generation, Granderson was the major league's Roberto Clemente Award winner in 2016. *Michael Baron*

Ken Griffey Jr. as a member of the Reds, wearing his hat backward, as he frequently did. Griffey was a baseball prodigy who lived up to his billing as the game's next great generational star. Griffey almost became the first unanimous Hall of Famer in 2016, when he received 99.3 percent of the vote. *Photo by Brad Schloss*

Mookie Betts is one of the game's great stars as the sport moves into the new decade. One of the most dynamic and consistent players in the sport, Betts has already won an MVP Award, three Silver Slugger Awards, and four Gold Gloves, and made four All-Star Teams in his first five seasons. *Photo by Keith Allison*

5

BIG HAIR AND KNOCKING DOWN MORE DOORS

ADDING FLAVOR TO THE NATIONAL PASTIME

The 1970s featured some of the most dominant and colorful teams in baseball history, and the same can be said about the individual players. It was during this decade that baseball broke through its long-standing traditions on decorum and appearance, and the players' personalities were able to shine through. There was an exuberance to Jackie Robinson's game, and that of Willie Mays, too, but most of the African American stars from previous decades were reserved and traditional. Players like Hank Aaron, Larry Doby, Frank Robinson, and Ernie Banks certainly had their own personalities, but they weren't as flamboyant as the stars of the '70s. Baseball is so ingrained in American culture that the sport had no choice but to change with the times.

Relaxed feelings toward facial hair and haircuts in general led to widespread Afros peeking out from underneath hats on baseball fields throughout the majors, and none were as prevalent as Oscar Gamble's. Gamble was discovered by Buck O'Neil when he was scouting for the Cubs and played on six different teams in the 1970s, including two stints with the Yankees. His Afro appeared to grow on a progression of baseball cards each year in that decade—two big poofs of hair poking out from each side of his cap, getting bigger each year Topps released a new set. It peaked on his famous 1976 Topps card, which pictures the newly traded Gamble in a Yankees uniform. He is centered neatly in the middle of the card, with his hair almost extending out of the picture on either side of him.

When he arrived in the Bronx for his first spring training in 1976, he didn't have a uniform in his locker. George Steinbrenner declared that he wouldn't get his pinstripes until his hair was trimmed, and there was a car waiting outside to take him for a haircut. Gamble's hair was so iconic that he had an endorsement deal with Afro Sheen, even though he had never been an All-Star player. That deal would go away if Gamble cut his hair. Steinbrenner upheld his team's strict policy on grooming and paid Gamble the endorsement money he lost out on. In an interview in 1978, Gamble said, "I sign those [baseball] cards all the time. When I've been at [Yankee] Stadium, they always put that big Afro on the scoreboard, and I get a good hand. I didn't know how famous it would get. A lot of people were wearing Afros."

Two days before the 1977 season opened, Gamble was traded to the White Sox, owned by Bill Veeck at the time. Veeck was the owner of the Indians in 1947, when they integrated the American League with Larry Doby. The White Sox were managed by Hall of Famer Bob Lemon, who was teammates with Doby and Satchel Paige in Cleveland. Gamble hit a career-high 31 home runs in 1977, and teamed with African American stars Ralph Garr and Chet Lemon to lead the White Sox to a dramatic turnaround. They went from losing more than 90 games the year before to winning 90 in 1977. As with just about any of Veeck's teams, they were as colorful as they were successful.

The speedy Garr earned the nickname "Road Runner" during his time with the Braves due to his speedy and exciting play. The Braves even went so far as to acquire rights from Warner Brothers to show *Looney Tunes* clips of the Road Runner on their scoreboard and play the trademark "beep-beep" sound effect when Garr reached first. Garr's speed had declined a touch in Chicago, as he was near the end of his career, but he remained a popular attraction and batted .297 in four seasons there. Chet Lemon was just as popular in Chicago as any of the top young all-around outfielders in the game about to turn into budding stars. He made two All-Star Teams in Chicago and put himself in contention for the title of best defensive outfielder in the game. In 1977, Lemon recorded 509 putouts in center field, a major-league record that stood until 2010. Doby was the team's hitting coach, and Chet Lemon credited him with his development. In 1978, the White Sox fired Bob Lemon and hired Doby as manager in June. Chet Lemon would go on to make his first All-Star Team that season.

Lemon was part of a core group of American League center fielders in the 1970s who carried the mantle as supremely talented defenders as Willie Mays and Vada Pinson began to show their age. The Orioles' Paul Blair and Amos Otis of the Royals combined to win 11 Gold Gloves, which explains why Lemon improbably never won a Gold Glove in his career. Blair and Otis were smooth-as-silk center fielders, the kind that people sometimes mistook for being too nonchalant because they made everything look so easy. Otis maintained the tradition of stellar outfielders to come out of Mobile, Alabama, started by Hank Aaron. Hall of Famer Billy Williams, Cleon Jones, and Tommy Agee also followed a path from Mobile to the majors before Otis. When the Royals established their franchise Hall of Fame in 1968, Otis was the first position player inducted.

The crop of center fielders in the American League allowed fans to argue about who was the best defensive center fielder of the decade, and really no answer was wrong between Blair, Lemon, and Otis. In the National League, the answer was more clear-cut. Garry Maddox's name may have well been etched onto the Gold Glove trophy before the season started each year of the decade. The fleet-footed Maddox earned the nickname "Secretary of Defense" and spurred the famous quote, "Two-thirds of the Earth is covered by water, the other one-third by Garry Maddox."

The decade wasn't rife with just African American star position players, however. Following in the vein of Vida Blue and Dock Ellis, there was a parade of exciting and successful African American pitchers in the decade, too. Blue Moon Odom's career in the majors was winding down during the decade, but he remained a popular and successful pitcher in the early 1970s. A graduate of the same high school in Georgia as Little Richard and Otis Redding, Odom was a talented pitcher and singer. He earned his nickname in grade school when a classmate determined that he had a head shaped like the moon. Odom embraced the nickname, and it fit right in with the Charlie Finley A's of the '70s.

Fergie Jenkins was an absolute workhouse throughout his career, hurling more than 300 innings five times. He won 178 games in the 1970s and became a member of Odom's "Black Aces" club for African American pitchers who reached 20 wins in a season. Jenkins did that seven times. Between 1967–1974, he finished in the top three in Cy Young voting five times, winning in 1971. Al Downing was a solid lefty pitcher for the Yankees in the mid-1960s until injuries derailed a promising career. Steely and determined on the mound, Downing's career was revived by a trade, and he won 20 games for the Dodgers in 1970, earning Comeback Player of the Year honors. Downing is also known for giving up Hank Aaron's record-breaking home run in 1975.

Luis Tiant, who battled through injuries after establishing himself as a star with the Indians, enjoyed a major revival beginning in 1972, when he led the American League with a 1.92 ERA. Tiant won 122 games for the Red Sox in eight seasons and was fantastic during the 1975 postseason. He energized Fenway Park, and his popularity eased some of the racial tensions that were prevalent in the city. He also had fans mimicking his windup in ballyards throughout the country. His performance and flair on the mound embodied the 1970s perfectly.

Another lefty pitcher who was a solid mainstay of the 1970s was Rudy May. A tall, hard-throwing lefty with a dangerous curve, May won 152 games in 16 seasons. As with many players, he developed his love of the game as a youngster growing up in California.

"When I was seven or eight years old, a major event happened in my life," said May, recounting early memories of the sport.

> My grandpa and father were great ballplayers; both were catchers. My grandpa came to visit us in California, and he wanted to take me to a baseball game. The House of David was like the Harlem Globetrotters of baseball, and they were playing against the Oakland Oaks. The big attraction was that Satchel Paige was pitching for House of David. I remember two things from that day. My father's side of the family were heavy drinkers, and we stopped to get drinks to bring into the game, which wasn't a good idea. They were drinking at the park and eventually got kicked out. I was crying because I wanted to stay and watch Satchel pitch and see him after the game. They let me stay as they left, and the fans around me looked after me. After the game, we waited outside the park because we heard Satchel was coming by. Sure enough, Satchel Paige came out of the park and walked right past us to his car and said he was going fishing.

Even though May was a talented player growing up in Oakland in the 1950s, he wasn't even the best player from his neighborhood. That honor would have to go to Joe Morgan. May and Morgan grew up playing ball together on the sandlots in Oakland and eventually were teammates at Castlemont High School in Oakland, with Morgan one year ahead of May. May recounted that Morgan's bedroom was a converted garage, and Morgan loved to sleep. May would have to drag him out of bed, and when he was successful in doing so, they would play basketball and baseball all day. May remembered how his path to becoming a successful pitcher started.

> I had two brothers, and I was a tall and wiry lefty growing up and was very clumsy. A bunch of the neighborhood boys always played baseball. I was always the last guy picked and was told to go stand in right field. One thing I always could do though was throw hard. One day when I was in ninth grade I was outside throwing alone when my homeroom teacher showed up. He asked me if I was a pitcher, and I told him I didn't know how to pitch. He invited me to come to school early and would show me how to pitch. We worked on my windup and my stretch, and I was still throwing hard. I remember, he told me that if I learned to get it over, I'd be a force to be reckoned with. I remember that, and it gave me confidence. One day, my teacher asked me if I had a television at home. I said I did, and he told me to watch the Dodgers–Giants series that was coming up. Sandy Koufax, Johnny Podres, and Johnny Antonelli were scheduled to pitch, three lefties. He told me to watch them and learn their mechanics. After I did, I asked my brother if he could help me. He said no because I threw too hard! I told him I just wanted to work on my motion, and he said that he would help, as long as I promised not to throw hard. I remember watching those guys and then practicing that motion and thinking, "I got it!"

May was fortunate growing up around baseball, and it was such a big part of his youth. He recounted how Willie Stargell, Frank Robinson, Ernie Broglio, and Vada Pinson used to work out at a local high school, and he and Joe Morgan would go watch them. His dad was a big baseball fan and a Willie Mays fan. While May played in the majors throughout the 1970s and half of the 1980s, he still faced prejudice at the start of his professional career. One of the last players to sign a professional contract before the draft was instituted, he signed with the Twins as an 18-year-old in November 1962. He faced discrimination from the start in the minor leagues. Said May,

When I broke into baseball, there was still a vast amount of prejudice. When I was with the Twins in my first spring training, I couldn't stay in the same hotel as the team; I had to stay in a house with a family. In the dugout, there was a water fountain for the white players. The black players had a pail of water that was kept behind the dugout, and we had to drink out of it with a ladle. The next year, I played in Portsmouth, Virginia, and we had seven black players in the starting lineup on Opening Day. Only the catcher and second baseman were white. The ballpark was segregated; there were separate seating areas for blacks and whites, and separate bathrooms. We had so many good black players though and drew so many black fans, they had to change that and opened the stadium to all. That was the summer of 1964, right in the middle of the civil rights movement. What a time to be living in the South.

As a 19-year-old, May dominated in the minors. He went 17–8, with a 2.61 ERA and 235 strikeouts in 207 innings, spread across single A and AAA. When he was promoted to AAA to play for the Indianapolis Indians, May ran into Bob Thurman, the scout who signed him with the Twins. Thurman was a former Negro League player who broke into the majors in 1955, as a 38-year-old with the Reds and hit 16 home runs as a part-time player in 1957. The two met for a drink in a hotel bar, and Thurman gave May some insight into the Twins organization. Remembered May,

We met at a hotel bar and I ordered a soda. Bob told me that it was a good thing I got away from the Twins. I asked him why as I didn't really have any bad experiences there. He told me that the Twins didn't want black pitchers and that they fined him for signing me. They had a good pitcher, Camilo Pascual, who was Cuban, but light-skinned. The Twins used Pascual to measure skin color. They wouldn't sign any pitcher who had darker skin than Camilo Pascual. Bob knew this and told the Twins I wasn't a pitcher. He figured that once they saw me pitch everything was fine. I didn't know any of this and nobody said anything to me when I was there, but Bob got fined for signing me and lying to them.

May's story is shared by many African American players who played during the 1970s, especially the early part of the decade. The players who fell into that category grew up in the 1950s pre–civil rights era. Depending where they played in the minors, they likely experienced different levels of racism and prejudice. But as their careers developed throughout the 1970s, they were playing in a different world than they grew up in. Three decades after Jackie Robinson's debut, African American ballplayers typically no longer had their race attached to them in newspaper articles. It was no longer, "Hank Aaron, the talented Negro ballplayer." Now it was just, "Hank Aaron, the baseball superstar." While there may be no line of demarcation for that change, as exists for the integration of baseball, the 1970s can be looked at as a coming-of-age era for African American ballplayers.

The decade saw the end of the careers of Willie Mays, Hank Aaron, Bob Gibson, Ernie Banks, and Frank Robinson. It brought the first African American manager in Major League Baseball and the first African American elected to the National Baseball Hall of Fame. It saw Aaron break Babe Ruth's career home run record and Lou Brock break Ty Cobb's career stolen base record. Gene Richards set a rookie stolen base record, topping a mark that had stood for 67 years. It saw Vida Blue and Reggie Jackson burst onto the scene with the A's and an avalanche of African American players whose personalities were as big as their game. There was the intimidating presence of Gibson and Dick Allen, the over-exuberant joy of Banks and Mickey Rivers. Players like Bill Madlock, Bob Watson, Dusty Baker, and Cecil Cooper were among the best pure hitters in the game.

There were the quirky stories, too. Ron LeFlore was signed out of prison by Billy Martin and the Tigers, and found himself in the All-Star Game just three years later. Herb Washington played 105 games for the A's in two seasons and never played the field or took an at-bat. He was a world-class sprinter signed by Charlie Finley to serve exclusively as a pinch-runner. The experiment didn't work, but Washington's legend lives on. George Hendrick was a supremely talented outfielder who is credited with being the first player to wear long baseball pants down to his ankles, covering his stirrups. He was nicknamed "Jogging George" for not running his hardest on easy ground outs. Lenny Randle was a solid player who made headlines late in the decade when he punched his manager Frank Lucchesi in the face three times in an altercation, hospitalizing the manager for a week. There was also the time Ellis Valentine, Reggie Smith, Dave Parker, and Dave Winfield decided to have an impromptu throwing contest before the 1977 All-Star Game, showing off the top outfield cannons of the day.

There were also a number of tragedies and bad breaks among African American players in the 1970s. Lyman Bostock was just 28 years old in 1978, and he was one of the best young hitters in the game. In 1977, he batted .336 with the Twins and held a .311 career average after just four seasons. He was shot and killed as a passenger in a car by a man who mistakenly thought Bostock was having an affair with his wife. The truth was that Bostock had just met the woman less than an hour before as part of a group of friends.

J. R. Richard wasn't killed, but he looked to be a surefire Hall of Famer before his career was cut short by a stroke. Richard was perhaps the most intimidating pitcher of the 1970s, taking the mantle from Bob Gibson when he retired. Richard became the first National League righty to strike out 300 batters in a season in 1978, and repeated the feat in 1979; however, in 1980, at the age of 30, Richard suffered a mysterious "dead" feeling in his pitching arm, as well as blurred vision. After weeks of trying to diagnose the problem, Richard was playing catch prior to a game when he suffered a massive stroke and collapsed in the outfield. Luckily, he survived, but he never again pitched in the majors.

There was plenty of African American representation throughout Major League Baseball. The Red Sox were the final team to integrate in 1959, a time when there were still teams with just a minimal number of African American players. Although it was just a short time between then and the colorful 1970s, it might as well have been a lifetime when calculating the progress in baseball. In four of the 10 seasons of the 1970s, at least 17.9 percent of active players were African American.

The African American stars of the 1970s came from all different backgrounds, had different levels of success, and featured as many different personalities as Satchel Paige had pitches. But they all had one thing in common. They all grew up watching baseball in the 1950s and early 1960s. That was the first era of the bustling, young African American baseball superstar. They grew up watching Hank Aaron, Ernie Banks, Willie Mays, and Frank Robinson establish themselves among the best players in the game. They grew up seeing a retired Jackie Robinson remain active in social justice and the class and resolve Roy Campanella showed while confined to a wheelchair. No matter where the stars of the 1970s looked for their baseball heroes, they had an abundance of young stars to look to and visual proof that African Americans could pursue fair opportunities in Major League Baseball if their talent allowed them to do so.

PROGRESS OFF THE FIELD

The summer of 1966 was a pivotal time in the United States. JFK had been shot three years prior, and Martin Luther King would be assassinated just two years later. The Civil Rights Act was not even two years old, and neither was the first march from Selma to Montgomery, Alabama. The Vietnam War raged on. On the afternoon of July 15, 1966, Ted Williams stepped to the podium for his Hall of Fame induction speech. Williams began his career in 1939, eight years before Jackie Robinson debuted and retired in 1960, one year after the Red Sox became the last team to integrate. Williams's speech was short, but it remains one of the more impactful speeches in the Hall of Fame's history, thanks to just four sentences toward its conclusion. After thanking the people who had afforded him the chance to be at the podium that afternoon, Williams lobbed some powerful words at the Hall of Fame itself. In his typical dignified but direct manner, he said,

> Baseball gives every American boy a chance to excel. Not just to be as good as anybody else, but to be better. This is the nature of man and the name of the game. I hope someday Satchel Paige and Josh Gibson will be voted into the Hall of Fame as symbols of the great Negro players who are not here only because they weren't given the chance.

Williams wasn't demanding or aggressive; he didn't have to be. His words and opinions carried weight, and he knew that. Joe Cronin, who was general manager of the Red Sox during the period when they refused to integrate, was one of the few Hall of Fame players who was there in attendance that day and was the American League president at the time.

The next day, sportswriter Jerry Nason wrote a column about Williams's remarks in the *Boston Globe*. Nason had been working for the *Globe* since 1942, and is one of the most respected sportswriters in Boston sports history. Nason said that Williams's comments "startled the baseball world" and then gave insight into the respect Williams had for Satchel Paige and other Negro League players.

Williams, arguably the game's greatest hitter, faced off against Paige 11 times in his career. By the time Paige faced Williams, he was an old man and was not the pitcher he was when he was dominating the Negro Leagues; however, he was still crafty and smart. Williams was just 1-for-10 against Paige in his career, a fact Williams was aware of when he faced Paige for what he figured would be the last time. The competitive Williams didn't want his career average to dip below .100 against a player he once saved up spare change as a kid to go see play on a barnstorming tour. Williams thought he picked up a tell from Page's delivery, a wiggle in the fingers at the top of his windup when he was going to throw a curve. Williams worked the count to 3–2, and as Paige reached the top of his windup, he spotted those fingers wiggling. As Williams geared up for a curve, Paige whistled a fastball by him with whatever speed he had left, sending Williams back to the bench on a strikeout.

Nason finished his article by stating that Jackie Robinson was the only African American player in the Hall of Fame, having been inducted in 1962. Roy Campanella just missed election in his second year on the ballot or he would have gone in with Williams. But ultimately, Nason concluded, "Unless they change the rule at the request of Williams, Paige and Gibson will forever remain legends—instead of realities—in the hall of plaques at Cooperstown."

Commissioner Bowie Kuhn formed the Official Negro Selection Committee for the Hall of Fame on February 3, 1971. The committee was helmed by Monte Irvin and consisted solely of former players and people associated with the Negro Leagues, notably Wendell Smith, the sports-writer for the *Pittsburgh Courier* who was at the forefront of the final push to integrate the major leagues. According to the initial bylaws, the committee would meet every year and elect one former Negro League player, as long as they got 75 percent of the committee's vote. One week later, it was announced that the committee had selected Satchel Paige as the first member of the Baseball Hall of Fame who had primarily played in the Negro Leagues. Kuhn's announcement came with a qualifier, how-ever. He said, "Technically, he's not in the Hall of Fame, but realistically the Hall of Fame is a state of mind." Kuhn's comments come off as segregationist in the vein of separate but equal, but the commissioner was just speaking on the rules set forth for the Hall of Fame stating that a player had to play 10 years in the major leagues to be inducted.

When the committee announced that Paige would be the first inductee but would be in a separate building as part of a Negro Leagues exhibit, the old righty took the news in stride publicly. Paige said, "I'm proud of wherever they put me in the Hall of Fame. Quite a few people told me if I was white, I would be playing in the big leagues, but I never did feel any bitterness." Paige continued, "I had a world of my own. I was having a lotta fun. We was making money out there, and we had some nice leagues out there, drawing some nice people. When the major leagues signed Jackie Robinson, I figured he was the man to take. They wanted a man with a college education."

Legendary New York sportswriters Phil Pepe and Dick Young addressed the fact of a separate place in the Hall for Negro League players in the *New York Daily News* the next day, and both supported this arrangement initially. Pepe wrote, "It's an academic point that the Negro stars will not be included in the same wing as other members of the Hall of Fame. They will be, nonetheless, Hall of Famers in their own right." Young also justified the initial decision to have a separate Negro League Hall of Fame within the Baseball Hall of Fame. He wrote,

> The criticism bound to be raised is that the Negro League stars are not being installed into the building reserved for the white stars. This would be an inaccurate objection. The Hall of Fame building is not reserved for whites. It is reserved for major-league stars. Jackie Robinson and Roy Campanella are enshrined in it, and shortly they will be joined by Willie Mays, Hank Aaron, Bob Gibson, and many others.

Young was prophetic that an objection would be raised about this separation, and after public backlash, Commissioner Kuhn stepped in a month before the formal induction to declare that all inductees, from both the Negro Leagues and major leagues, would be enshrined together.

Young changed his tune about the separation as the induction drew closer. One week before Paige's induction, Young wrote another column with a completely opposite opinion from what he had stated six months prior. Young hypothesized that if the Hall of Fame went through with their "preposterous plan of separatism, a few uninvited guests, quite black and quite noisy, might appear at the induction ceremony, carrying signs and making unfriendly sounds." Young then credited the Baseball Writers' Association of America, a group he belonged to, with pushing for full inclusion. Young was one of the most preeminent sportswriters of the time, and he was right to give credit to the baseball writers; however, he failed to state that he was one of the people trumpeting the division in the first place.

The New York press conference announcing Paige's induction was exactly what someone who knew Paige would expect. Paige was known to work according to his own schedule, but he was the headliner at this press conference and needed to be there as scheduled. Monte Irvin was tasked with getting Paige there on time. He called his old friend at 9:30 that morning, two hours before the press conference was set to begin, emphasizing the importance of being on time. Ray Dandridge, the former Newark Eagles star, escorted Paige and his wife Lahoma to the event to make sure. Upon arriving, Paige was greeted by his former Indians teammate, Larry Doby, who was a batting coach with the Expos at the time. When Doby congratulated the 65-year-old Paige, his response was, "Thanks, do you think they'll remember me?"

Paige was given instructions on how the press conference would go. Bowie Kuhn was set to greet the press and give some introductory statements. There was a big, covered portrait of Paige in his St. Louis Browns uniform at Kuhn's side, ready to be revealed as Paige was announced as the latest Hall of Famer. According to the plan, Paige was supposed to enter the room just as his portrait was being revealed to an ovation from those in attendance. When Kuhn made the formal announcement and unveiled the portrait, heads turned toward the door, but no one walked through the doorway. Kuhn paused. He allowed some time for Paige to enter, but there was still no movement. Finally, Kuhn said, "Satchel and Mrs. Paige are with us, and I ask them to come forward now." At that point the mercurial Paige came forward to be recognized and interviewed by the press. Paige worked on his own schedule.

The formal ceremony to induct Paige was scheduled for August 10. In addition to Paige, a group of seven players, mostly turn-of-the-century stars, were also inducted. The baseball writers announced their voting results in January, a month before Paige was selected, and they did not vote a single player in on the regular ballot. This was somewhat shocking considering such players as Yogi Berra, Ralph Kiner, and Duke Snider were eligible. It was Berra's first year on the ballot, and he would be inducted the following year. In his comments about being snubbed, Berra wasn't too upset and pointed out that at that time, there had been only four first-ballot Hall of Famers after the initial class. Those players were

Ted Williams, Stan Musial, Bob Feller, and Jackie Robinson. Robinson was the first position player to be inducted on his first ballot when he was enshrined in 1962.

In the next six years, eight more former Negro League players were inducted into the Hall of Fame. Paige was a slam dunk as a first-year candidate, and the following year, everyone knew the inductee would be Josh Gibson, the "Black Babe Ruth." He was inducted unanimously by the nine-person committee, a result as sure as the sun rising that morning. What was surprising was that Buck Leonard also gained enough votes for election. Originally, the committee was to select one player per year, but that was changed to include anyone who received at least seven votes from the nine-person committee. It was appropriate that former teammates Leonard and Gibson went in together.

Gibson was likened to Ruth due to the frequency and distance of his home runs. Leonard was often referred to as being similar to Lou Gehrig on the strength of his dependability, smooth fielding, and high batting average. Gibson was a mythical figure the same way Ruth was. Leonard and Gibson teamed up on the Homestead Grays and were the most feared combo in Negro League history. As of 2020, there were 35 players enshrined in the Hall of Fame by various Negro League committees, including a field of 17 former players and influential figures in 2006.

MORE BARRIERS TO BREAK

When Satchel Paige was inducted into the Baseball Hall of Fame in 1971, he was the headline attraction. Approximately 2,500 people attended the event and heard Paige talk about his career and call himself the "proudest man on Earth." Paige also expressed hope for a future in baseball as a manager. He said, "I could manage easy. I've been in baseball 40 years. And I would want to manage." On an otherwise happy occasion, Paige spoke his truth. He continued, "I don't think the white is ready to listen to the colored yet. That's why they're afraid to get a black manager—they're afraid everybody won't take orders from him. You know there are plenty of qualified guys around."

In September 1974, Frank Robinson was sold by the Angels to the Indians for a $20,000 waiver price. At the time, Robinson was 39, and winding down an iconic career. He was fourth all-time in career home runs, trailing only Hank Aaron, Babe Ruth, and Willie Mays. He was widely respected as a cerebral and fierce player, and was always viewed as a future managerial candidate. His final days with the Angels were embattled, and some felt he was campaigning to take over the managerial role. On the day he was sold to the Indians late in the pennant race, United Press International reporter Milton Richman wrote an editorial with the headline "Robinson: First Black Manager?"

Just three years after Paige said at his induction ceremony that he didn't think players were ready for an African American manager, Robinson was on the precipice of breaking this barrier. Richman started his article by saying that the trade brought Robinson closer to becoming a manager. It seemed like an obvious plan that Robinson would play the role of veteran leader through the end of the year and then take over as a player-manager the following spring if the Indians fell short of the pennant. Richman cast his doubts about that, however. He pointed to a contentious relationship that had been standing between Robinson and Indians general manager Phil Seghi since their days in Cincinnati.

Two weeks after the Indians acquired Robinson, the team was showing no new signs of life. On September 27, manager Ken Aspromonte was told his contract wouldn't be renewed, furthering speculation that Robinson would take over. He had been managing in the winter leagues and publicly expressed interest in managing in the major leagues. On October 2, the Indians faced off against the Red Sox in the last game of the season. Robinson homered in his final official at-bat of the season against Dick Pole to give the Indians a lead they would not relinquish. Even with the win, Aspromonte's fate was sealed, and it didn't take the Indians long to fill their vacancy. The very next day, Frank Robinson was named the first African American manager in Major League Baseball history.

Robinson's press conference wasn't the typical managerial press conference. It was called a "gala press conference" by *New York Daily News* columnist Dick Young, who was in attendance for the announcement in Cleveland. The event was so historic, Robinson received a congratulatory telegram from President Gerald Ford. In part, the telegram read, "Your selection as player-manager is welcome news not only for the Indians, the American League, and all of baseball, but also for baseball fans across the nation." Ford lauded his athletic skills and unsurpassed leadership in the sport as well.

Ford didn't congratulate Robinson on becoming the first African American manager, he just congratulated him on becoming a major-league manager, and that's how Robinson wanted to be seen. At his press conference, he said, "I hope I have been named as a baseball man, and not because I am black. I am the first black manager only because I was born black. If I start nine black players one day, or nine white players, it will be because they are the best I have, and only for that reason." Throughout his career, Robinson was known for being a levelheaded but headstrong player. He was a no-nonsense person who believed everyone should be treated fairly. He spoke up if he didn't think that was happening as a player, and now he had the power to put that into action as a manager. Robinson said, "I am not going to demand respect. You think you can demand respect, that doesn't mean you're going to get it. You earn respect." If there was anyone who could speak on earning respect, it was certainly Robinson, one of the most respected figures in the sport.

At his press conference, Robinson also addressed a thought that is on most managers' minds when they get hired: "What happens when I get fired?" Few managerial careers end on a high note. Most end in firings, while some end with the manager being nudged into a different position in the organization or retirement. The nature of the job is that they don't generally go out on their own accord. In speaking about this, Robinson said,

> I don't see any big problem firing me or any black manager if he's not doing the job. If they are not satisfied, fire me. I don't think there will be any repercussions. The public, they're pretty smart. They're the first ones to know you're not doing the job. If I'm fired at the end of the year, or before then, I'd probably be the first to say, fire me.

Robinson's Indians showed slight improvement in his first year at the helm. His team improved five games in the loss column, and Robinson contributed sparingly in his last active year as a player. His final home run came in the final game he played against the Angels team he felt wronged him. On July 6, against the Angels, Robinson inserted himself as the designated hitter, batting third in the first game of a doubleheader. He belted his 586th and final home run in his first at-bat and singled his next time up before calling on Orlando Gonzalez to run for him.

The Indians were expected to take a step forward in 1976, but a second straight fourth-place finish put Robinson on the hot seat going into

1977, even after leading the Indians to their first winning record since divisional play began in 1969. The Indians started slowly in 1977, and Robinson was fired after 57 games. At the time, articles cited such issues as ongoing feuds with players like Rico Carty and Larvell Blanks, in addition to the Tribe's on-field performance. Robinson showed up to the ballpark on June 19, to say goodbye to his players and meet the press. As expected, he handled the situation with honest answers, accountability, and class.

Robinson said,

> I haven't really had a chance to think about much of anything. Surprised? Yes and no. This thing has been hanging for quite some time. I tried to make the situation workable, and I have no animosity toward anyone here. In fact, I want to thank the players, the press, and the fans for the way they've treated me here.

Robinson's .509 winning percentage in 1976 was topped by only the Indians once between 1966 and 1994. Robinson would go on to managerial stints with the Giants and Orioles, and was at the helm of the Expos when they relocated and became the Nationals. He won the Manager of the Year Award in 1988, and finished his career with more than 1,000 wins.

Robinson's elevation to first African American major-league manager was a long time coming. The discussion of who would become the first African American manager was almost two decades old by the time he took charge of the Indians. There was always speculation that Jackie Robinson would break that color barrier as well, but after his retirement as a player, he never pursued coaching or managerial jobs. The first African American coach on a major-league staff was Buck O'Neil, who became a Cubs coach in 1962, after a successful run as a scout. Through no fault of his own, O'Neil was part of one of the biggest administrative blunders in baseball history.

After years of futility and shuffling through managers, Cubs owner P. K. Wrigley decided to employ a "college of coaches" system starting in 1961. Wrigley hired eight separate coaches who would rotate responsibilities haphazardly throughout the organization. For periods of time, there would be one "head coach" while the others served in different capacities. Just as a relief pitcher would be brought into games, relief managers would rotate in and take turns as the head coach. This proved to be disastrous, and the Cubs continued to struggle mightily despite having such Hall of Famers as Ernie Banks, Billy Williams, and Ron Santo. During this time, O'Neil was a successful scout and a constant presence at Wrigley Field; however, he wasn't allowed to remain in the dugout during games because he wasn't officially on the coaching staff. He could have remained if an opponent agreed, but most teams wouldn't allow it, realizing that having O'Neil on the bench would be an advantage for the Cubs. In May 1962, the Cubs hired O'Neil as a scout/coach and opened a spot on the bench for him by reassigning Vedie Himsl to the minor leagues.

O'Neil never did get a chance to manage in the majors, however. While he was part of the college of coaches, he was not part of the rotation of head coaches. O'Neil managed the Kansas City Monarchs successfully for eight seasons and in intrasquad games in spring training for the Cubs, but his position as scout/coach would be the highest the Cubs would let him climb. The closest he came to managing was during a doubleheader in 1962. Cubs manager Charlie Meto was ejected in the first inning of a game, forcing Elvin Tappe to take over. Tappe was subsequently ejected, and O'Neil should have been the next person in line. Instead, pitching coach Fred Martin was assigned to take over for Tappe. O'Neil counted that missed opportunity as one of his few baseball letdowns.

In his book *I Was Right on Time*, O'Neil wrote about the day. He said,

> After 40 years in baseball and 10 as a manager, I was pretty sure I knew when to wave somebody home and when to make him put on the brakes. I would have gotten a huge thrill out of being on a major-league field during game. Not going out there that day was one of the few disappointments I've had in over 60 years in baseball.

Cubs All-Star outfielder George Altman agreed. In an interview years later, he recalled O'Neil's missed opportunity. Altman said,

> He should've gotten an opportunity to manage that year because of the fact that he was the best manager of the group. He had experience and knowledge—and the players all took to him, even as a coach. He was a fiery guy. In the dugout, you could hear his booming voice giving encouragement to players and so forth. Everybody loved Buck.

While O'Neil's opportunity to manage never materialized and Jackie Robinson's chance didn't happen on his own accord, there was another African American pioneer who also had been knocking at the door of being a managerial trailblazer. He was a familiar face as an integration pioneer, and although he missed being the player to integrate the sport by three months, two decades later he was at the forefront of breaking yet another barrier. Larry Doby, the first African American player in the American League, was building an impressive resume as a coach, scout, and manager in the Venezuelan winter leagues immediately after his retirement as a player.

Doby worked with Gene Mauch and the Expos as a hitting coach and minor-league instructor, and his coaching received positive reviews from players. In 1974, he took a job as the Indians first base coach, which brought him one step closer to a managerial job. With Ken Aspromonte's Indians struggling, a managerial change was rumored in Cleveland for a long time, and Doby was a possibility for the job. He had been an All-Star outfielder for the Tribe for 10 seasons and key member of the 1948 World Series team. Doby was also popular among Indians fans and management; however, when Aspromonte was fired in 1975, it was Frank Robinson who took over, not Doby.

By this time, Bill Veeck had purchased the Chicago White Sox and hired Doby as his batting coach. Veeck was the Indians owner when Doby integrated the American League and had remained close with his former star. The White Sox showed considerable improvement offensively under Doby, but overall, the team struggled. In June 1978, Veeck fired manager Bob Lemon and named Doby the manager for the remainder of the season. Once again, Doby became the second African American to integrate an aspect of the baseball world.

THE DESCENDANTS OF THE 1970S

In the United States, the World War II generation is known as the "Greatest Generation." After the war was over, the United States experienced a growth in population, spurring the onset of the next generation, the "Baby Boomers." Of course, a generation of baseball players was born during that era, and fans of 1980s and 1990s baseball reaped the rewards. While there are hundreds of baseball stars who are part of the Baby Boomer generation, the years between 1957–1960 are of particular interest to baseball fans. During that short span of time, Hall of Famers Rickey Henderson, Tony Gwynn, Tim Raines, Harold Baines, and Lee Smith were born. Other stars, like Dave Stewart, Lou Whitaker, Jesse Barfield, and Willie McGee, were born as well. These were the stars of baseball that would lead the game from the celebrated '70s to the underappreciated '80s.

The year in which they were born is significant when looking back at the baseball stars who dominated the sport while these players were growing up. Having heroes to emulate during childhood can have a significant impact on impressionable youth, and there was no shortage of superstars for these future greats to look up to. Players born at the end of the baby boom were about eight years old when Bob Gibson authored one of the best pitching seasons in baseball history. They were in their teens when Hank Aaron surpassed Babe Ruth. For many, it was probably one of the defining moments of their youth. Bob Kendrick, president of the Negro Leagues Baseball Museum, was in his formative years and described the impact of Aaron's record-breaking home run on a young African American sports fan.

Kendrick said,

> I grew up in Crawfordville, Georgia. When I was a kid, the town was still segregated. I remember watching Hank hit number 715 in my mother's living room when I was 11 years old. When Hank hit that ball, I circled the bases with him in my living room. I went from the couch, to the TV, to the recliner, and to home. I circled the bases with Hank 90 miles away.

It's impossible to quantify how many young African American sports fans and future major leaguers had a similar experience that night. Childhood moments like that hook a young fan for life.

While Aaron's home run was the seminal baseball moment of the 1970s, it was the colorful nature of the sport and the abundance of African American players and large personalities that provided an incredible reason for young fans to watch the sport. As Rickey Henderson was growing up, Lou Brock was setting basepaths ablaze. When Tony Gwynn was in high school, Joe Morgan was winning back-to-back Most Valuable Player (MVP) Awards. Jesse Barfield turned 12 years old less than two weeks after Roberto Clemente uncorked one of the greatest throws from right field in baseball history when he fired a one-hop bullet to home from the warning track at Memorial Stadium. Years later, Barfield's throwing arm would be likened to Clemente's.

Young African American athletes of the Baby Boomer generation got to watch diversity in baseball explode right in front of their eyes in the 1970s. There was someone for everyone to look up to. Fans who liked the long ball watched Reggie Jackson and George Foster terrorize pitchers during the decade. If you liked speed, there was Brock, Morgan, and Mickey Rivers. If you wanted a combination of both, Bobby Bonds was doing it all. Young pitchers could look up to Vida Blue and Fergie Jenkins, and if you wanted to be a catcher, Elrod Hendricks was a key member of the great Orioles teams of the era. The African American stars of the '80s were part of the first generation of players to grow up in an era where African American players were no longer being identified as "Black major leaguers"; they were just major leaguers.

The 1980s featured the highest level of participation from African American ballplayers. The '80s came at the perfect time in history. Players from that decade played just before the widespread globalization of the sport. It's the only decade in which each year at least 16.5 percent of the players were of African American heritage. In five of the 10 years in the '80s, at least 18 percent of the league consisted of African American players, including an all-time high-water mark of 18.7 percent in 1981. It's not a stretch to think that having so many influential African American players to look up to as kids resulted in higher participation in the sport for African American players of future generations. The participation of African American players in the 1980s was a dividend of the fantastic era in which they grew up.

As Hank Aaron and Willie Mays took the baton from Jackie Robinson and Larry Doby, it was time for the stars of the 1970s to cede their way to a new generation of players. By 1980, Aaron, Mays, Gibson, and Frank Robinson were gone. Joe Morgan and Willie Stargell were aging fast. As with life, the culture of African American baseball continued to perpetuate, however. Dave Winfield, Jim Rice, and Dave Parker were established stars, and there was a fantastic group of youngsters waiting to join them.

In 1977, the top three place winners in the American League and National League Rookie of the Year Award voting were African Americans. By 1980, their paths were already starting to diverge, but two of them stayed on a track to Cooperstown. Andre Dawson and Eddie

Murray were the Rookie of the Year Award winners in 1977. Dawson beat out Steve Richards and Gene Richards, while Murray outdistanced Mitchell Paige and Bump Wills in the American League.

Dawson started as a hotshot center fielder for the Expos, blessed with great athletic skills that manifested in a fantastic throwing arm, great range, and a powerful bat. But playing this brand of baseball on the punishing Olympic Stadium turf quickly took its toll on Dawson's knees. In 1984, he moved to right field, where he continued to be a Gold Glove defender. Dawson stole at least 25 bases in six straight seasons before moving to right but then never topped 18 for the rest of his career. He carried his nickname, "The Hawk," from childhood to the majors and was a popular player with his hometown fans. He won eight Gold Gloves and four Silver Slugger Awards, and became the first MVP from a last-place team as a Cub in 1987, when he led the National League with 49 homers and 137 RBI. Dawson had two previous runner-up MVP finishes and was inducted into the Hall of Fame in 2010.

Just as fearsome in the American League was Eddie Murray. Murray ended his 21-year career as one of the best switch-hitters to ever play the game. He followed up his 1977 Rookie of the Year campaign by garnering top-10 MVP finishes in seven of the next eight seasons, including runner-up finishes in 1982 and 1983. Although he spent some time as a designated hitter early in his career, Murray won two Gold Gloves playing first base. He was quiet but intense, and his greatness is somewhat underappreciated; however, when you start stacking up Murray's accomplishments, it's clear he stands among the greats in the sport. When Murray belted his 500th home run in 1996, he joined Hank Aaron and Willie Mays as the only players with 500 home runs and 3,000 hits. As of 2021, he still holds the record for RBI for switch-hitters, with 1,917. No active major-league switch-hitter is within 1,000 RBI of Murray's record.

Nicknamed "Steady Eddie," Murray was incredibly clutch and reliable throughout his career. Upon his retirement, he was second to Lou Gehrig with 19 career grand slams and set a record by hitting home runs from both sides of the plate in the same game 11 times. Murray remains second to Mickey Mantle in all-time switch-hit home runs, with 504. As of 2021, the closest active player, Carlos Santana, had less than half of Murray's total. Murray became a first-ballot Hall of Famer in 2003, and should be appreciated for exactly what he was, a player so unique and talented that there have been just a handful of players able to do the things he did in the game.

Jim Rice is another star of the era who had a playing style similar to that of Dawson and Murray. Rice could be surly, and many point to that fact as one reason why he had to wait until his 15th and final year on the ballot to be elected to the Hall of Fame. But for a period of time, he was the most feared slugger in the game. His 1978 season ranks among the best offensive seasons of the second half of the twentieth century. Rice pounded the ball for 46 home runs and 139 RBI, leading the American League in both categories. He also banged out a league-high 15 triples, and if he would have gotten one additional hit every two weeks, he would have won the Triple Crown.

As Murray, Dawson, and Rice were establishing themselves as three of the hottest young stars in the game, two more all-time greats broke into the majors. While Murray, Dawson, and Rice were quiet, hot-blooded competitors with a toughness to their games and personalities, a couple of young, flamboyant players were capturing the imagination of fans as the decades converged. At the start of the 1978 season, a skinny little short-stop was quietly breaking through with the Padres. Ozzie Smith was the starting shortstop on Opening Day in 1978, after just one minor-league season. The Padres only had been in existence for nine years when Smith debuted for them, and the franchise had never won more than 73 games in a season. They were the outpost of the National League and a traditional doormat. A year later, Rickey Henderson was called up to the A's in late June of 1979, at 20 years of age, and he stayed an active major leaguer until 2003. Henderson and Smith remained two of the most electric players throughout the 1980s.

By the onset of the 1980s, Mobile, Alabama, had a legitimate claim as the top producer of baseball talent in the country. Hall of Famers Hank Aaron, Willie McCovey, Satchel Paige, and Billy Williams were all born in Mobile. Another Mobile native, Ozzie Smith, was already showing signs that he would be adding to the lore of those native sons. In just his 10th major-league game for the San Diego Padres, Smith pulled off per-haps the most improbable play of his sparkling defensive career. Jeff Burroughs smoked a one-hop line drive toward the middle of the di-amond. Smith ranged to his left and timed a dive to try to pick it up on one hop. The ball hit a rock in the infield and shot back behind Smith, who was already in midair. What should have been a bad hop single turned into one of the great defensive plays in baseball history when Smith reached back with his throwing hand while still in the air. He snagged the ball, hit the ground, bounced up, and fired to first to nail Burroughs by a step. Smith's career was defined by his glove, but he didn't need a glove to make the most remarkable play of his career.

Smith won his first of 13 consecutive Gold Gloves in 1980, when he set the major-league record for most assists by a shortstop, with 621. He made his first of 12 straight All-Star Games the next season and picked up an appropriate nickname that would follow him all the way to his plaque in Cooperstown. In 1981, the *Yuma Daily Sun* wrote a feature article about Smith during spring training and dubbed him "The Wizard of Oz." The name would eventually be shortened to "The Wizard," as no further clarification was needed in the baseball world to know who that adjective was attached to.

Jerry Reuss faced Ozzie Smith in 25 games throughout his long career and was always in awe of his defensive prowess. Reuss reflected,

> Ozzie was a highlight waiting to happen anytime he walked on the field. I was with the Dodgers, and we went to St. Louis for two series a year. I made a point to get onto the field early just to watch Ozzie practice. I watched him field grounders and work on his footwork. He'd be two steps into the outfield making long throws to first. I just loved watching him field grounders and watch the feeds he gave to his teammates. Ozzie wasn't just great himself, he made his teammates better. Because he covered so much ground, Tommy Herr could cheat a little towards first because Ozzie covered so much ground up the middle. He made a great infield even better. You can see why the Cardinals had the success they did during those years.

Smith and Dave Winfield should have been budding young stars for the moribund Padres to build around, but it wasn't meant to be. Winfield left San Diego on bad terms after the 1980 season. In the spring of 1980, Winfield made a proposal to the Padres seeking a 10-year contract with a base salary of $1.3 million, which was just about unheard-of at the time. The Padres not only balked at the offer, but also made Winfield's request public, knowing that fans would turn against their superstar. Padres management was correct in predicting the fans' resentment, which made it an easier pill for them to swallow when Winfield left in free agency, headed to the Yankees. At a time when free agency was in its infancy and player movement minimal, Winfield signed with the Yankees a week before Christmas in 1980, for a shocking $1.5 million, the richest contract in baseball history.

Almost a year to the day, Smith exited San Diego as well. Although he was born in Mobile, Smith moved to California when he was six and grew up there. He was high school teammates with Eddie Murray at Locke High School in Los Angeles and drafted out of Cal Poly San Luis Obispo. He wanted to commit to the Padres for his entire career and approached Padres management with an offer—a lifetime contract with the Padres, which would tie him to the franchise for 25 years at a little less than $1.5 million a year. The Padres failed to make a counteroffer and turned down Smith's request. As they did with Winfield, the management leaked Smith's contract demands to the public, further deepening the rift between the two parties. On December 10, 1981, Smith was shipped to the Cardinals in a six-player trade. The main piece coming back to the Padres was Garry Templeton, another of the game's exciting young shortstops.

Smith took his image as an emerging star a level higher in St. Louis, where he could make a case as the flashiest player in the league. His trademark cartwheel-and-flip entrance onto the field may have originated in San Diego at the behest of Padres employee Andy Strasberg, but it became folklore in St. Louis. In an instant, Smith went from one of the worst franchises to one of the best and was thrust into the spotlight, which played perfectly for his bright personality. The Cardinals couldn't have been a better fit.

Smith was one of the fastest players in the game and possibly had the quickest first step of any infielder in baseball history. He played his home games at Busch Stadium, where the smooth, hard turf provided nothing but true hops for him. Moreover, playing on the turf was a boon to his quickness. In his book *Wizard*, Smith also noted that the Busch Stadium turf helped his offensive game, along with some prodding from manager Whitey Herzog. According to Smith, Herzog proposed that every time Smith hit a ball on the ground, Herzog owed him a dollar. Every time Smith hit a fly ball, he owed Herzog a dollar. That helped Smith hit the ball on the ground, taking advantage of his speed and the quick turf of Busch Stadium. It also helped Smith develop into one of the toughest players to strike out in the decade. Twice while playing in St. Louis,

Smith struck out less than 20 times the entire season. He surpassed 40 strikeouts only once, in 1988.

While Smith created a legacy of wizardry at the shortstop position, his postseason heroics in St. Louis were based on one of the most improbable home runs in major-league history. In a pivotal Game 5 of the 1985 National League Championship Series, Smith hit a solo home run with one out in the bottom of the ninth to give the Cardinals a walk-off win. In 3,009 at-bats, that was the first home run the switch-hitting Smith ever hit left-handed. The home run spurred Hall of Famer Jack Buck's "Go crazy, folks" home run call and remains one of the defining moments in Cardinals history. Smith was named MVP of the National League Championship Series. They moved on to the World Series but ultimately fell to the Royals in the World Series in seven games. Smith appeared in four postseasons for the Cardinals, including three World Series, winning one in his first season there.

As flashy as Smith was in the National League in the 1980s, there was another star in the American League doing things the game had never seen. Rickey Henderson was born in Chicago but grew up in Oakland, where he developed into one of the great prep athletes in the country. Henderson was a natural lefty but learned to bat right-handed growing up because he modeled himself after his friends, who were all right-handed. He was an accomplished baseball player at Oakland Technical High School but also an All-American running back who could have taken his talents to any college in the country. The hometown A's drafted him in the fourth round of the 1976 draft and literally put Henderson on the fast track to the major leagues.

In 1978, Henderson was playing for the AA Jersey City A's as a 19-year-old. The A's played their home games at Roosevelt Stadium, in Hudson County, New Jersey. It was the same stadium where Jackie Robinson made his professional debut in 1946, while playing for the Montreal Royals. Henderson batted .310 and stole 81 bases for the A's that season. Incredibly, his 81 steals were 14 less than he had the previous season in single A. Henderson started the next season in AAA but was called up to the A's that June. In his first game, Henderson batted leadoff against the Rangers, whose own leadoff hitter was Bump Wills, the son of stolen-base legend Maury Wills. Henderson doubled in his first at-bat and singled in his next.

Henderson made his first of 10 All-Star Games in his first full season in 1980, when he torched the basepaths for 100 stolen bases, good enough for an American League record. He was just the third player to reach that milestone, joining Lou Brock and Maury Wills. In 1981, Henderson lost more than 50 games to a players' strike, but in 1982, he set a record that is not likely to be approached anytime soon, if ever. That year, Henderson stole 130 bases, a total higher than nine of the other 13 teams in the American League that season combined. Henderson had 84 stolen bases at the All-Star break. No player since 1988 has stolen 84 bases in an entire season. He topped 50 steals 14 times, including 66 as a 39-year-old in 1998. Henderson finished his career with 1,406 stolen bases, which is 468 more steals than anyone else in Major League Baseball history. The career stolen-base gap between Henderson and Lou Brock, who is in second place, is the same as between Brock and Jimmy Rollins, who stands in 46th place all-time. As of 2020, the closest active player to Henderson is Dee Gordon, who has 330 career steals.

Henderson's game was more than just stolen bases, however. He retired with three major career records: 81 home runs leading off a game, 2,295 runs scored, and 2,190 walks (which has since been surpassed by Barry Bonds). The most impressive thing about Henderson's numbers are that pitchers spent his entire career trying not to walk him and then trying to keep him stationary when he was on base. Everyone knew when Henderson was going to steal, and they still couldn't stop him.

While Henderson's play spoke for itself, his unique personality only added to his legend. He frequently spoke in the third person and had a good-natured relationship with the media. To put it in Henderson's own words, "People are always saying 'Rickey says Rickey.' But it's always been blown way out of proportion. Rickey says it when Rickey doesn't do what Rickey needs to be doing. Rickey uses it to remind himself, like, 'Rickey, what you doing, you stupid.' Rickey's just scolding himself." Even when he was on the wrong side of history, Henderson was ready with a memorable quote. When he became Nolan Ryan's 5,000th strikeout victim, Henderson said, "If you haven't been struck out by Nolan Ryan, you're nobody."

Henderson lasted in the majors for 25 years, but his desire to play extended longer than that. He played in 30 games for the Dodgers in 2003, and hoped to return the next year. Henderson also played independent ball, and his success there drew attention. In 2007, Henderson still expressed a desire to play. A's general manager Billy Beane was considering offering him a one-day contract so he could play one final game for his hometown A's. Henderson rebuffed the rumored transaction, saying he wanted a chance to play on a full-time basis. He said he didn't want to take anyone's roster spot and to give him a fair chance to prove himself. Henderson even offered to play for the major-league minimum and said he'd donate every penny of his salary to charity. That's how much he loved the game.

Henderson never did get to prove himself again in the majors, even if he was still contending he could play when he was in his 50s. He was still a superior athlete, and few people doubted that he could still steal bases in the majors. Henderson skated into the Hall of Fame, earning 94.8 percent of the ballot in 2009. His induction speech was highly anticipated due to his reputation for Yogi Berra–level doublespeak. Fans also wondered if he would confirm any of the stories of his antics that had become folklore throughout time, like the time he allegedly took his $1 million signing-bonus check and framed it on the wall instead of cashing it. Instead, Henderson did what he always does—the unexpected.

When Henderson topped Lou Brock's stolen-base record, he gave a short, planned speech in which he declared himself the "greatest of all-time." It was meant as a nod to Muhammed Ali but was taken by fans and the media of a slight of the quiet and classy Brock. This misconception haunted Henderson for years, as he had a respectful, long-standing friendship with Brock. Brock even allegedly helped Henderson write the speech. On July 26, 2009, Henderson found himself right where he was most comfortable, with the spotlight of the baseball world on him. He gave a funny, heartfelt induction speech as fans waited for that braggadocious comment they knew was coming. As Henderson was wrapping up, he appeared to be ready to deliver a callback line to his stolen-base record speech. In Cooperstown that day, Henderson said, "I am now in the class of the greatest players to ever play the game. And at this moment, I am . . . very, very humble." It was a redemptive line, perfectly fitting for a star who was sometimes misunderstood as selfish but who was humble and flamboyant at heart.

Henderson and Smith weren't the only African American stars of the 1980s who played the game in the spirit of their flashy brethren from a decade earlier. Tim Raines reached 70 stolen bases in six straight seasons, a feat Henderson never accomplished. If not for Henderson's historic feats during the era, it would have been Raines who was the heir apparent to Lou Brock. Jerry Reuss, who was teammates with Brock, spoke about the stolen-base threat from the perspective of a pitcher. "With the elite guys, it's not enough to just keep them close. I tried to pick them off," said the veteran of 22 major-league seasons.

> When I had any runner on first, the mindset still has to stay on getting the hitter out. You have to know the tendencies of the runners though. There were a handful of guys that really concerned me. Rickey Henderson, Davey Lopes, Joe Morgan, Tim Raines, Vince Coleman. Guys like that you have to pay special attention to but not so much that you lose focus on the batter. It's a game within a game. Lou Brock was the best; he's elite for a reason. Lou once said to me that it's easy to steal third on a pitcher on the next pitch after stealing second. He said after giving up a steal, a pitcher has a tendency to think that "game within a game" has been lost, so they let their guard down on the next pitch. Average guys might just stay put, happy that they stole second. But the elite guys like Brock and Henderson aren't satisfied. They're still looking to go.

The decline in stolen bases in the modern game has taken this drama from the sport. It also has had an effect on African American participation in Major League Baseball. Players like Henderson and Raines would have a place in any era, but players who typically hit single-digit home run numbers while consistently stealing 50 bases no longer have a place in the sport. Historically, the players who fit that description typically have been African American players. By removing the stolen base as a featured weapon, it removes not only a level of excitement from the game, but also those specialized players.

Today's well-rounded stars can still steal a base when needed, but that would be just a small portion of their game. Although he never walked at the rate as those who believe in modern analytics would like, Kirby Puckett would fit into that category. Puckett was a bowling ball of a center fielder and incredibly popular in the sport. The improbably gifted Puckett was an All-Star in each of his final 10 seasons. His production was surpassed by only the unbounding enthusiasm with which he played and a smile that could light up the Metrodome. The beloved Puckett saved his signature moments for the postseason.

Puckett led the Twins to the 1987 World Series title against the Cardinals, batting .357 in the Fall Classic. In 1991, he did even better. A year after the Twins finished in last place, Puckett won American League Championship Series MVP honors after batting .429 in a five-game series win against the Blue Jays and then turned in one of the most legendary postseason performances of the decade in the World Series against the Braves. With the Twins down three games to two and the World Series on the line in Game 6, Puckett provided his two signature moments in one of the biggest games in franchise history.

Puckett's leaping catch of a deep fly ball off the bat of Ron Gant early in the game remains the signature defensive play in Twins history. Then, in the 11th inning, with the Twins' season on the line and the game tied, 3–3, Puckett launched a 2–1 pitch over the left-center field fence to send the series to Game 7. Jack Buck, who was on the call for Ozzie Smith's improbable postseason home run in 1985, again provided the soundtrack for the historic moment. Against the backdrop of a frenzied Metrodome crowd, Buck simply said, "And we'll see you tomorrow night." The tomorrow night Buck was talking about ended up being anther signature moment for a Hall of Famer, as Jack Morris threw 10 shutout innings to lead the Twins to their second World Series in four seasons. It wouldn't have been possible without Puckett's heroics in Game 6.

In New York, the Mets of the early 1980s resembled the Mets of the early 1960s, which is to say they weren't very good. The reward for their terrible play was being able to draft at the top of the Major League Baseball Draft on a regular basis. The Mets nailed two of their draft picks by picking Darryl Strawberry first overall in 1980, and Dwight Gooden fifth overall in 1982. The two players not only produced on the field, but also lit up New York City, threw the franchise on their backs, and pulled the team out of the depths of the National League. The excitement provided by these rising young stars was bolstered by the acquisition of Keith Hernandez and Gary Carter, and together, the four of them led the Mets to a World Series title in 1986, after a couple of years battling the Cardinals for National League supremacy.

As with the 1970s, many of the top performances of the decade were provided by African American players. Tony Gwynn won four of his eight batting titles in the 1980s and batted .332 for the decade. Dave Stewart broke through as a dominant pitcher when he joined the A's in 1986. He developed a forkball and worked with pitching coach Dave

Duncan to transform himself from a journeyman swingman into a full-blown ace with an intimidation factor close to that of Bob Gibson. Stewart won 20 games in four straight seasons in Oakland and led the A's to the 1989 World Series title, capturing MVP honors for the Series along the way. It was the second of three rings he would win in his career and the first of his three postseason series MVP Awards.

Eric Davis was a rail-thin center fielder for the Reds who established himself as an MVP candidate in his first full season in 1986. He hit 27 home runs and stole 80 bases while playing Gold Glove–level defense. Davis followed that up with a season that could have gone down as one of the best all-around performances of the decade if he hadn't missed 33 games due to injury. Despite missing a month's worth of games, Davis still belted 37 homers and drove in 100 runs while stealing 50 bases. He was one of the most exciting young players to come into the game in a long time, but he just couldn't stay healthy. He topped 130 games played only five times in his career, but for that short period of time, Davis seemed to be on the fast track to Cooperstown.

While Davis was battling through injuries, a new star emerged in the American League whose superhuman feats surpassed Davis's or anyone else's for that matter. In the mid-1980s, Bo Jackson was known to most fans as the Heisman Trophy–winning running back from Auburn who was a clear favorite to emerge as the top pick in the National Football League (NFL) Draft. What a lot of people didn't realize was that he was also a baseball and track star for Auburn, and had been drafted by the Yankees in the second round of the 1982 Major League Baseball Draft, sandwiched between Barry Bonds and Barry Larkin. None of the three signed, but they would all find their way to stardom. Jackson didn't even play baseball his senior year at Auburn, as the NCAA ruled him ineligible after a visit to the Tampa Bay Buccaneers violated his amateur status. Jackson claimed that the Buccaneers misled him into thinking they had NCAA approval for the visit so that he would be ineligible for baseball, making the decision to play football an easy one.

Despite stating that he wouldn't play for the Bucs, they still drafted him first overall. Jackson turned down a five-year, $7.6 million predraft contract offer from Tampa Bay and instead signed a three-year, $1.07 million contract with the Royals with a commitment to play baseball. Despite this, Al Davis and the Raiders still drafted Jackson in the seventh round and offered him a five-year, $7.4 million contract that would allow him to play the entire full baseball season before joining the Raiders after his baseball commitment was done. Jackson played parts of four seasons with the Raiders and, in 1989, became the first person ever to be selected for both an NFL Pro Bowl and a Major League Baseball All-Star Game.

Jackson spent just 53 games in the minor leagues in 1986, before being called up for a 25-game trial with the Royals at the end of the season. After taking his senior year off from baseball and with little minor-league preparation, Jackson only batted .207 in those 25 games. He proved to be a solid player the next two seasons, playing all three outfield positions, before he broke through to his peak in 1989. That season, Jackson hit 32 homers and drove in 105 runs while performing superhuman feats on a nightly basis. Whether it was making improbable throws from the outfield, breaking bats over his knee and head, or running up the outfield wall after a catch, he frequently wowed on their field no matter what he was doing.

The peak of Jackson's career can be pinpointed to July 11, 1989. He was the leadoff batter for the American League in his only All-Star Game appearance and blasted the second pitch he saw from Rick Reuschel over the center-field fence. President Ronald Reagan was in the broadcast booth as a guest and on the call for the shot. After Cal Ripken grounded out for the final out of the inning, NBC debuted their famous "Bo Knows" commercial. The ad had been planned to run in that spot, and the timing couldn't have been any better.

Jackson followed that season with another solid year in Kansas City, but he suffered a severe hip injury playing for the Raiders the following January that ultimately resulted in hip replacement surgery. Despite a new hip, Jackson returned to baseball after missing the entire 1992 season. After his surgery, he promised his mother he would return to the majors and hit a home run for her. Jackson's mother died before she saw him make it back to the majors, but when he did return in 1993, with a new hip, he homered to right in his first at-bat back. Despite being robbed of almost all his athleticism due to the injury, Jackson returned to play two partial seasons for the White Sox and Angels. In what amounted to the equivalent of one full season, he hit 29 home runs and drove in 88 runs before retiring.

When fans remember baseball in the 1980s, they picture Rickey Henderson running wild on the bases and Darryl Strawberry's moonshot home runs. They think of Mookie Wilson's grounder trickling past Bill

Buckner in the 1986 World Series and Dave Stewart glaring over his glove at a helpless batter. They remember Ozzie Smith, Vince Coleman, and Willie McGee playing that distinct brand of exciting ball Whitey Herzog was known for. They remember the classy professionalism of Tony Gwynn, Lou Whitaker, and Harold Baines, and the outright dominant seasons of Dwight Gooden, Eric Davis, and Andre Dawson. Players like Reggie Jackson, Joe Morgan, and Willie Stargell retired during the decade, while such young future Hall of Famers as Barry Bonds and Barry Larkin got their start. The period was capped with the arrival of the next great superstar who would lead the game through the final decade of the twentieth century: Ken Griffey Jr.

The game of baseball was in great shape to move forward. The sport has just gone through a 20-year period of growth and excitement that was unprecedented. Players were now larger-than-life personalities, and salaries were skyrocketing exponentially. The 1980s started with Dave Winfield being vilified by fans for requesting a salary that topped $1 million annually and ended with the top players making close to $3 million and no one batting an eye. There was, however, one trend that wasn't necessarily picked up on at the time but can now be looked at in retrospect as the advent of the decline of African American participation in Major League Baseball. In the 1989 season, 16.5 percent of the league was made up of African American ballplayers. That figure had only decreased by less than 1 percent, but it was the third straight year in which there was a decrease in participation. It was the first time in baseball history that participation had shrunk three years in a row and represented a low-water mark that hadn't been seen since 1972. At the same time, participation of Latino players was at 13.2 percent and trending upward. It may not have been noticed at the moment, but the slow decline in the number of African American Major League Baseball players had already begun.

6

FIGHTING AGAINST A CHANGING BASEBALL CULTURE

THE STEADY DECLINE

In Major League Baseball, the 1990s were ushered in by a host of new young stars. Barry Bonds won the first of his seven Most Valuable Player (MVP) Awards in 1990, Barry Larkin had taken over the mantle as the National League's top shortstop from Ozzie Smith, and Fred McGriff was establishing himself as one of the top lefty power sources in baseball. Frank Thomas debuted with the White Sox to much fanfare and more than lived up to the hype. By the time Thomas's career was over, fans could make an argument that he was the best designated hitter of all time. The decade saw Cecil Fielder hit two homers in the final game of the 1990 season to become the first person to hit 50 homers since George Foster in 1972. Dwight Gooden redeemed his derailed career by pitching a no-hitter, and Joe Carter hit the only walk-off, come-from-behind home run in World Series history. Derek Jeter emerged as a captain in the Bronx, and Albert Belle enjoyed a short peak as a feared slugger that rivaled just about any hitter in major-league history. Make no mistake about it, however, the decade belonged to Ken Griffey Jr.

The name Ken Griffey was familiar to baseball fans because it had been only about 15 years since someone by that same name had been a key component in the Big Red Machine teams of the 1970s. In fact, Griffey was back with the Reds and served as a productive pinch-hitter, even at the age of 40. But young fans knew a different Griffey. Ken

Griffey Jr. was the first pick of the 1987 Major League Baseball Draft, and after two productive minor-league seasons that saw him shoot to the top of the top-prospects list, he was on the precipice of making the majors in 1989, at the age of 19. Griffey made the Mariners Opening Day roster and doubled in his first career at-bat, against Dave Stewart. One week later, Griffey homered in his first home at-bat. It was clear this Griffey had a flair for the dramatic. Griffey Jr. finished third in the American League Rookie of the Year voting, his case submarined by missing a month in the middle of the season. Even at 20 years old, it was clear he was something special.

In 1990, Griffey made his first All-Star Game and won his first Gold Glove. He was already ingrained in American culture as well. This was the peak of baseball card collecting, and Griffey had the most sought-after card of the time. He was turning into a lefty Willie Mays in front of everyone's eyes and quickly became the face of the sport. His infectious smile and bubbly personality, mixed with his intensity during games, made him an instant role model for young fans. Griffey was a player for a new generation, someone who wore his cap backward during batting practice, to the chagrin of baseball lifers. He was the player whose swing kids were emulating. Even righties would flip around and do their best Griffey swing from the left side. He made highlight-reel catches on a nightly basis, stealing home runs and ranging far in the gap to run down a sure double. He was the perfect player for the age of growing media coverage.

In 1990, Ken Griffey Sr. was released by the Reds and quickly signed with the Mariners. It was the first time in the history of Organized Baseball that a father and son played on the same major-league team. Everyone was excited, but the Mariners and the Griffeys wanted to be clear this wasn't a publicity stunt. Manager Jim Lefebvre said, "We are very honored to have them both here, but he's here to make a contribution—not just for the father–son thing. We wanted him because he's a winner, a leader who will play and make a contribution." Griffey Sr. concurred, saying, "This is the number-one thrill for me in all my years in the game."

Two days after Griffey signed with the Mariners, he found himself in the same starting outfield as his son. Senior batted second and Junior third. Griffey Sr. singled in his first at-bat, and Griffey Jr. followed with a single of his own. They each scored runs in the inning as well. Griffey Sr. played regularly and became revitalized in his new setting. He raised his average almost .100 points in less than two weeks and hovered at about .300 on September 14. That was the day father and son made more history.

Harold Reynolds led off a game against the Angels with a walk, and Griffey Sr. followed with his third homer since joining the Mariners. Junior and Senior had batted back-to-back in the lineup since Senior's arrival, so the possibility that they could hit back-to-back homers was always there, although chances were slim. Junior wasn't really a home run hitter yet, and Senior was never a home run hitter to begin with and was 40 years old. Junior took the first three pitches for balls in his next at-bat after his father's home run, but then when Kirk McCaskill grooved a 3–0 fastball, the young Griffey swung away and hit a home run near the exact spot his father had just four pitches earlier. It was one of the major milestones in cementing Griffey as the next generational sports superstar, in the same mold as Michael Jordan and Bo Jackson.

Griffey made the All-Star Game each year in the decade and had seven top-10 MVP finishes in the 10-year span. He peaked in 1997 and 1998, when he hit 56 home runs in back-to-back seasons while topping 145 RBI both years. He was the American League MVP in 1997 and, along with Edgar Martinez, probably saved baseball in Seattle. At about the same time as Griffey's emergence, Mariners ownership wanted a new stadium. The measure finally came to a public vote, but a 1 percent sales tax increase to fund a new stadium was voted down by the public. Upset, the ownership turned to government officials for help and said if they didn't receive public funds, a sale of the team and probable relocation would ensue.

Two weeks after the vote, the Mariners found themselves in the 1995 American League Division Series against the Yankees. Griffey and Martinez powered the Mariners to a 16–5 finish on the season and a one-game playoff win over the Angels. Down 5–4 in the bottom of the 11th inning of the deciding Game 5 of the American League Division Series, the Mariners rallied and won on a walk-off two-run double by Martinez. The image of Griffey motoring around the bases and sliding into home just ahead of the throw with the winning run is one of the lasting images of the decade. After Griffey slid safely into home, he popped up, only to be mobbed by Vince Coleman and his teammates, setting off a wild celebration in the Kingdome. Soon thereafter, local officials met to approve funding for the construction of what would become Safeco Field. This was not a coincidence.

Griffey left Seattle in a trade to the Reds following the 1999 season after expressing a desire to be closer to his family. He vetoed a trade to the Mets, saying he only wanted to play for his hometown Reds, his father's old team. Despite leaving Seattle, he remains a hero there and among baseball fans league-wide. The 10 years he spent in the majors after leaving the Reds didn't come close to measuring up to his accomplishments in Seattle. He had trouble staying healthy as he aged. He hit 398 home runs during his first 10 years in the majors and then just 232 in the next decade. Griffey returned to Seattle as a free agent and played two partial seasons there before retiring on June 2, in the middle of the 2010 season. It was this natural downward trajectory of his career that keeps Griffey as one of the few superstars of the era that doesn't have the stigma of steroids attached to him. He played through the height of the steroid era and never showed the physical changes or "reverse aging" of other superstars whose performances were buoyed by steroid use. Griffey was one of the few clean superstars of the time and is still looked at fondly as "The Kid" who saved baseball in Seattle.

Griffey's definitive seasons may have come in 1997 and 1998, but things could have been much different in the baseball world had the strike of 1994 not happened. Griffey was leading the American League with 40 home runs in just 111 games when the season came to a grinding halt. He was almost on pace to break Roger Maris's home run record, alongside Matt Williams, and knowing Griffey's competitive nature, few people would have bet against him. At the time, the single-season home run record was arguably the most coveted record in sports. Griffey was the ideal person to claim the same throne that had been passed from Babe Ruth to Maris. If things had ended differently in 1994, there is no telling what the steroid era would have looked like.

While there is no direct correlation, the 1994 season was the start of a 16-year period of declining participation among African Americans in Major League Baseball. In the strike-shortened season, African American players made up 17.2 percent of the league, in line with the previous two decades. When baseball returned after the strike, participation among African Americans dropped to 16.1 percent in 1995. By the end of the decade, the percentage of African Americans in Major League Baseball had reached levels not seen since the 1960s, and six years later, that percentage would drop to single digits. At the same time, baseball was globalizing, and the number of Latino players was growing exponentially. At the time of the strike, the rate of participation among Latino players was 17.8 percent, similar to African Americans. That percentage had grown to 24.7 percent by 2000, and for the next 20 years, the number of Latino players in the sport hovered at approximately 25 percent.

This should have been an era of continued prosperity among African American players, and there are many theories as to why the opposite happened. African American athletes who were adults in the 1990s and 2000s grew up watching some of the most exciting baseball ever played by people who looked like they did, who they could relate to. There was no shortage of stars and role models, and no matter whether you were a slugger, pitcher, basestealer, or defensive whiz, there was an African American player for kids to look up to. There are many theories circulating about what caused the decline in the number of African Americans in Major League Baseball.

The data in the Society for American Baseball Research's demographic study about the increase in Latino and Asian players certainly plays a role. The evolution of the sport and the resulting roster construction also have had an effect. Historically, the most underrepresented positions among African American players have been pitcher and catcher. Typically, the number of African American pitchers has been less than 5 percent. The percentage of African American catchers is even lower. As teams have become more reliant on bullpens, active pitching staffs in the modern game have 15 pitchers. Going back to 1980, teams typically carried nine pitchers. With approximately 60 percent of roster spots taken up by pitchers in the modern game compared to about 35 percent two generations earlier, there has been a decrease in African American players, while the percentage of African American pitchers has remained largely unchanged.

Perhaps the biggest factor, however, is the demographic change in the sport. Throughout much of the twentieth century, baseball was a sport played largely on sandlots and playgrounds in the spring and summer, until kids traded their gloves and bats for a football. In the late 1980s and early 1990s, baseball started transitioning to a "country club sport." Travel teams, private lessons, and expensive high-tech equipment started becoming mandatory for serious young players, outpricing urban players at a young age. The best athletes in the neighborhoods didn't need baseball when they had basketball. As big of stars as Ken Griffey Jr. and Bo Jackson were, they still weren't on the level of Michael Jordan. The National Basketball Association (NBA) went through a renaissance in the 1980s and 1990s, on the backs of Magic Johnson, Larry Bird, and Michael Jordan, and with the growing costs and declining opportunities to play baseball, young African American athletes had a new set of heroes to emulate.

As popular as the NBA was at this time, the National Football League (NFL) had it beat. There was a time when the top sport in the United States was unquestionably baseball. Football and basketball were closer to being fringe sports than they were to challenging baseball's crown. That shifted as the millennium ended. The NBA had an unprecedented run of stars and exponential growth while still only requiring a ball and rim to play. The NFL had taken over as the king of all sports, pushing baseball to second place, at best. The cost of excelling at football remained steady during this growth, too. Teams always provided equipment; the players just needed to train on their own, which could be done for little cost. These factors pushed a lot of the best African American athletes away from baseball and toward basketball and football.

Andrew McCutchen and LaTroy Hawkins cited accessibility for African American youngsters as the main factor in the decline. Speaking at an MLB Network Roundtable in 2017, McCutchen said, "It starts at a young age in the game of baseball. If you can't afford it, you can't pay for it, we're thrown out, we move onto something else." Hawkins agreed, commenting, "A lot of stuff I learned on my own and from watching TV. We didn't have to worry about being on a travel team back then where it is only the kids who can afford it. Today's minorities and underserved area kids have to worry about it, but the exposure is not there."

Another factor that comes into play is NCAA scholarship allotments. In 2018, there were 64 NCAA Division I baseball programs, and just 6 percent of the players were African American. NCAA baseball teams offer about 12 total scholarships per team, while Division I football teams can offer 87. When you consider that NCAA football and basketball have a higher profile in American culture in 2021 than baseball, and add in the NCAA scholarship opportunities, it makes sense that the best athletes are turning away from baseball as youngsters. Imagine a baseball world where Reggie Jackson had chosen football, Bob Gibson had stuck with basketball, and Jackie Robinson had opted to pursue track and field. Dave

Winfield was drafted by the Vikings in the NFL, the Hawks in the NBA, and the Utah Stars in the American Basketball Association, in addition to being the Padres' first-round draft pick in 1973. Even though he was the MVP of the College World Series that year, it's possible, if not likely, that Winfield would have chosen the quick millions of the NBA or NFL over the struggle and uncertainty of having to work his way through the minor leagues in today's American sports setting.

Andre Robertson, who played shortstop for the Yankees in the 1980s, believes the number of African Americans who have the ability to play multiple sports on a professional level is prevalent. Granting them the ability to develop as young baseball players is essential in helping them choose baseball as a path. Robertson said,

> When you see the Bo Jacksons, Deion Sanders, and Brian Jordans as African Americans who actually played football and baseball at the same time, it's evident that there could be a lot more [young African American athletes] playing baseball. Also, Dave Winfield getting drafted in three sports. If you look at the ones who chose the sport of baseball, they are some of the best to ever play, with several being installed in the Hall of Fame. Football and basketball are just higher on kids' agendas now.

Robertson grew up in Orange, Texas, a football hotbed, and listed football as his favorite sport; however, he chose baseball as his path instead. Although he grew up in the 1960s and 1970s, there were still racial barriers for him to break in baseball, even if he didn't realize it at the time. "At the time I was playing, I didn't realize I was a pioneer," said Robertson, who was the first African American baseball player to receive a scholarship to play at the University of Texas. "As time went on, it became clearer that it opened the door for other minorities to get there. Being inducted into the University of Texas Athletics Hall of Honor in August of 2019 cemented the fact that I was seen as a trailblazer. This year's team (2020) is the most diverse in school history."

There are other factors in the decline of African Americans playing baseball, although most of the evidence is circumstantial, yet logical. There has been an overall drop in participation among youth baseball in all demographics, meaning less teams to compete on. In 2015, a National Sporting Goods Association study found that the number of kids playing baseball between 2002–2013 decreased by 41 percent. With the decline in participation, teams merged or disappeared, which meant more travel and more money for kids who wanted to participate on organized high-level teams. There is also a "cool factor" that comes into play. Throughout most of the twentieth century, the biggest sports celebrities were baseball players. That has shifted with younger generations, who now favor basketball and football heroes over baseball stars. The marketing of baseball and its heroes to America's youth has come under fire in the age of social media.

THE AFRICAN AMERICAN STARS OF THE NEW MILLENNIUM

The lack of marketing of Major League Baseball's stars to America's youth, specifically among African Americans, is baffling, as there has been no shortage of outstanding role models to play the sport in the past two decades. Going into the 2021 season, Mookie Betts remained one of the best and most marketable stars in the sport. Betts grew up in Tennessee as a baseball and basketball star, and was even the Tennessee State Bowler of the Year in 2010. He eschewed an offer for a baseball scholarship from the University of Tennessee after being drafted by the Red Sox in the fifth round of the 2011 Major League Baseball Draft. Betts quickly rose through the system and was called up in June 2014. He was installed as right fielder for the Red Sox at the age of 21, and batted eighth in his first game. By the end of the season, he had been installed as the leadoff hitter and clearly was a star on the rise.

By 2018, Betts, along with Mike Trout, was being called baseball's best player. While stats and accomplishments indicated it was Trout, there was more of a debate between Trout and Betts than between Betts and anyone who would be considered the next best player behind him. With the added pressure and recognition, Betts captured the most hardware of any player in the sport's history for one season. In 2018, he was the American League MVP, while also winning the Silver Slugger and Gold Glove awards. He won the American League batting title and capped it off by leading the Red Sox to a World Series title. He was the first player in baseball history to have all those accomplishments in one season.

In addition to his on-field performance, Betts's personality and fun-loving nature also make him an ideal candidate as the face of the sport, especially considering that he chose baseball over basketball in a climate where such a choice is rare among African American athletes. Betts has finished in the top 10 in MVP voting in each of the past four seasons, and after the 2019 season, he was traded to the Los Angeles Dodgers, which is even with New York as far as marketing opportunities.

The Dodgers have been the top team in the National League coming into the new decade, and Betts is primed to be the biggest name on a team that features some of the game's greatest young stars. His Dodgers debut has been delayed by the U.S. shutdown due to the Coronavirus pandemic, but when he has the chance to get on the field for the Dodgers, fans throughout the country will no doubt be ready to embrace him.

Betts hasn't been the only marketable African American star of this era. Andrew McCutchen, Jimmy Rollins, Ryan Howard, and Giancarlo Stanton joined Betts in winning MVP Awards in the past 15 years, and Aaron Judge, Prince Fielder, Stanton, and Howard have each hit 50 home runs in a season during that time. Just as Betts and his outfield mate, Jackie Bradley Jr., have led the Red Sox to a World Series title, Rollins and Howard did the same for the Phillies.

Jason Heyward and Dexter Fowler also played a huge role in the Cubs winning perhaps the most historically significant World Series in decades. David Price has been a fixture in the postseason and Major League Baseball All-Star Game, while also winning the 2012 Cy Young Award and coming close three other times with second-place finishes. The percentage of African American players in Major League Baseball may have declined, but the abundance of Black superstars and role models has not.

In 2019, the percentage of African American players on Opening Day rosters was 7.7 percent. That number was the same as the previous year and represented a high-water mark that hadn't been seen since 2011. It was the third-highest total of the past decade, being eclipsed in only 2010 (7.8 percent) and 2011 (7.9 percent). There is no telling what effect the delayed 2020 baseball season will have on participation, on both long-term and short-term basis, but the decline seems to have steadied with some encouraging advances along the way. During the past 20 years, about one-quarter of Major League Baseball players have been Latino. Throughout the peak of African American participation between

1975–1995, about 12 percent of major-league ballplayers were Latino. With the steady persistence of Latino players in the sport, coupled with the globalization of baseball and the popularity among the Latino culture, it's unlikely that African American participation will return to the previous levels, but a more proportionate percentage is possible.

The growth in Latino players and globalization of the sport seems to stem from increased international scouting and baseball academies that sprung up in the 1980s. Tony Barbone, a baseball lifer who is now director of athletics at Jackie Robinson's alma mater, Pasadena City College, was a coach and manager in the minor leagues when the fruits of the Latino baseball academies and expanded international scouting started making their way into the professional ranks. Barbone said, "I started with the Expos in 1998 [as manager of the Class A Vermont Expos], and each of my teams had high percentages of Latino players. That may be a result of the academies starting to blossom as many of these young men started coming to the academies in their early teens. Thus, by 18 or 19 years old, they were ready to leave the rock, so to speak."

Even before his stint as manager of the Vermont Expos, Barbone saw the globalization of the sport start to influence the minor leagues. He brought up an interesting connection with the Olympics as well. Baseball was a demonstration sport in the Olympics from 1908–1988, before becoming a medal sport in 1992. The 1984 Olympics featured a full tournament for the first time, and because it was played in the United States, it drew a lot of attention. Barbone was the hitting coach for the Butte Copper Kings, the Rangers Rookie Ball affiliate in 1992, and believed the globalization of the sport was already underway at that point.

Barbone said, "I was with the Texas Rangers in the early 90s, and we had a plethora of Latino players, as the Rangers were one of the first organizations to dig into the global population and participation in baseball." He continued, "1988 was the final year the Olympics had baseball as a demonstration sport before becoming a medal sport. This caused various countries to develop their baseball programs, which led to higher development of players. So, I think the Olympic movement played a role, too."

Jim Campanis Jr. was a member of Team USA in 1988, and spoke on the development academies he experienced outside the United States. He said,

I've traveled to many countries to play baseball over the years [in the 1980s]. It amazed me seeing 20 kids in a Latin American country like Mexico, Puerto Rico, or the Dominican Republic, playing great baseball on a dirt lot wearing no shoes, hitting a beat-up ball, creating a makeshift glove out of a cardboard box, all while using a broken bat held together by tape and nails. The kids in these countries looked at baseball as a way to get out of the extreme poverty in their families' lives so they practice and practice. In fact, MLB teams in most Latin American countries offer Baseball Academies with free schooling, coaching, baseball training, equipment, even room and board if they try out and make it. These players can sign pro contracts at 16 years old, and now Latin American players make up nearly 30 percent of the players in the game. This "Baseball Academy" concept is working well in Latin American countries and could be replicated in the United States with the same type of success in urban settings.

In the United States, by the late 1980s there was already a movement starting to urge more inner-city youths to play baseball, thanks to the vision of former major leaguer John Young, who deserves more credit for his pioneering career. Young was drafted in the first round of the same 1969 draft that produced J. R. Richard. He ascended to the majors quickly, earning a call-up from the Tigers in late 1971. He debuted as a pinch-hitter against the Yankees on September 9, and then on September 25, he pinch hit for Hall of Famer Al Kaline and stayed in the game, going 2-for-3, with a double. Young returned to AA the next year and never made it back to the majors. He became a minor-league instructor upon his retirement and then got into scouting. In 1981, he became the first African American to become director of scouting for an organization when the Tigers hired him in that capacity.

In 1986, Young noticed a dearth among African Americans when he was preparing for the Major League Baseball Draft as a scout for the Orioles. He brought this to the attention of Orioles general manager Roland Hemond and Peter Ueberroth, who was the commissioner of baseball at the time. He and Ueberroth approached Los Angeles mayor Tom Bradley and proposed starting a program in Young's hometown of Los Angeles to try to spark interest and provide opportunity for inner-city youths to play baseball. The city provided some financing for the effort, as did Eric Davis and Darryl Strawberry, two of the top stars in the game at the time, who were from Los Angeles. With their financial backing,

Young founded the RBI (Reviving Baseball in the Inner Cities) Program and had it up and running by 1989.

The RBI Program began as a 12-team league with 180 players who were 13 or 14 years old and enjoyed immediate success. The league returned the following year and flourished from there. Along with Young, Major League Baseball assumed operation of the RBI Program in 1991, with an eye toward expansion. RBI added programs in Harlem, Kansas City, and St. Louis in 1992. By 2003, the program had grown to 300 programs in 200 U.S. cities and added junior and senior divisions, as well as a softball branch for girls 18 years of age and younger. The league expanded from Young's original vision of a single 12-team league of 13- and 14-year-olds to serve children ages six to 18, and has had more than 230,000 participants since its inception, and hundreds of those participants have been drafted by major-league teams.

RBI expanded internationally, adding programs in Canada, the Caribbean, and South America. Major League Baseball provides scholarships for RBI participants annually as well. Many Major League Baseball All-Stars started out in the RBI Program, including Justin and B. J. Upton, Carl Crawford, CC Sabathia, Jimmy Rollins, and Coco Crisp. The program boasts at least 15 major leaguers as alumni. Recent Major League Baseball Drafts have shown an increase in African American players among high-level picks, as progress seems like it is being made on these levels.

THE CHALLENGE AHEAD

During the past decade, participation among African American, Latino, and Asian players has stabilized in Major League Baseball. The three groups have steadily comprised 35 percent of players who participate in any year during that time period. Going into the 2020 season, the percentage of African American players increased slightly compared to the previous two seasons. That number is likely to be affected by the interruption of play due to the Coronavirus in 2020. Even so, the trend is moving in the right direction. Much of that has to do with the rise in the percentage of African Americans among high draft picks.

At the 2017 Major League Baseball Draft, Commissioner Rob Manfred noted the increase. He said,

Prior to this year, about 20 percent of our first-rounders were African American, and those academies have been built in communities largely African American. Almost all of those kids had some touch with one of our academy programs or with the Elite Development Invitational, and we believe that the bigger we make those programs, the more diversity we will attract to the game.

Manfred noted this after eight of the first 26 players picked in the draft were African American, including the top two picks, Royce Lewis and Hunter Greene. It was also the first time that three African American players were taken in the top 10 picks since 1992, when five were selected, one of whom was Derek Jeter.

Greene was selected second overall by the Reds, who attempted to make the supremely gifted athlete a two-way player a year before the Angels did it with Shohei Ohtani. That spring, Greene had been the 13th high school athlete to appear on the cover of *Sports Illustrated* on the strength of his 102-mile-per-hour fastball and prolific hitting. On the cover, Greene peered menacingly, and the text posed the question, "Baseball's Lebron or the new Babe?" An accompanying feature detailed Greene's talent in baseball, violin, and art, among other things. It painted him as not only someone who had a 100-mile-per-hour fastball who could hit 450-foot home runs, but also a ready-made superstar who could influence a movement among young African American baseball players.

Greene received a $7.2 million signing bonus and reported to the Rookie League, where he pitched and was a designated hitter. Unfortunately, in 2018 Greene suffered an arm injury and underwent Tommy John surgery in 2019. The setback was disappointing, but there is still hope that he can develop into the type of player he was projected to be. Greene will still be only 21 at the start of the 2021 season, after spending the 2020 season in the Reds development camp pitching without restriction. In addition to Greene, any top prospects list in 2020, was rife with potential young African American superstars. Jo Adell, Royce Lewis, C. J. Abrams, Jeter Downs, Kristian Robinson, and Taylor Trammell found themselves among baseball's top prospects going into the 2021 season, with some breaking through to make their debuts. When Major League Baseball handed out their awards after a truncated 2020 season, both winners of the Rookie of the Year Award, Devin Williams and Kyle Lewis, were African Americans. This was the first time a pair of Black ballplayers won the award in the same season since Dwight Gooden and Alvin Davis did so in 1984.

Another name to keep an eye on in the future is Ke'Bryan Hayes, a first-round pick who is the son of former major-league third baseman Charlie Hayes. Despite the decline in participation among African Americans, there has never been a shortage of superstars from one generation to the next. Just as Jackie Robinson and Larry Doby passed on the torch to Willie Mays and Hank Aaron, the young minor-league stars of today will take the baton from the previous generation. In a collegiate and high school season shortened by COVID-19, African American youngsters like Kumar Rocker, Braylon Bishop, and Tyree Reed established themselves as potential top-five prospects for the 2021 Major League Baseball Draft. Then there is the case of 2021 Iowa high school prospect Ian Moller.

Moller was projected as a first-round draft pick as early as his junior year of high school and has dreams of making the majors in the rarest of situations for an African American: as a starting catcher. In this millennium, the only two African American catchers who have caught at least 70 games in a season are Charles Johnson and Russell Martin. Even as a high school junior, Moller is aware of those statistics and has already developed a relationship with Johnson. He is also aware of the implications if he can fulfill his dream.

"Becoming the highest-drafted black catcher is definitely a goal of mine," Moller said in an interview with *Prospects Live* in 2020. "It's important to me because it would represent a good, huge start for the black community. It would be easier for me to promote black baseball if that happened. I want to get black kids involved."

From the day Robinson debuted with the Dodgers until today, there have always been prominent African American players for fans to look up to. The challenge ahead is increasing interest and opportunity among the African American community. In addition to the RBI Program, Major League Baseball established Urban Youth Academies with the same goal in mind. The first Urban Youth Academy was formed in 2002, in Puerto Rico, followed by numerous locations throughout the United States. One of the goals of the Urban Youth Academy is tackling one of the huge obstacles for underprivileged youth: the rising costs of participating in the sport at a high level. It is this socioeconomic barrier that most agree has suppressed participation among African Americans.

Jim Campanis Jr. recognizes this obstacle and believes the academies can help. He commented,

Baseball equipment is very expensive. This is not just an African American issue, it's an economic issue across all demographics. A good aluminum bat costs $350, a dozen baseballs are $75, a decent glove is $100, baseball spikes are $100, baseball pants and jerseys are $100, a helmet is $40, batting gloves are $35. Playing in youth tournaments against other teams is in the $600 per team range, paid equally by the players. Add in team monthly fees, private trainers, cage time, travel expenses for away tournaments like gas, food, hotel, and then the tournament fees—it's common for middle and high school–aged families to pay over $1,000 a month just to play.

This is where the Urban Youth Academy comes into play. The academy provides free equipment and instruction to underprivileged youths between the ages of six and 18. The success of the academies was touted by Major League Baseball's vice president of youth and facility development, Darrell Miller, when a new academy broke ground in Cincinnati in 2013. The academy was the seventh one opened in the country, and at that time, it had already produced more than 100 draftees. Miller also noted that in 2013, five players drafted in the first two rounds that year were Urban Youth Academy alumni, and he estimated that thousands of alumni had gone on to play in college. That is important, as the Urban Youth Academy is working to strengthen the bridge from high school to college for underprivileged youngsters. The academy offers SAT and ACT prep courses, as well as life lessons, at no charge to those who attend.

Bob Kendrick, president of the Negro Leagues Baseball Museum, sees participation at higher-level colleges as a bridge from the amateur level to the pros, ultimately helping to increase participation at the professional level among African Americans. Kendrick declared,

There are a limited number of college baseball scholarships. So, you think about this, particularly in these urban communities, if I am a single parent household and there's an interest in sports, I'm going to steer my child to the sport that I know has a possibility of getting his education paid for. We've got to figure out a way to increase the number of scholarship opportunities at the collegiate level.

I spent time with the baseball teams at Vanderbilt University and the University of Michigan, and they probably have more African Americans playing on the Division I level on their squads than any other Division I universities. They get it. They created a program where they are looking to try and bring ethnic diversity to their program and developing great talent along with it. I have to commend Major League Baseball and the Major League Baseball Players Association for recognizing that there is an issue here that needs to be addressed, and they tried to put in measures to see it reverse itself. Like anything else though, it will take time, and we have to be patient. The problem didn't occur overnight, and the solution won't occur overnight. That's the nature of baseball.

It's a methodical process.

The methodical process to slow the decline of African Americans in Major League Baseball seems to be well underway. It is now time to reverse the trend with the goal of building a steady, sustainable increase in participation. John Young was a visionary who recognized the declining participation, and he should be credited with starting the movement by founding the RBI Program in 1989. His single 12-team league has evolved into multiple academies and organizations throughout the country that have received millions of dollars in support. The opportunities are now there for many disadvantaged youths in major cities in the United States, and those academies have certainly proven fruitful.

The next step is reaching other low-income areas that aren't in the proximity of major cities. Additional work is also needed to fill the gaps along the trail of development. As the levels of sports increase from youth to the pros, players naturally filter out of the sport due to many factors. Players who do not have the physical ability to make the next step, whether it's from recreation to high school or college to the pros, are going to fall off as they advance in life. Baseball needs to focus on those other reasons that cause African American players to give up the sport. At each step up the ladder, African American players face different obstacles. They need the opportunities, equipment, and instruction as youngsters to compete with children who have the financial means to cover those costs on their own. As all players advance through high school and into college, academics play a major role in athletics. Failing to meet academic standards forces many talented players out of the sport during their development. Incorporating academic support into the Urban Youth

Development program is a good step toward mitigating some of these issues, but more widespread support is needed.

The baseball academies that sprung up in the 1980s in Latin America paid long-term dividends at the major-league level years later, and participation among Latinos in Major League Baseball is stronger than ever. Those academies incorporated academics from the start. For many talented youngsters growing up in Latino and Caribbean countries, they saw baseball as a way out of poverty. Moreover, there wasn't a socioeconomic chasm weeding out players from less financially stable families, as has happened in the United States in the past 30 years. The academies in the United States have surpassed what existed in Latin America a generation ago, but they must expand beyond the major cities. Such players as Ernie Banks, Bob Gibson, and countless other African American pros grew up poor with little, if any, formal instruction. It makes one wonder if they would have fallen by the wayside had they been from a later generation. It also makes one wonder how many talented players have suffered that exact fate. Bob Kendrick addressed the socioeconomic changes the sport has seen throughout the generations, as well as a change in youth culture.

"Baseball went from being a blue-collar sport to almost being a country club sport," started Kendrick.

It's sad to say, and I don't want to be right about this, I hope I'm wrong, but the days of sandlot baseball are gone. It's over with. There was a time when you didn't have to have nine kids on a team to play baseball. However many kids you had, you divided them up, and then you made up your rules to go along with it. When I was a kid, you split them up, and if you hit the ball in Mrs. Jones's yard, you were out. We've lost that. As this game became more organized, which is what it has to be now for kids to play, it became extremely expensive. The equipment is expensive, the league fees, the specialization.

You've got to have a hitting coach. If you want to stay competitive and be in that conversation to be looked at for those very limited number of college scholarships and the potential of getting drafted into the major leagues, it's extremely expensive. It has priced out a lot of kids. Then the other sports, basketball and football, really did outmarket Major League Baseball. I tell people all the time, the thing that you love about baseball is its tradition. The thing that has hurt baseball is its tradition.

The paradox Kendrick alluded to is the crossroads at which baseball finds itself today. No fan base of any major sport is more protective of its history and traditions than in baseball. In baseball, every rule change that seems radical at the time generates rumblings among the sport's core fan base. While the sport has changed significantly throughout generations, those changes have resulted in an evolution that has made the game less attractive to many young fans when compared with other major sports. NFL and NBA games are almost entirely different today than they were 30 years ago. The changes made provided a fertile ground to generate more offense and excitement in those sports. Baseball's changes have taken that excitement and fast action out of the game. Stolen bases, hit-and-runs, squeeze plays, manager arguments, and even the occasional brawl generated drama, and now they're almost absent from the sport as teams rely more and more on analytics. Drama is high during the postseason and in big games in a pennant race, but a vast majority of baseball games are chess matches where teams "play by the book" with little to no surprise or creativity. Young fans, especially young African American fans, would much rather watch NBA players run up and down the floor, hoisting three pointers, as opposed to baseball games where teams are content with swinging for the fences while walks and strikeouts pile up. Baseball must find a way to evolve while still honoring the fantastic traditions of the great sport.

Kendrick also brought up an interesting point about modern-day American culture. In today's world, more than ever, youngsters seek immediate gratification. Of all the professional sports, that hinders baseball participation the most. Basketball and football players can make an immediate leap from college to the highest level of play, while even the best baseball players spend years developing in the minor leagues. Even though the pool of professional players is significantly larger in baseball than in other sports when you take into consideration the minor leagues, the dream of the big stage remains equal across all sports. Speaking on this, Kendrick said,

> The lure of what we perceive to be instant wealth with basketball and football has also hurt baseball. Baseball has a very arduous, time-consuming move through the minor leagues to get to "the show," and that doesn't appeal to people because we live in a microwave society where we want it right now. We want it instantly. We're fighting against all of those things.

While people debate the changes and the current state of baseball, there is one element that can be easily addressed and is building a personal connection between the game's stars and its young fans. While Mookie Betts probably can't stroll the streets and play pickup stickball games with the neighborhood kids the way Willie Mays did, there are other ways to make that connection, and baseball is beginning to make that effort. It's that personal connection that Kendrick believes was key in the popularity of the Negro Leagues.

"The Negro Leagues, to me, from a marketing standpoint was similar to the NBA and NFL. They're not afraid to market their stars," Kendrick said.

> Baseball has this tradition where it's always about the team. And it is about the team. But, as Buck Leonard would say, the [Kansas City] Monarchs were always a good team. When Satchel [Paige] was on the mound, they were a great team. When they publicized the Monarchs coming to town, it was "Satchel Paige and the Kansas City Monarchs are coming to town." So, baseball must market these stars and put them out there so kids want to emulate them. They compare themselves, and they want to be like them. You see that with basketball and football. I do think we'll see these numbers reverse themselves. We have to be patient, and we're not a patient society.

CULTIVATING A SUCCESSFUL GRASSROOTS EFFORT

More than any other sport, baseball prides itself and thrives on its incredible history. The sport was referred to as the national pastime as early as 1856, and its origins can be traced nearly a century before a baseball craze swept the Northeast United States in the 1850s. The history of African American players dates back just as far, you just have to look for them in different places throughout the game's history. A man born a slave in 1804, named Henry Rosecranse Columbus Jr., was interviewed by the *Daily Freeman* in 1881, and recounted his youth in New York playing baseball. He spoke of the recreational activities African American youth enjoyed while he was growing up, saying, "Colored men raced horses on Peter Sharpe's lane. The bosses used to come and bet on the horses, and they had a great deal of fun. After the races, they used to play ball for eggnog." When the reporter pressed Columbus about whether it was baseball "as now played," Columbus replied that it was similar, only the ball was softer and they had more fun. Frederick Douglass even mentioned playing baseball in his famous *Narrative of the Life of Frederick Douglass, an American Slave.*

As the game developed into a profession, African Americans were shunned from the sport, as a Black man taking a paid spot from a white man was unheard-of. That didn't stop African Americans from playing, however. A scant few cracked the professional ranks before the color line was drawn, while others simply enjoyed the sport as recreation. Generations after that would follow suit. Fans fell in love with the sport by playing as youngsters and having baseball heroes to look up to. Baseball is a generational game; the legends are passed down as parents educate their children about the heroes they grew up watching. It instills a feeling in young fans that they are carrying on a great tradition, and every time they go out and play ball on a playground, they are part of this great history people speak of.

It's that connection to history that Bob Kendrick spoke about when talking about the Urban Youth Academy that opened in Kansas City, adjacent to the Negro Leagues Baseball Museum, where he serves as president. Kendrick related,

> We're so excited to have an Urban Youth Baseball Academy right behind the Negro Leagues Baseball Museum. Kudos to Dayton Moore, general manager of the Kansas City Royals, who had the foresight to want to lead this effort to build what was then baseball's seventh Urban Youth Baseball Academy, but to also build it in an area that has the Negro Leagues Museum. So, you essentially have a museum attached to this, so as these urban kids are being introduced to our sport, nurtured in our sport, and hopefully fall in love with our sport, they also have a museum where they can come in and see people who look just like them who played this game as well as anyone has ever played this game. Not only did they play the game, they owned the teams, they were managers, coaches, team physicians, traveling secretaries. They fulfilled every aspect of the business of the game of baseball. That's all vitally important that you see yourself in this sport.

The opportunity for African American youngsters to see themselves in the sport at the major-league level was absent for the first half of the twentieth century, but from that void grew the Negro Leagues. Despite being shut out of the majors, African American players formed their own successful and entertaining professional leagues. Their heroes were just as sensational as the major-league stars of the time and more entertaining. Baseball remained segregated until 1946, but throughout that time, generations perpetuated the sport along parallel unequal color lines. When Jackie Robinson finally broke through professionally with the Montreal Royals, the Dodgers AAA affiliate, in 1946, the two baseball worlds started to come together as one. The road to full integration was slow and ugly, but at least a diverse group of players were now playing together. This allowed young boys of every race to look up to heroes in the same league.

There was never a shortage of African American role models in the sport, and there still isn't today. There was never a point in time when African Americans weren't among the best players in the United States. Even during segregation, players like Satchel Paige, Josh Gibson, Martin Dihigo, and Cool Papa Bell were every bit the heroes to youngsters as were Babe Ruth, Jimmie Foxx, and Walter Johnson. That remained true as different generations were led by the likes of Jackie Robinson, Hank Aaron, Willie Mays, Bob Gibson, Reggie Jackson, Ozzie Smith, Tony Gwynn, and Ken Griffey Jr. In the new millennium, such stars as Mookie Betts, Andrew McCutchen, Curtis Granderson, and CC Sabathia, among others, carried that torch, and there's a new crop waiting in the minors to carry on for them.

In 2020, during the summer of heightened racial unrest in the United States, African American athletes in every sport were pushed to the forefront of the sports news cycle. Many spoke out, most visibly Dominic Smith of the Mets and Andrew McCutchen of the Phillies, and almost every player in Major League Baseball banded together in support of one another. A nonprofit organization called the Players Alliance was founded by both former and current African American Major League Baseball players, with Curtis Granderson, CC Sabathia, Edwin Jackson, and Dee Gordon taking the lead. Almost instantly, more than 100 former and current African American players became part of an organization with a mission statement to "use our collective voice and platform to create increased opportunities for the black community in every aspect of our game and beyond."

The Players Alliance announced its arrival with a viral video in which African American players galvanized and made their voices heard for a new generation. The video was a call for unity and a hopeful line in the sand to create change in the game and continue to bring awareness to the obstacles faced by young African American boys and men playing the sport of baseball. On the Friday Major League Baseball celebrated Jackie Robinson Day in 2020, and on the Thursday before, many African American players donated their game check to the Players Alliance.

When the 2020 Major League Baseball season got underway after a lengthy COVID-19 shutdown, the number of African American players in the major leagues continued to show a slight improvement. It was the first time in 12 years that at least 8 percent of the league consisted of African American players. The big difference was that this time, the trend was moving upward, while in 2008, it was taking a downward trajectory. The movement to increase participation among African Americans in Major League Baseball has never been stronger than it was at the conclusion of the 2020 Major League Baseball season. Players are united, there is a crop of incredible young African American players in the minor leagues and college, and more and more African American players are being given a voice as media outlets cover the ways in which baseball is dealing with the cultural climate in the United States. Once again, baseball is tied directly into modern society and American culture of the time.

At the start of the 2021 season, as fans reflect on baseball history, they'll see Organized Baseball populated with African American players, despite players of other races having a 70-year head start. The single-season home run record and the career home run record, the two most revered records in the sport, are held by Barry Bonds. The undisputed greatest leadoff man in baseball history is Rickey Henderson. In 2021, the title of greatest living player belonged to Willie Mays or Hank Aaron. When a pitcher of any color or race has a fierce streak to his game, he's compared to Bob Gibson. For today's generation, the standard bearer of baseball champions is Derek Jeter. Ozzie Smith is in the discussion as the best fielding infielder of all time, and when you move to the outfield, it's usually a debate between Willie Mays, Roberto Clemente, Ken Griffey Jr., and Andruw Jones. The era of free agency was brought forth by Curt Flood and his legal challenge of the reserve clause—a moment so important in the game's history that it's justifiable that Flood sacrificed his career for it. Jackie Robinson breaking the color barrier and Hank Aaron topping Babe Ruth's career home run record aren't just watershed moments in baseball history, they're two moments that transcend the sport and became ingrained in American culture. A familiar refrain about Robinson is that his Dodgers debut did more to advance civil rights than just about any other moment of the era.

Toward the end of the twentieth century, as the game became big business on every level, African Americans migrated away from the sport as they were priced out by the game's development. As society changed, baseball became a victim of its own tradition. Games became more methodical and less imaginative, and were played at a much slower pace. At the same time, the NFL and NBA did the unthinkable and unseated baseball as the most popular sports among America's youth. For generations, kids developed into great baseball players on the sandlots and high school teams. Now they hone their skills through private instruction, expensive equipment, and exclusive travel teams. When economically challenged kids had to choose between sticking with baseball or moving to basketball or football, it wasn't a choice at all. Even if they had the talent, they largely didn't have the money or opportunity to compete with their more privileged peers. This wasn't a situation that was exclusive to African Americans either, but a disproportionate number of your African American athletes gave up pursuing baseball at a higher level.

It has been a quarter-century since Jackie Robinson's debut, and a concerted grassroots effort to increase participation among African American players seems to be showing dividends. The percentage of African Americans in Major League Baseball remains low, but it has leveled off after years of decline. Coinciding with this plateau is the exponential growth of development academies geared toward underprivileged youths. The academies started small, with just one league in the Los Angeles area, but have boomed to become part of a multimillion-dollar operation that has assisted thousands of young players. Just as the baseball academies in Latin America in the 1980s developed a large crop of players who reached the majors in the 1990s, boosting the number of Latino players in the major leagues during that era, the hope is that the modern-day baseball academies in the United States will start to pay similar dividends.

While the academies have gone a long way to help African Americans in some inner cities receive the opportunities, instruction, and equipment they would otherwise have no access to, it's just one piece of the puzzle. Baseball needs kids to evolve to the point where they fall in love with the sport again. Most passionate baseball fans today got hooked on the sport learning about the game's past from older generations, going to games with their families, collecting baseball cards, and playing ball with their friends. The path for many African American kids to become professional baseball players became muddied as the sport became more specialized and expensive. The Players Alliance has partnered with African American youth baseball academies to push the movement forward. The academies work to provide opportunities and coaching, while the Players Alliance supports financial efforts and also markets the game and gives current African American players a voice. It's more complex than that, but the potential exists for significant advancement in the movement.

Only a small number of people will become professional baseball players, and as that pool has become smaller throughout the years, so has the number of smaller groups in that pool. It was easy for African American kids to migrate away from baseball toward basketball and football. Basketball and football were less expensive to play and had the cool factor that baseball had lost for this generation. While the path isn't always clear and there are still countless kids who have to give up the sport because of the growing costs associated with playing, progress is being made. Major League Baseball has a long way to go, but it appears to be making a concerted effort to connect with this generation of fans.

The idea is to foster growth in young players and clear the path for their development. The ones who have the supreme talent and motivation to become major leaguers need to have a path that is free of obstacles, and the sport is making gains. It takes patience, attention, and care for results to bear themselves in the major leagues. This history of African Americans in Major League Baseball is incredibly rich, historic, and colorful. Participation may have faded since its heyday, but it's not going away by any means. When it comes time for Aaron Judge, Mookie Betts, and Andrew McCutchen to retire, there will be a new crop of young African American stars ready to take over. The hope is that the overall pool of African American players is bigger in the next generation than it is now. In an interview in 2016, Hank Aaron said, "Jackie Robinson held his head up high, Willie Mays, myself, and Frank Robinson, all of us. And now baseball is a dying sport as far as African Americans. It's got to be turned around." A road map has been developed, and now it's up to the baseball world to cultivate increased participation so those possessing talent see baseball as their most desirable path toward athletic success.

BIBLIOGRAPHY

"1946 Montreal Royals Statistics." *Baseball-Reference.com.* Available at https://www.baseball-reference.com/register/team.cgi?id=7d25f8c5 (accessed January 10, 2020).

Acocella, N. "How Jackie Robinson Made Baseball History in Jersey City." *Njmonthly.com,* April 13, 2016. Available at https://njmonthly.com/articles/jersey-living/jersey-celebrities/jackie-robinson-baseballs-finest-moment/ (accessed November 5, 2019).

"All-Star Baseball Poll." *Chicago Tribune,* July 5, 1948, p. 37.

"All-Star Baseball Teams Announced." *Carlsbad Current,* July 3, 1949, p. 6.

"American Indian Major League Baseball Players." *Baseball-almanac.com.* Available at https://www.baseball-almanac.com/legendary/american_indian_baseball_players.shtml (accessed November 28, 2019).

Anderson, Dave. "Demand for Blind Loyalty by Cincinnati Could Cause Reds Stars to Go Bidding." *Courier-Journal,* November 26, 1976, p. 39.

Anstine, Dennis. "Griffeys Become Baseball's First Father–Son Teammates." *Tyrone Daily Herald,* August 30, 1990, p. 4.

Armour, M., and D. Levitt. "Baseball Demographics, 1947–2016." *Society for American Baseball Research.* Available at https://sabr.org/bioproj/topic/baseball-demographics-1947-2012 (accessed October 5, 2019).

"The A's Super Trade, Another World Title?" *San Mateo Times,* April 3, 1976, p. 15.

"A's to Bring Up 1966's Top Draft." *Lancaster New Era,* June 8, 1967, p. 51.

"Barnstorming Hurts Standing of Clubs." *Evening Star,* 1910, p. 14.

Barr, D. "Negro Leagues Players Played Major Role in World War II." *MLB.com,* November 11, 2014. Available at https://nlbm.mlblogs.com/negro-leagues-players-played-major-role-in-world-war-ii-4bc5cb125b7f (accessed December 29, 2019).

"Baseball Writers Fail to Vote Any Player into Hall of Fame." *Fort Myers News-Press,* January 22, 1971, pp. 2A, 2C.

Belson, K. "Apples for a Nickel, and Plenty of Empty Seats." *New York Times,* January 6, 2009. Available at https://www.nytimes.com/2009/01/07/sports/baseball/07depression.html (accessed December 13, 2019).

"Billy, Reggie Pals in Victory." *Bridgeport Post,* October 10, 1977, p. 46.

Birtwell, Roger. "Sox Recall Pumpsie." *Boston Globe,* July 22, 1959, pp. 25–26.

———. "Ted Batted Only .091 vs. Boyhood Idol Paige." *Boston Globe,* July 26, 1966, p. 25.

"Black Famous Baseball Firsts by Baseball Almanac." *Baseball-almanac.com.* Available at https://www.baseball-almanac.com/firsts/first8.shtml (accessed November 23, 2019).

"Blades or Martin to Succeed Durocher as Dodgers' Manager." *Bergen Record,* April 4, 1947, p. 30.

Bock, H. "Teammates and Opponents Remember Jackie Robinson." *AP News*, April 4, 1997. Available at https://apnews.com/8fe6e46ab70004ab375d5243aecca1ba (accessed January 19, 2020).

Booth, S. "The Story of Kindly Old Burt Shotton." *Hardball Times*, February 4, 2011. Available at https://tht.fangraphs.com/the-story-of-kindly-old-burt-shotton/ (accessed January 19, 2020).

Broeg, B. "Short Waves." *St. Louis Post-Dispatch*, February 6, 1947, p. 22.

"Brooklyn Signs Negro Player, First in Organized Baseball." *Baltimore Sun*, October 24, 1945, pp. 1, 24.

Bryson, B., Sr. "No Law?" *Des Moines Tribune*, July 6, 1962, p. 16.

Burgos, A. "El Profe: Cubans' Big-League Arrival." *La Vida Baseball*, 2018. Available at https://www.lavidabaseball.com/cuba-pioneers-marsans-almeida/ (accessed November 15, 2019).

———. *Playing America's Game*. Berkeley: University of California Press, 2007, pp. 111–117, 122, 143–145, 233.

Burick, Si. "What Trade Means to Reds' Anderson." *Dayton Daily News*, November 30, 1971, p. 14.

"Cards Had Planned Strike against Jackie Robinson." *Ottawa Citizen*, May 9, 1947, p. 30.

Carrington, Walter. "The Red Sox Were the Last Baseball Team to Integrate. This Is How It Happened." *Wbur.org*, July 17, 2019. Available at https://www.wbur.org/cognoscenti/2019/07/17/red-sox-last-team-in-baseball-to-integrate-pumpsie-green-walter-c-carrington (accessed February 8, 2020).

Carroll, D. "Playing the Field." *Montreal Gazette*, April 15, 1946, p. 16.

———. "Royals Set Precedent, Sign First Colored Ballplayer." *Montreal Gazette*, October 24, 1945, pp. 14–15.

"Chandler Suspends Durocher for 1947 Baseball Season." *Arizona Republic*, April 10, 1947, p. 16.

"Charlie Grant Almost Broke Color Line." *Cincinnati.com*, April 18, 2015. Available at https://www.cincinnati.com/story/news/history/2015/04/18/cincinnatis-charlie-grant-came-close-breaking-baseballs-color-line/25821705/ (accessed November 2, 2019).

Chesterton, Eric, and Mike Bertha. "Jackie Chose Retirement Over Playing for Giants." *MLB.com*, April 14, 2020. Available at https://www.mlb.com/cut4/jackie-robinson-traded-to-giants/c-159535328 (accessed May 6, 2020).

Ciammachilli, Esther. "Baseball Makes an Early Pitch to Catch the Interest of Black Players." *Npr.org*, February 12, 2020. Available at https://www.npr.org/2020/02/12/804463301/baseball-makes-an-early-pitch-to-catch-the-interest-of-black-players (accessed May 6, 2020).

"Cleveland Reported Set to Fire Robinson." *Greenville News*, June 19, 1977, p. 2C.

Corbett, Warren. "Bill White." *Society for American Baseball Research*, 2013. Available at https://sabr.org/bioproj/person/c3eea582 (accessed February 26, 2020).

Dent, Mark. "The Story of John Kennedy, the Phillies' Forgotten First Black Player." *Billy Penn*, February 1, 2017. Available at https://billypenn.com/2017/02/01/the-story-of-john-kennedy-the-phillies-forgotten-first-black-player/ (accessed February 20, 2020).

Dick Cavett Show, The. January 26, 1972. ABC.

"Dock Ellis Goes Wild." *Piqua Daily Call*, May 2, 1974, p. 15.

"Dodger 'Who's on First' Script Not Giving Robinson a Break." *Passaic Herald-News*, April 4, 1947, p. 16.

Dolan, Steve. "Padres Stop Short of Finishing a Deal." *Los Angeles Times*, December 11, 1981, pp. 2, 11.

Dolson, Frank. "Martinez Jackson, 89, Tailor, Reggie's Father." *Philadelphia Inquirer*, April 29, 1994, p. 59.

Doyle, J. "Ian Moller Looks to Spearhead the Black Baseball Movement." *Prospects Live*, July 2020. Available at https://www.prospectslive.com/mlb-draft/2020/7/2/ian-moller-looks-to-dismantle-black-baseball-stereotypes (accessed February 20, 2020).

Dunn, Bob. "A Bargain, and Bye-Bye Basement." *SI.com*, August 8, 1977. Available at https://vault.si.com/vault/1977/08/08/a-bargain-and-byebye-basement (accessed April 4, 2020).

Dunn, S. "September 17, 1953: Ernie Banks Breaks Color Barrier for Cubs." *Society for American Baseball Research.* Available at https://sabr.org/gamesproj/game/september-17-1953-ernie-banks-breaks-color-barrier-cubs (accessed February 8, 2020).

Eck, F. "Baseball in '46 Was Kinda Screwy." *Sioux Falls Daily Argus-Leader*, December 28, 1946, p. 3.

Edes, G. "George Digby and Willie Mays, the One Who Got Away." *ESPN.com*, May 3, 2014. Available at https://www.espn.com/blog/boston/red-sox/post/_/id/36622/george-digby-and-willie-mays-the-one-who-got-away (accessed February 8, 2020).

Engelmann, L. "Barnstorming with Gehrig and the Babe." *Los Angeles Times*, October 26, 1987, pp. 16–17.

Erion, Greg. "Blue Moon Odom." *Society for American Baseball Research*, 2015. Available at https://sabr.org/bioproj/person/e57a5b30 (accessed February 8, 2020).

Fatsis, S. "The First Black Player in Major-League History." *Slate Magazine*, April 22, 2013. Available at http://www.slate.com/articles/sports/sports_nut/2013/04/william_edward_white_was_a_little_known_19th_century_man_the_first_black.html (accessed October 20, 2019).

———. "Mystery of Baseball: Was William White Game's First Black?" *Wall Street Journal*, January 30, 2004. Available at https://www.wsj.com/articles/SB107541676333815810 (accessed October 20, 2019).

Feinsand, Mark. "Game's Blossoming Diversity Evident at Draft." *MLB.com*, June 13, 2017. Available at https://www.mlb.com/cubs/news/mlb-s-growing-diversity-on-display-at-draft-c236124942 (accessed October 20, 2019).

"Feller All-Stars vs. Paige's in 'Racial Rivalry.'" *Sports Collectors Digest*, December 28, 2007. Available at https://www.sportscollectorsdigest.com/fell_paige_all_stars/ (accessed December 29, 2019).

Ferguson, Jim. "May, Helms Not Surprised Over Being Dealt to the Astros." *Dayton Daily News*, November 3, 1971, p. 14.

Fleitz, D. "Cap Anson." *Society for American Baseball Research*, January 4, 2012. Available at https://sabr.org/bioproj/person/9b42f875 (accessed October 29, 2019).

Francis, B. "At Home on the Road." *Baseball Hall of Fame.* Available at https://baseball-hall.org/discover-more/history/barnstorming-tours (accessed December 19, 2019).

Goldfarb, I. "1947 Dodgers: Spring Training in Havana." *Society for American Baseball Research*, 2012. Available at https://sabr.org/research/1947-dodgers-spring-training-havana (accessed January 11, 2020).

Goldstein, D. "Doby Hits Homer in Last Game with Newark Club." *Paterson Evening News*, July 5, 1947, p. 16.

Goodman, J. "The Final Childhood Summer of the Say Hey Kid." *Alabama.com*, January 13, 2019. Available at https://www.al.com/sports/2017/06/on_willie_mays_his_father_and.html (accessed February 8, 2020).

Goren, H. "Dodgers Differ on Robinson, Negro Player, as Teammate." *Star Press*, March 3, 1947, p. 8.

Hand, J. "A's Continue to Dog Footsteps of Front-Running Tribe." *Sandusky Register*, July 10, 1948, p. 6.

———. "Will All-Star Game Be Another Farce?" *Albuquerque Journal*, July 7, 1950, p. 22.

Hermann, M. "Newcombe Calls for Robinson Holiday." *Atlanta Constitution*, April 10, 1997, p. D1.

Hill, Herman. "Connie Mack Vague on When Negros Will Crash Majors." *Pittsburgh Courier*, December 16, 1944, p. 12.

Hill, J. "Traveling Show: Barnstorming Was Commonplace in the Negro Leagues." *MLB.com.* Available at http://mlb.mlb.com/mlb/history/mlb_negro_leagues_story.jsp?story=barnstorming (accessed December 19, 2019)

Hogan, L. "The Negro Leagues Discovered an Oasis at Yankee Stadium." *New York Times*, February 12, 2011. Available at https://www.nytimes.com/2011/02/13/sports/baseball/13stadium.html (accessed December 29, 2019).

Holbrook, Bob. "Pumpsie's Chances Good of Staying Up with Sox." *Boston Globe*, March 25, 1959, pp. 25–26.

———. "Red Sox Send Pumpsie Green to Minors." *Boston Globe*, April 7, 1959, pp. 1, 33, 35.

Holmes, T. "A Colored Pitcher Joins the Dodgers." *Brooklyn Daily Eagle*, August 26, 1947, p. 11.

———. "Dodgers Lack Luster in Latest NL Fiasco." *Brooklyn Daily Eagle*, July 13, 1949, p. 19.

Howard, C. "MLB Announces Highest Percentage of Black Players since 2012." *Sportingnews.com*, April 11, 2018. Available at https://www.sportingnews.com/us/mlb/news/mlb-percentage-African American-players-african-american-highest-increase-2012/133a8iikqfdswza7v25usmj5x (accessed May 23, 2020).

Hruby, Patrick. "OTL: The Long, Strange Trip of Dock Ellis." *ESPN.com*, August 24, 2012. Available at http://www.espn.com/espn/eticket/story?page=Dock-Ellis&redirected=true (accessed April 9, 2020).

Husman, J. "August 10, 1883: Cap Anson vs. Fleet Walker." *Society for American Baseball Research*, 2013. Available at https://sabr.org/gamesproj/game/august-10-1883-cap-anson-vs-fleet-walker (accessed October 15, 2019).

———. "June 21, 1879: The Cameo of William Edward White." *Society for American Baseball Research*, 2013. Available at https://sabr.org/gamesproj/game/june-21-1879-cameo-william-edward-white (accessed October 18, 2019).

"If Brooklyn Plays Robinson Over Stanky, We'll Win." *Passaic Herald-News*, March 19, 1947, p. 19.

"Jackson Ends His Four-Week Holdout." *Great Falls Tribune*, May 1, 1976, p. 16.

Jackson, James. "Reggie Jackson Happy to Be Chosen by A's." *Baltimore Sun*, June 8, 1966, pp. C1, C5.

Jordan, D., L. Gerlach, and J. Rossi. "A Baseball Myth Exploded." *Society for American Baseball Research*, 1998. Available at https://sabr.org/cmsFiles/Files/Bill_Veeck_and_the_1943_sale_of_the_Phillies.pdf (accessed October 26, 2019).

Jordan, David M. *The A's*. Jefferson, NC: McFarland, 2014, pp. 128–132, 137.

"Josh Gibson and Leonard Voted into Hall of Fame." *Simpson's Leader-Times*, February 9, 1972, p. 19.

"Judge Landis Dies." *Mason City Globe-Gazette*, November 25, 1944, p. 9.

"Just Like Frankie Robinson." *Mansfield News-Journal*, April 6, 1958, p. 20.

Kaese, Harold. "Isolated Pumpsie Wonders If He Will See Boston." *Boston Globe*, March 16, 1959, pp. 23–24.

Kaiser, D. "A Troubling Myth about Jackie Robinson Endures." *Time.com*, April 15, 2016. Available at https://time.com/4294175/jackie-robinson-burns-landis-myth/ (accessed December 29, 2019).

Kashatus, W. C. "Chief Bender's Tragic Story." *Historylive.net*, October 13, 2003. Available at https://www.historylive.net/op-eds-bill-kashatus/chief-benders-tragic-story/ (accessed November 28, 2019).

Keeney, S. "Blurring the Color Line: How Cuban Baseball Players Led to the Racial Integration of Major League Baseball." *Society for American Baseball Research*, 2016. Available at https://sabr.org/research/blurring-color-line-how-cuban-baseball-players-led-racial-integration-major-league-baseball (accessed November 28, 2019).

Kirst, S. "Struggles of a Baseball Pioneer: In Syracuse, the Trials of Fleet Walker." *Syracuse.com*, March 23, 2019. Available at https://www.syracuse.com/kirst/1994/02/in_syracuse_the_trials_of_flee.html (accessed October 23, 2019).

Klein, Gary. "Program Brings Baseball Back to Inner City." *Los Angeles Times*, May 22, 1990. Available at https://www.latimes.com/archives/la-xpm-1990-05-22-sp-208-story.html (accessed October 23, 2019).

Lamberty, Bill. "Amos Otis." *Society for American Baseball Research*, June 1, 2019. Available at https://sabr.org/bioproj/person/588ccedb (accessed October 23, 2019).

"League Meeting: Gathering of the Magnates at the Hotel Garde." *Hartford Courant*, July 18, 1908, p. 10.

Macht, N., R. Crepeau, and L. Lowenfish. "Does Baseball Deserve This Black Eye?" *Baseball Research Journal* 38, no. 1 (2009): 5–14.

Maher, Charles. "Jackson KO's Dodgers on Three Swings." *Los Angeles Times*, October 19, 1977, pp. 1, 4.

Malloy, J. "Out at Home." *National Pastime: A Review of Baseball History* 2, no. 1 (Fall 1982): 14–29. Available at http://research.sabr.org/journals/files/SABR-National_Pastime-02.pdf (accessed October 26, 2019).

Manoloff, Dennis. "One on One with Rickey Henderson, Future Hall of Famer." *Baseball Digest*, February 1, 2003, n.p.

Maxon, S. "The Red Sox Could've Signed Jackie Robinson. They Gave Him a Sham Tryout Instead." *Slate.com*, May 4, 2017. Available at https://slate.com/culture/2017/05/the-red-sox-couldve-signed-jackie-robinson-they-gave-him-a-sham-tryout-instead.html (accessed January 4, 2020).

Mays, Chris. "Eight Times Hank Aaron Faced Racism: #3, Integrating the Sally League." *Talking Chop*, April 29, 2009. Available at https://www.talkingchop.com/2009/4/29/858774/8-times-hank-aaron-faced-racism-3 (accessed February 8, 2020).

McAlester, Keven. "High Times." *Houstonpress.com*, June 23, 2005. Available at https://www.houstonpress.com/news/high-times-6549194 (accessed April 4, 2020).

McCarron, Anthony. "NY Daily News—We Are Currently Unavailable in Your Region." *NYdailynews.com*, November 16, 2008. Available at https://www.nydailynews.com/sports/baseball/yankees/oscar-gamble-life-to-and-fro-article-1.336569 (accessed February 8, 2020).

McCarty, Bob. "From the Sidelines." *Tribune*, May 11, 1958, p. 14.

McClary, Mike. "Chet Lemon." *Society for American Baseball Research*, 2019. Available at https://sabr.org/bioproj/person/e57a5b30 (accessed February 8, 2020).

McKenna, B. "Charlie Grant." *Society for American Baseball Research*, 2019. Available at https://sabr.org/bioproj/person/bd564010 (accessed October 30, 2019).

McMurray, J. "Larry Doby." *Society for American Baseball Research*, 2009. Available at https://sabr.org/bioproj/person/4e985e86 (accessed January 28, 2020).

Metcalf, M. "Organized Baseball's Night Birth." *Society for American Baseball Research*, 2016. Available at https://sabr.org/research/organized-baseball-s-night-birth (accessed December 9, 2019).

Morgan, J. "Doby Was AL's First African American Player." *ESPN.com*, June 26, 2003. Available at https://www.espn.com/classic/obit/s/2003/0618/1570127.html (accessed January 29, 2020).

Neyer, Rob. *Rob Neyer's Big Book of Baseball Blunders*. New York: Touchstone, 2014, pp. 106–11.

"No Pirates on All-Stars." *Pittsburgh Sun-Telegraph*, June 29, 1947, p. 22.

"Oakland A's Top Tigers, 2–1, to Gain World Series." *Rutland Daily Herald*, October 13, 1972, p. 22.

Ofgang, E. "Brooklyn Dodger Ralph Branca Recalls Friendship with Jackie Robinson and Baseball's History of Racism." *WestchesterMagazine.com*, March 26, 2014. Available at https://westchestermagazine.com/life-style/brooklyn-dodger-ralph-branca-recalls-friendship-with-jackie-robinson-and-baseballs-history-of-racism/ (accessed January 21, 2020).

O'Keefe, M. "Document from 1945—Two Years before Jackie Robinson Broke MLB Color Barrier—Saying Black Players Couldn't Make It in Baseball Is Up for Sale." *NYdailynews.com*, January 14, 2015. Available at https://www.nydailynews.com/sports/baseball/document-45-dismissing-black-baseball-players-sale-article-1.2076973 (accessed November 28, 2019).

Parrott, H. "Brooklyn Fans Yell Louder but Don't Know Baseball, Says Dizzy." *Brooklyn Daily Eagle*, October 18, 1934, pp. 22, 24.

Pepe, Phil. "Old Negro Greats Get Crack at Hall of Fame." *New York Daily News*, February 4, 1971, p. 90.

"Pirates Field First All-Black Starting Team." *Tyrone Daily Herald*, September 2, 1971, p. 5.

Posnanski, J. "The Integration Timeline." *JoeBlogs*, July 11, 2015. Available at https://joeposnanski.substack.com/p/the-integration-timeline (accessed February 7, 2020).

Puerzer, Rich. "September 1, 1971: Pirates Field First All-Black Lineup in Baseball." *Society for American Baseball Research*, 2018. Available at https://sabr.org/gamesproj/game/september-1-1971-first-all-black-lineup (accessed February 7, 2020).

"Pumpsie Appears Vastly Improved as 2d Baseman." *Boston Globe*, April 23, 1959, p. 31.

"Pumpsie Case Charges Heard by State." *Boston Globe*, April 14, 1959, p. 44.

Queen, Bob. "From Majors to Class B in Minors Is Fate of Phillies' John Kennedy." *Pittsburgh Courier*, May 18, 1957, p. 24.

Reichler, Joe. "Can't Miss Tag Hung On Conley." *Marshfield News-Herald*, January 21, 1954, p. 16.

"Remembering Jackie Robinson." *MiLB.com*, 2015. Available at http://www.milb.com/milb/features/jackie_robinson.jsp?mc=timeline (accessed January 9, 2020).

Richman, Milt. "Satchel Arrives." *Escondido Times-Advocate*, February 10, 1971, p. 16.

Rickey, B. *Branch Rickey Papers*. Library of Congress, Branch Rickey Papers, Washington, DC, 1952–1960.

Ringolsby, Tracy. "RBI Program Creator John Young Dies at 67." *MLB.com*, March 8, 2016. Available at https://www.mlb.com/news/john-young-rbi-program-creator-dies-at-67-c177039186 (accessed January 9, 2020).

"Robinson Wins Slugging Honors." *Oakland Tribune*, January 3, 1947, p. 7.

Rogosin, Donn. *Invisible Men: Life in Baseball's Negro Leagues*. Lincoln, NE: Bison Books, 2007.

Rosen, S. "Cincinnati's Charlie Grant Came Close to Breaking Baseball's Color Line." *Cincinnati Enquirer*, April 19, 2015, p. 8AA.

Rosenberg, H. "Fantasy Baseball: The Momentous Drawing of the Sport's Nineteenth-Century 'Color Line' Is Still Tripping Up History Writers." *Atavist*, 2016. Available at https://howardwrosenberg.atavist.com/racism-bbhistory (accessed October 22, 2019).

Saccoman, J. "Willie Mays." *Society for American Baseball Research*, January 4, 2012. Available at https://sabr.org/bioproj/person/64f5dfa2 (accessed February 8, 2020).

"Sandy Nava: BR Bullpen." *Baseball-reference.com*, 2016. Available at https://www.baseball-reference.com/bullpen/Sandy_Nava (accessed November 16, 2019.

"Satchel Paige Inducted into Baseball Hall of Fame." *Times Record*, August 10, 1971, p. 22.

"Satchel Paige Signs Contract with Cleveland." *Chicago Tribune*, July 8, 1948, p. 49.

Sauer, P. "The Year of Jackie Robinson's Mutual Love Affair with Montreal." *Smithsonian Magazine*, April 6, 2015. Available at https://www.smithsonianmag.com/history/year-jackie-robinsons-mutual-love-affair-montreal-180954878/?no-ist (accessed January 10, 2020).

"Second MVP for Joe, New Uniform for Doyle." *Press and Sun-Bulletin*, November 24, 1976, p. 22.

"Selection of McCovey Continues Domination of NL Rookie Award." *Pittsburgh Courier*, November 28, 1959, p. 25.

"Sixteen Teams to Compete in Semipro Tournament Here." *Michigan Herald-Press*, June 10, 1952, p. 10.

Smiles, J. *Bucky Harris: A Biography of Baseball's Boy Wonder*. Jefferson, NC: McFarland, 2011, pp. 263–69.

Smith, Ozzie, and Rob Rains. *Wizard*. Chicago: Contemporary Books, 1988.

Smith, W. "Brooklyn Dodgers Admit Negro Players Rate Place in Majors." *Pittsburgh Courier*, August 5, 1939, p. 16.

———. "Discrimination Has No Place in Baseball—These Cubs Agree." *Pittsburgh Courier*, August 12, 1939, p. 16.

———. "No Need for Color Ban in Big Leagues." *Pittsburgh Courier*, September 2, 1939. p. 16.

———. "Owners Will Admit Negro Players If Fans Demand Them." *Pittsburgh Courier*, August 18, 1939, p. 16.

———. "Smitty's Sports Spurts." *Pittsburgh Courier*, August 15, 1942, p. 17.

———. "The Sports Beat." *Pittsburgh Courier*, September 29, 1945, p. 12.

"Sporting: Baseball." *Chicago Tribune*, June 22, 1879, p. 7.

Stilley, A. "Wid Matthews." *Society for American Baseball Research*. Available at https://sabr.org/bioproj/person/wid-matthews/ (accessed February 8, 2020).

Stitt, A. "Positive Trend Shows More African American Players on MLB Rosters." *Forbes*, August 14, 2020. Available at https://www.forbes.com/sites/anthonystitt/2020/08/14/positive-trend-shows-more-black-players-on-mlb-rosters/#4b5070ef1b5b (accessed February 8, 2020).

Streeter, Harold. "McCovey Hits 'Em Left, Right—Also Center—in Giants Debut." *Sacramento Bee*, July 31, 1959, pp. D1, D4.

Swain, Rick. "Bob Thurman." *Society for American Baseball Research*, January 4, 2006. Available at https://sabr.org/bioproj/person/23f9d960 (accessed February 8, 2020).

Thorn, John. "Did African American Slaves Play Baseball?" *Our Game*, December 26, 2012. Available at https://ourgame.mlblogs.com/did-african-american-slaves-play-baseball-1b63bed0fd26 (accessed February 8, 2020).

———. "Jackie Robinson's Signing: The Real Story." *Our Game*, April 15, 2012. Available at https://ourgame.mlblogs.com/jackie-robinsons-signing-the-real-story-6e685f8e42de (accessed January 4, 2020).

Thornton, Patrick K., et al. *Sports Ethics for Sports Management Professionals*. Burlington, MA: Jones & Bartlett Learning, 2012, pp. 60–61.

Trujillo, Gary. "The Origins of the 'Mustache Gang.'" *Coco Crisp's Afro, MLB Blogs*, April 24, 2015. Available at https://cococrispafro.wordpress.com/2015/04/24/the-origins-of-the-mustache-gang/ (accessed January 4, 2020).

Twombly, Wells. "Vida Blue: His Life Is A Series of Scenes, Bright and Electric." *Palm Beach Post-Times*, August 1, 1971, p. 64.

"Vida Blue of Oakland Most Valuable in AL." *Napa Valley Register*, November 17, 1971, p. 10.

"Waitkus to Remain in Hospital Four More Days." *Camden Courier-Post*, June 29, 1949, p. 18.

Wancho, Joseph. "Mudcat Grant." *Society for American Baseball Research*, January 4, 2015. Available at https://sabr.org/bioproj/person/ba7b1b4d#footnote3_junw14o (accessed January 4, 2020).

Ward, Robert. "Reggie Jackson In No-Man's Land." *Sport*, June 1977. Available at http://www.thestacksreader.com/reggie-jackson-in-no-mans-land/ (accessed January 4, 2020).

Warnemuende, Jeremy. "Reds Break Ground on New Urban Youth Academy." *MLB.com*, July 3, 2013. Available at https://www.mlb.com/reds/news/cincinnati-reds-and-major-league-baseball-open-first-urban-youth-academy-in-midwest/c-52569874 (accessed January 4, 2020).

Werner, D. "Baseball and the U. S. Navy: All Who Play Win." *Sextant*, November 9, 2018. Available at https://usnhistory.navylive.dodlive.mil/2018/11/09/baseball-and-the-u-s-navy-all-who-play-win/ (accessed December 29, 2019).

Young, Dick. "Robinson . . . New Indian Chief." *New York Daily News*, October 4, 1974, p. 88.

Zoss, J., and J. Bowman. *Diamonds in the Rough*. Lincoln: University of Nebraska Press, 2004, pp. 138–46.

INDEX

ABOUT THE AUTHOR

Rocco Constantino is a lifelong baseball fan and historian who has worked as a writer in a number of capacities. He is lead writer for Ball-Nine, a baseball multimedia website that operates under the mantra "History, Humor, and Hot Dog," a site he cofounded with his old Little League batterymate, Chris Vitali. Previously, he was a feature columnist for Bleacher Report and a history and breaking news writer for Baseball Hot Corner. Constantino published his first book, *50 Moments That Defined Major League Baseball*, in 2016, with Rowman & Littlefield, with representation from Curtis Russell, president and principal agent of P.S. Literary Agency. Outside of writing, Constantino serves as director of athletics at Santa Barbara City College in Santa Barbara, California, one of the largest and most successful two-year college athletics programs in the country. He also serves on the Board of Directors for the Santa Barbara Foresters, the seven-time National Baseball Congress summer collegiate World Series champions.

A lifelong Mets fan, Constantino developed his love of baseball as a kid through collecting baseball cards, learning about the sport from his family, and trekking to Shea Stadium on the hottest of summer days in the family station wagon. He was lucky to grow up in Belleville, New Jersey, playing wiffle ball in his yard, stickball at Number Five School, and recreation baseball for the 1986 champion Indians, who were coached by Lou Conte and Rich and Steve Romano. While playing high school baseball for the Belleville Buccaneers, Constantino had the honor of playing in Hinchcliffe Stadium in Paterson, New Jersey. Hinchcliffe was the historic home stadium for the New York Black Yankees in the

Negro National League for more than a decade, including the 1941 team that featured Hall of Famers Satchel Paige and Mule Suttles. Constantino resides in Santa Barbara, California. He is the son of Rocco and Irene; brother to Daniel, James, Glora, and Jennifer; and proud uncle to Eva, Daniel Jr., Rocco, and Juliana.